Spotlight SCIENCE

9

Keith JOHNSON ★ Sue ADAMSON ★ Gareth WILLIAMS

With the active support of: Lawrie Ryan, Phil Bunyan, Roger Frost, Helen Davis, Simon Read, Adrian Wheaton, Janet Hawkins, Susannah Wills, Cathryn Mellor, John Bailey, Ann Johnson, Graham Adamson, Diana Williams.

SPIRAL EDITION

OXFORD
UNIVERSITY PRESS

OXFORD
UNIVERSITY PRESS

Great Clarendon Street, Oxford, OX2 6DP, United Kingdom

Oxford University Press is a department of the University of Oxford. It furthers the University's objective of excellence in research, scholarship, and education by publishing worldwide. Oxford is a registered trade mark of Oxford University Press in the UK and in certain other countries

First published by Stanley Thornes Ltd in 1995
This edition first published by Nelson Thornes Ltd in 2001

British Library Cataloguing in Publication Data
Data available

978-0-7487-8457-8

10 9 8

Printed in China

Acknowledgements

Illustrations: Barking Dog, Jane Cope and Angela Lumley
Page make-up: Tech-Set

Picture research by johnbailey@axonimages.com

The authors and publishers are grateful to the following for permission to reproduce photographs:

Ace Photo Agency: Latin Stock 44T, 93T, Take Stock 131C, Lazlo Willinger 148TR, Roger Howard 172T, PL1, 201C; Action Plus: 30T, 53BL, 123tr, TL, 148BR; Adams Picture Library: 74; Allsport: Gary M Prior 53TR, Bob Martin 53BR, Tony Duffy 56, Dan Smith 57, Bob Martin 59, Michael Fauquet 62R, Dave Rogers 64T, Tom Hevezi 68; Ancient Art and Architecture Collection: 194R; Ann Ronan Photolibrary: 50, 82TL, 124; Ardea: J L Mason 170BR; Associated Sports Photos: 86TC, George Herringshaw 86TCR; Axon Images: 139TR A Yeoman; Biophoto Associates: 95B; BOC: 135C; Bodleian Library: 16; Britstock IFA: 60B; Bruce Coleman: J Fennel 8T, Dr Frieder Sauer 12T, Peter Davey 22B, Nicholas de Vore 44BL, Frank Greenaway 81BC, Hans Reinhard 154BL, 169, Jane Burton 198CBR, 209B; BT Pictures: 118R; Bubbles Photolibrary: Ian West 28BR, Lois Joy Thurston 150T; Camera Press: Karsh of Ottowa 82B, Neil Morrison 123B; Colorsport: 30BL, Andrew Cowie 173B; Collections: 135BR, 139B; Corbis Stockmarket: Zefa 210C; Ecoscene: Eva Miessler 179T, Anthony Cooper 206BL; Empics: John Marsh 30BR, Tony Marshall 122; Eye Ubiquitous: TRIP/TRIP 121BL, NASA/TRIP 121BR; Frank Lane Picture Agency: 15T, R Wilmhurst 26BL, 81BL, R Bender 154BR, S Jonasson 201B, Celtic Picture Agency 203B; Geophotos: Tony Waltham 204T, C, 205T, 209TC, 210R; Geoscience Features Picture Library: 4CC, 36CC, 198TR, TL, CTL, CTC, 200, 201TL, TC, TR, 202L, CL, CR, R, 203 TL, TR, 204 BL, BR, 208L, 209TL, TR, C, 210L, 218; Greenpeace: 4CL; Holt Studios International: N Cattlin 4BL, 9B, Michael Mayer 31B; Hulton Getty: 32R, 82TR, 102B; Hutchison Picture Library: 60T; ICI: 48T, 207TC; Image Bank: J P Frankhauser cover, 19, Paulo Curto 88T, S Marks 94T; Image State: 35; Impact Photos: 87CL, 92B, 93B, 162T; J Allen Cash Photolibrary: 13CL, 90T, 91B, 105, 131TR, 198BC; James Davis Worldwide Photographic Travel Library: 197; Kanehara & Co. Ltd: 74B (Ishihara's Tests for colour blindness cannot be conducted with this material); Kemira Agro UK Ltd: 177; Last Resort Picture Library: 49C, 86CL, 198BR, Dick Makin 206T; Leslie Garland Picture Library: 206BR; Magnum Photos: David Hurn 4CBL, Chris Steele Perkins 4CBR, W Eugene Smith 9T, Paul Lowe 100B; Martyn Chillmaid: 4CTR, 11B, 26T, 29BR, 31TL, 34, 36CL, B, 37BL, BC, BR, 40TL, B, 41, 42L, CL, CR,44 BC, BL, BR, 45, 46T, B, 47, 49B, 52TR, TL, C, B, 59T, C, 61T, 71, 74, 76, 78, 80, 95T, 108, 109, 128, 130L, CL, CR, 131CB, BL, 132 TL, TR, BL, BR, 133T, C, 134, 135BL, BC, 136TL, TC, TR, BR, BC, BL, 138, 139TL, CL, CR, 140T, B, 141, 142CC, TL, TR, BL, BC, BR, 143TL, BR, 146, 148BL, 149, 154T, 162 b, c, d, e, f, g, h, i, j, B, 163, 164, 165L, C, R, 166T, B, 167TL, TC, TR, B, 168L, R, 170 a, b, c, d, e, BL, BC, 172B, 173TL, TC, TR, 175, 180, 182, 183, 188; Mary Evans Picture Library: 32L, 37T, Devany 196; Milepost 9½: BR Archive 132C; Mike Read: 6; Natural History Museum, London: 208R; Natural Visions: Heather Angel 13TR, TL, 15B, 30CR; New Media: 179B; News International: Michael Powell 4T; Nick Cobbing Photography: 157C, B; Oxford Scientific Films: K A Larsson 5T, Kim Westerskov 11B, P Gathercole 13CR, C Milkins 13BL, J A L Cooke 13CBR, John McCammon 14B, Doug Allan 15CT, Mike Hill 15CB, M Chillmaid 18T, J A L Cooke 153T, 160T, Michael Fogden 212, Papilio Photolibrary: Robert Gill 30CR, Parke-Davis: 66; Pepsi Co International: 127; Photographers Library: 129T, 130TR; Photolibrary International: 119BL; Planet Earth Pictures: N Downer 4BR, F C Millington 8B, J Lithgow 10T, Barry Gorman 114; Popperfoto: 131BR, 144; QCA: 211; Rex Features: Jonathan Player 156T, 178T, 194L; Robert Harding Picture Library: 28R, Walter Rawlings 48B, 86TR, Toav Levy 101B, FPG International 104T, 106, 133B, M H Black 155, M Leslie Evans 171B, Roy Rainford 184, 207TL; Sally and Richard Greenhill: 92C; Science and Society Picture Library: 39, 178BL, BR; Science Photolibrary: G Williams 29BL, Charles D Winters 36TR, Klaus Guldbrandsen 44BCR, 55TL, TCL, D C R Salisbury 55TCR, A Pasieka 55TR, Department of Clinical Radiology, Salisbury District Hospital 55B, Dr R Clarke and Mr Goff 62L, 64C, Oscar Burriel 72, Francois Gohier 81C, 94BR, BL, Dr Gopal Murti 96T, 97, NIBSC 101T, R Ressmeyer 118L, ESA 119T, ESC 119BC, NRSC 119BR, J Sanford 120, NASA 121T, R Fowell TL, Adam Hart Davis 135T, CNRI 150B, 151B, 156B, Division of Computer Research and Technology, National Institute of Health 158T, A Barrington Brown 158B 161, G Tompkinson 174B, S Fraser 190, Martin Bond 192, Sinclair Stammer 198CR, R de Giulemo 198CBL; Shout Pictures: 80TL, TR, 81TL; Sporting Pictures: 111; Stone: Oliver Strewe 21, Eric Hayman 40TR, Terry Vine 61B, 64B, Chris Warbey 69, 81 BR, P Correz 85, J Causse 86BR, Dan Smith 87TL, Jo McBride 87BL, 104B, L A Peck 147, 134, Richard Kaylin 142 TC; Telegraph Colour Library: 29T, 86T, 87TR, CR, BR, 92T, 99, 129C, VCL, 193R, 198BL, Colorific Andrew Holbrooke 100T; Topham Picture Point: 26BC, 137, 151T, 171T, 174T; Transport Research Laboratories: 107T; TRIP: NASA 81TR; Viewfinder: Adrian Carrol 28BL; Wellcome Institute: 102T; Wildlife Matters: 5B; www.JohnBirdsall.co.uk: 65, 88B

Although we have made every effort to trace and contact all copyright holders before publication this has not been possible in all cases. If notified, the publisher will rectify any errors or omissions at the earliest opportunity.

Contents

Against all odds

This little boy stood for hours in the cold in London:
He wanted to tell people what had happened to his local river.

What do you think could have happened to the river?

This is just one example of **pollution**.
What do you think we mean by pollution?
Write down some of your ideas.

Pollution is when we do things that harm our environment.

What's causing the pollution?

Look at these photographs:

▶ Copy the list below of the types of pollution shown in the photographs.
Match each one with the correct effects from the other list:

Type of pollution	Effects of pollution
• dumping radio-active waste	• damages body cells
• oil spills	• lung diseases
• dangerous tips	• kills trees and water life
• smog	• kills sea-birds
• detergents	• harmful chemicals leak out
• acid gases	• too many water plants grow

Signs of pollution

When fossil fuels burn, they make acid gases like **sulphur dioxide**.
These dissolve in water in the clouds to make acid rain.
Acid rain can kill plants and fish.

Black spot is a mould that grows on roses. The mould cannot live if there is sulphur dioxide in the air.

a What does it tell you if roses do not have black spot?

Lichens are plants that are sensitive to sulphur dioxide in the air.

b Look at the shrubby lichens in the picture.
What do you think the air is like?

Who says the rain's to blame?

Does acid rain really damage plants?

Plan an investigation to see how acid affects the growth of cress seeds.

- What will you change?
- How will you make it a fair test?
- What will you measure to see if the seeds have grown?
- Your investigation should last about a week.
  How often will you record your results?

Show your plan to your teacher before you try it out.

No real answer

In Sweden, they are fighting acid rain by spraying lime on lakes.

c   What do you think the lime does to the acid?

Experts say that it is "like taking aspirin to cure cancer".

d   What do you think the experts mean by this?
e   What would be a better way to cure acid rain?

1   Copy and complete:
Pollution occurs when . . . . put harmful . . . .
or energy into the . . . . When fossil fuels are
burned, they give off gases like . . . .
These gases dissolve in water to give . . . .
. . . . The effects of acid rain can be reduced
by adding . . . . to lakes.

2   Each day millions of cars pour poisonous
exhaust fumes into the atmosphere.
Pollutants in the fumes include lead, carbon
monoxide and nitrogen oxides.
a) Try to find out what effects these
    chemicals have on our bodies.
b) How can these chemicals be reduced in
    exhaust fumes?

Things to do

3   Why do you think that people in
Norway blame factories in Britain for
acid rain pollution?
How could our factories give out less
sulphur dioxide?

4   Why do oil slicks appear on the sea?
What effect does oil have on sea-birds and
other coastal life?
How are oil slicks treated to make them less
harmful?

Exploring pyramids

Food chains can show how food (and energy) pass from one living thing to another.

Write out this food chain in the correct order:

owl, oak leaves, shrew, caterpillar

a   Where do the oak leaves get their energy from?

How many?

Food chains cannot tell you **how many** living things are involved.
It takes lots of leaves to feed a caterpillar, and lots of caterpillars to feed one shrew.

▶   Look at the diagram:

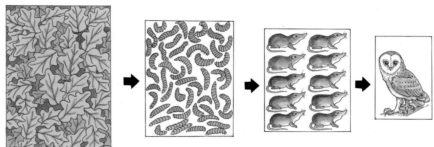

b   Why are there more plants than there are herbivores?

c   Why are there more prey than there are predators?

Up the pyramids

Look at the numbers in this food chain:

owl	1
shrews	10
caterpillars	100
oak leaves	300

You can show this information in a **pyramid of numbers**.
The area of each box tells us how big the numbers are.
Start with the plants on the first level and build it up:

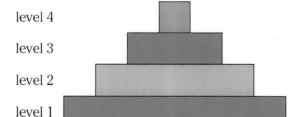

level 4
level 3
level 2
level 1

▶   Copy the diagram and label each feeding level.

d   What happens to the **numbers** of living things as you go up this pyramid?

e   What happens to the **size** of each living thing as you go up this pyramid?

f   Why are the plants always on the first level?

▶   Now try drawing a pyramid of numbers for each of these food chains:

	producer	*herbivore*	*carnivore*	*top carnivore*
g	5 cabbages	20 slugs	5 thrushes	1 cat
h	1 oak tree	100 caterpillars	5 robins	100 fleas

A top carnivore

Funnel fun

You can find very small animals in leaf litter using a **Tullgren funnel**.

Phew!... too hot and dry up there for me.

- Set up the funnel as shown:
- Place a sample of leaf litter onto the gauze.
- Switch on the light and leave it for 30 minutes to work.
- ***Be careful not to over-heat your sample and kill your animals.***
- Use a lens to look at the tiny animals that you have collected.

i What two things made the animals move downwards**?**

j Why should the light not be too close to your leaf litter**?**

k Why should your layer of leaf litter not be too thick**?**

Your teacher can give you a Help Sheet to identify your animals. It also tells you what they eat.

- Make a count of each of your animals and record it in a table:

Animal	Number found	Herbivore or carnivore?
mites springtails symphylids		

- Draw a pyramid of numbers for the animals you have collected.

Things to do

1 Copy and complete:
Pyramids of . . . . can tell us about the numbers of living things at each feeding . . . . Plants are always put in the . . . . level because they make food by . . . . and so bring energy into the food chain. As you go up the pyramid, the numbers of animals get . . . . and the size of each animal gets . . . .

2 a) Draw a pyramid of numbers from these data:

sparrowhawk 1
blue tits 5
bark beetles 50
beech tree 1

b) How is it that one tree can support so many herbivores?

c) Why do you think this is called an 'inverted pyramid'?

3 Instead of using numbers to draw pyramids, scientists sometimes use **biomass**. This is the weight of living material.
a) What would the pyramid of numbers in question 2 look like as a pyramid of biomass?
b) Draw and label it.

4 Look at the Help Sheet that you used in the activity on this page.
Choose 5 of the animals and make a key that you could use to identify each one.
Get a friend to try it out.

Dicing with death

Pesticides are chemicals that farmers use to kill **pests**.

a   What kinds of plants and animals might be pests to a farmer?

b   Why do you think farmers need to kill pests?

The main farm pests are insects, weeds and moulds.
Farmers need to control them because they destroy crops.

Nasty stuff

DDT is a pesticide. Only a small amount is needed to kill *any* insect.
It was used to kill plant pests and the mosquitoes that spread **malaria**.
However, DDT does not break down quickly. It stays in the soil for
a long time. So it can be passed along food chains. This is dangerous.

This lake in California was sprayed with DDT to control midges.
Look at the diagram to see what happened:

c   How does DDT get into this food chain?

d   What happens to the concentration of DDT as it passes along
the food chain? Try to explain this.

e   Why are the fish-eating birds the first to be killed by DDT?

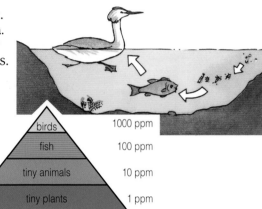

birds	1000 ppm
fish	100 ppm
tiny animals	10 ppm
tiny plants	1 ppm

pyramid of numbers

Who killed the sparrowhawk?

In the 1960s, seeds were often dipped in pesticide to protect them from pests.
Soon birds of prey, like the sparrowhawk, started dying.
Their bodies had large amounts of pesticide in them.
They also laid eggs with thin shells.

f   How do you think the pesticide got from the seeds into the sparrowhawk?

g   Why was it less concentrated in the bodies of seed-eating birds?

h   Why do more birds die if their eggs have thin shells?

Pesticides, like DDT, are now banned in many countries.

The perfect pesticide?

A pesticide must be effective, but it must also be safe.
Discuss, in your groups, what makes a good pesticide.

- Which insects should it kill?
- For how long should it be active?
- Should it dissolve in water? Why?
- How will it get into the insect's body?
- On which part of the body will it act?
- How will it be safely used?

Write down your ideas.

Disaster in Minamata

Minamata is a fishing village in Japan. In 1953 there was a disaster.
Fifty people died and hundreds were very ill. They were poisoned
by mercury.

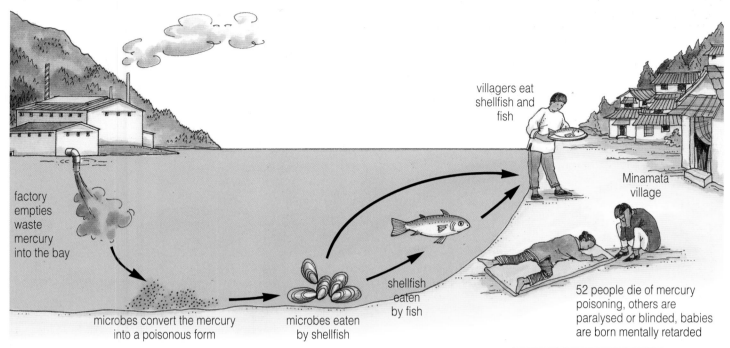

villagers eat
shellfish and
fish

Minamata
village

factory
empties
waste
mercury
into the bay

microbes convert the mercury
into a poisonous form

microbes eaten
by shellfish

shellfish
eaten
by fish

52 people die of mercury
poisoning, others are
paralysed or blinded, babies
are born mentally retarded

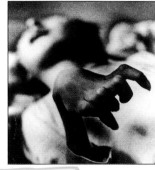

▶ Look at the picture above.

i Where did the mercury come from?

j How do you think the mercury got into the food chain?

k Explain why the concentration of mercury was higher in the people than
in the fish.

l What parts of the body are most affected by mercury poisoning?

---

1 Copy and complete:
Chemicals that kill pests are called . . . . Pests
that can damage crops are . . . . , moulds and
. . . . Some pesticides do not . . . . down easily.
They can enter food . . . . and, as they are
passed on, they become . . . . concentrated.
Animals at the . . . . of the food chain are the
first ones to die.

2 A new pesticide has been made to kill
weeds.
The manufacturer wants to know at what
concentration to sell it.
If it is too strong, it will kill the crop and
harm wildlife.
If it is too weak, then it will not kill the
weeds.
Plan an investigation to find out the best
concentration of pesticide.

3 Some insects can develop **resistance** to
a particular pesticide.
a) What is likely to happen to the farmer's
crop if this happens?
b) What could the farmer do about it?

4 In Holland, they are using ladybirds to
kill off lice on trees. The ladybirds are
imported from California. Sixty million are
being sold to Holland this year. The US
suppliers say "Unlike pesticides, they are
environmentally-friendly and real cute too!".
a) This is an example of **biological control**.
What do you think this means?
b) What are the advantages of using
ladybirds instead of pesticides?

Things to do

Cycles

Can you remember what happens to dead plants and animals?
They rot away. We say that they **decompose**.
The microbes that make dead things rot are called **decomposers**.
The most important microbes are **fungi** (moulds) and **bacteria**.

▶ Look at the diagram:

a How do plants take up nutrients?

b How do nutrients get into animals?

c How do nutrients get back into the soil?

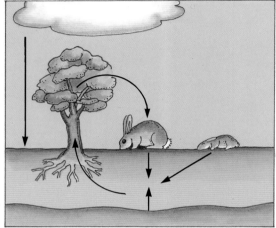

The natural roundabout

When plants and animals die, they decompose.
Nutrients are then put back into the soil.
Without fungi and bacteria, the dead material would never
decompose.

▶ Look at the diagram:

d Which process makes soil nutrients part of green plants?

e What are the living things that return nutrients to the soil?

We call the movement of nutrients a **nutrient cycle**.
This takes place on land, in fresh-water and in the sea.

f Where do you think the decomposers are found in the sea?

g Can you name 3 of the most important nutrients?

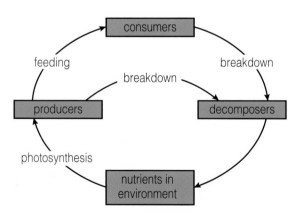

Natural or chemical?

Chemical fertilisers contain the nutrients **nitrogen**, **phosphorus**
and **potassium**. They are easy to store and to use. The farmer also
knows exactly how much of each nutrient is being used. However,
sometimes chemical fertilisers get washed out of the soil into rivers.
Some farmers prefer to use **natural fertilisers** like manure. They
rot down slower and add **humus** to the soil to improve it.

h Can you give 2 advantages of organic fertilisers?

i Can you give 2 advantages of chemical fertilisers?

Breaking the cycle

Humans share the Earth with millions of other living things.
Unfortunately some human activities destroy wildlife.
They disrupt the natural cycle of life that keeps environments in balance.

- Pollution can harm our environment in many ways.
- Clearing land for crops, housing, roads, factories and mines destroys the habitats of plants and animals.
- Over-fishing can cause the collapse of fish stocks.
- Hunters and poachers are threatening the survival of rare species.

Do some research into ways in which we can protect living things and their environments.
You could find information in books, ROMs or on the internet.

Make a leaflet aimed at convincing others of the need to protect the environment.

Your ideas should:

- be workable and able to be enforced;
- not threaten the livelihood of people, like fishermen;
- use the idea of **sustainable development**, such as replacing trees that have been felled for timber or not taking so many fish out of the oceans that they cannot be replaced by natural reproduction

---

1 Copy and complete:
Decomposers are microbes that . . . . down dead things. The most important decomposers are . . . . and bacteria. The nutrients in the soil are replaced when . . . . and animals die and . . . . Plants take up these nutrients and use them during . . . . Three important nutrients for plant growth are . . . . , phosphorus and . . . .

2 Recycling means using materials again.
a) Make a list of materials that can be recycled.
b) What effect could recycling of these materials have on:
  i) The raw materials used to manufacture goods?
  ii) The energy needed to manufacture these goods 'from scratch'?
  iii) Landfill sites?

3 35% of all our waste comes from packaging.
a) Make a list of the different types of packaging that we take away from shops.
b) In what ways does this packaging cause us problems?
Every year every person in the UK uses up one tree's worth of paper.
c) How would the recycling of paper help our environment?

4 Use books, ROMs or the internet to find out how the following help conservation in the UK:
a) National Nature Reserves (NNRs)
b) Sites of Special Scientific Interest (SSSIs).
c) Nitrate sensitive areas.
d) Heritage Coasts.
e) Set-aside.
f) Tree preservation orders.

Things to do

Poison algae

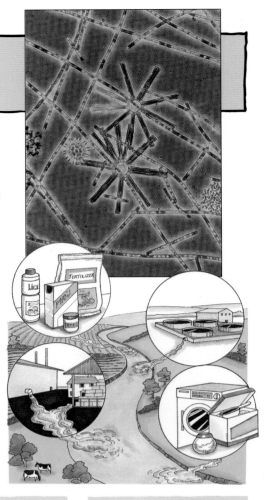

Algae are tiny plants. They live in lakes, rivers and seas.

Look at this food chain:

algae ➡ water fleas ➡ small fish ➡ large fish ➡ people

a Why are algae found at the start of the food chain?

b Can you name 3 things that algae need to grow?

c Why are fisheries often found where there are lots of algae?

Algae grow well when there is light, warmth and lots of **nutrients**.
Nutrients, like **nitrates** and **phosphates**, make algae grow best.

d What do you think will happen if *lots* of nutrients get into the water?

▶ Look at the picture:
Write down the ways in which *extra* nutrients get into the river.

Too much of a good thing

More nutrients mean more plant growth – in this case, lots of algae.
This can cause problems for animals and other plants in the water.

▶ Write out these sentences in the correct order.
They will tell you what can happen when too much algae grows.

Algae die and sink to the bottom of the lake or river.	Extra nutrients in the water make the algae grow fast.	The lack of oxygen in the water kills fish and other water animals.	Dead algae are broken down by microbes which use up lots of oxygen.

A soapy story

Detergents contain phosphates. These are plant nutrients.
In this experiment, you can find out the effect of detergent on the growth of algae.

- Label 6 test-tubes 1 to 6.
- Add 5 cm^3 of nutrient solution to each tube.
- Using a clean dropper, add 5 drops of algae water to each tube.
- Using clean droppers, add the following amounts of detergent solution and distilled water.

Test-tube	Drops of detergent solution	Drops of distilled water
1	0	5
2	1	4
3	2	3
4	3	2
5	4	1
6	5	0

- Leave all 6 test-tubes in a well-lit place.
- After a few days, shake each tube and see how green it is.
Compare the growth of algae in each one.
- Record your results in a table.
- Discuss your results and write down your conclusions.

Living indicators

We can use water animals to tell us how pure the water is:

- Come on in, the water's fine!

Mayfly larvae and stonefly larvae need clean water.

- It's getting worse!

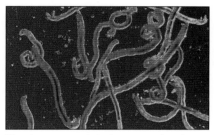 

Freshwater shrimps and water-lice can stand some pollution.

- The dirty duo!

Blood worms and sludge worms just love pollution!

e If you find a stonefly larva in a water sample, what would it tell you about the water?

f Which animals do you think could survive in the water in test-tube 6 in your investigation?

g Can you think of any other ways of testing the water for pollution?

---

1 Copy and complete:
Algae are . . . . that live in water. To grow well, they need light, warmth and . . . .
Two of the nutrients which increase the growth of algae are . . . . and phosphates.
If too much algae grow, they die and . . . . rot them down. The microbes use up a lot of . . . . and this means that fish and other water animals will . . . .

2 Are farmers poisoning our water supply?
Some of the nitrates in fertilisers wash out of the soil and trickle down into the bed-rock. Very slowly, the nitrates are moving nearer to water that we use to drink.
a) Try to explain the 'nitrate time bomb'.
b) Find out what effects nitrates can have on our health.

3 a) Should chemical fertilisers be banned?
b) What would happen to the world's food production if they were?
c) What could we use instead of them if they were banned?

Clearing weeds from a canal

Things to do

Biology at Work

Deforestation

a What do you think we mean by the word 'deforestation'?

b Why do you think humans are cutting down and clearing large areas of tropical rainforest? Try to think of *3* reasons.

Forests help to maintain the balance of the gases in the atmosphere.

c How do forests affect the carbon dioxide in the atmosphere?

d How do forests affect the oxygen in the atmosphere?

e What effect will deforestation have on the concentration of each of these gases in the atmosphere?

f Sustainable timber production could conserve our forests.
Give *2* ways in which this could happen.

Glasshouse production

To produce a high yield of crop, a grower needs photosynthesis to occur at maximum rate.

g What conditions are needed for photosynthesis?

▶ Look at the diagram of the glasshouse:

h How are the crops kept at the right temperature in the winter?

i Give *2* ways in which the temperature in the glasshouse is controlled in summer.

j How is the carbon dioxide concentration increased inside the glasshouse?

k How is the amount of sunlight inside the glasshouse controlled   i) in winter?   ii) in summer?

▶ Look at the photograph:

l How are crops watered in modern commercial glasshouses?

Conditions inside glasshouses allow plants to:
- grow earlier in the year,
- grow in places where they would not normally grow.

m How do these 2 things help the crop grower?

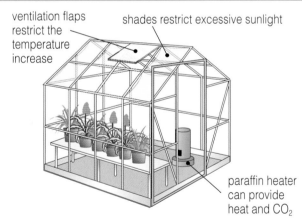

ventilation flaps restrict the temperature increase

shades restrict excessive sunlight

paraffin heater can provide heat and CO_2

Fish farming

Many fish species are **over-fished** and some are at the point of extinction.

n Give *2* ways in which fishermen have become more efficient at catching fish.

International agreements could control the amount of fishing.

o What controls could be put into place?

Another answer to the over-fishing problem is **fish farming**. Fish, like salmon and trout, are kept in large cages.

p Why do you think the fish are:
   i) fed on a high protein diet?
   ii) treated with chemicals that kill microbes?

q There are worries that fish farming can cause pollution. How do you think this could happen?

Conservation

Zoos are able to breed wild animal species in captivity.

r How do you think that zoos are able to:
   i)   increase the numbers of a particular species in the wild?
   ii) show people that wildlife is worth preserving?

Many zoos have **captive breeding programmes** for endangered species.

s What do you think is involved in a captive breeding programme?

t Why is it important that zoos also ***attract*** people?

The Arabian Oryx has been bred in Phoenix Zoo and released into the wild.

Botanic gardens and seed banks

Scientists believe that 25% of the world's plant species could be extinct in the next 50 years.

u What are the main threats to plants in the wild?

v How can botanic gardens help conserve plant species?

Seed banks are cold stores of seeds.
The seeds can be kept at $-40\ ^{\circ}C$ for 200 years.

w How can this help conserve endangered plant species?

The Millennium Seed Bank has been constructed in the UK. The building stores seeds from about 10% of the world's estimated 250 000 wild flowering plants. The project stemmed from Britain's signing of the 1992 Convention of Biodiversity in Rio.

x Use books, ROMs and the internet to find out more about the Rio Convention.

Environment

Webs and pyramids

Charles Elton was responsible for many of the ideas that formed the science that we call **ecology**. Ecology is the study of how living things interact with each other and with their environment.

In 1921, he took part in an expedition to Spitsbergen in the Arctic Circle and made a survey of the animal life there. As a result, in 1927 he wrote his classic book *Animal Ecology* in just 3 months! In it he set out his ideas about food chains, food webs and pyramids of numbers. These ideas were based upon his close observations of the animals that he had seen in the Arctic.

But Charles also introduced scientific method into his study of natural history.

His conclusions were not based upon his observations alone, he also made counts of the numbers of animals found in an area.

Elton first pieced together **food chains** based upon the feeding relationships that he observed. Here is an example:

plant plankton ➡ krill ➡ squid ➡ leopard seal

The plant plankton is eaten by the krill, which, in turn is eaten by the squid, which is eaten by the seal. Elton noticed that predators are usually larger than their prey. So organisms increase in size as you go along the food chain.

But communities are not made up of just one food chain. For instance, krill also forms the food of penguins, fish, seals and a number of whales. So a more realistic picture of the feeding relationships in a community can be shown in a **food web**.

Elton was able to piece together a complex food web for the living organisms on Bear Island. A food web shows a number of interlocking food chains. Here is an example of a seashore food web:

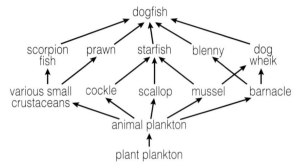

Food webs do not tell us **how many** individuals are involved in a community. Elton noted that, 'animals at the base of the food chain are relatively abundant, while those at the end are relatively few, and there is a progressive decrease between the two extremes'.

This was the basis upon which Elton constructed **pyramids of numbers**. (See p 6).
Unlike food chains and webs, pyramids of numbers show the actual number of organisms involved at each feeding level. Elton took samples of the living organisms in a community and divided them into producers, herbivores and carnivores. He drew a horizontal bar-chart, with the area of each bar being proportional to the number of individuals at each feeding level.

Questions

1 What do you think is meant by the word 'ecology'?

2 What are food chains able to show?

3 In the arctic food chain, name: a) the producers b) the herbivores c) the top carnivores.

4 Why do food webs give 'a more realistic picture of the feeding relationships in a community' than do food chains?

5 Look at the seashore food web. a) What are the producers? b) What do starfish feed on?

c) If the dog-whelks were all killed by pollution, what would happen to the populations of
i) mussels? and ii) animal plankton?

6 What is meant by a pyramid of numbers?

7 What advantages do pyramids of numbers have over food chains?

8 Try to find out more about the life and work of Charles Elton using books, ROMs and the internet.

Revision Summary

Environment

- A habitat is a place where a plant or animal lives.

- Plants and animals can only survive in a habitat if they have all the things they need for life and reproduction.
  For example, plants need light, water, suitable temperature and nutrients if they are to survive.

- Different animals and plants are adapted to survive in different habitats.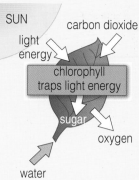
  Many plants and animals are adapted to daily and seasonal changes in their habitats.
  Some plants are able to survive the winter as seeds.
  Some animals survive the winter by hibernating (going to sleep) or by migrating (flying to warmer countries).

- A **population** is a group of animals or plants living in the same habitat.

- Some factors can limit the growth of a population, e.g. predators, disease, climate.

- Living things compete for resources that are in short supply, e.g. food, space.
  Living things that compete successfully survive to produce more offspring.

- Predators are adapted to kill other animals (their prey) for food.
  Many prey species have adaptations to avoid being caught, e.g. camouflage.

- **Food chains** show what an animal eats and how food energy is passed on.

- A food web is made up of many food chains.

- A pyramid of numbers shows the numbers of plants, herbivores and carnivores in a habitat.

- There is a flow of food energy from the producers to the final organisms in the food chain.

- Poisonous chemicals can increase in concentration along food chains.

- It is important to protect and conserve living things and their environment.

- Sustainable development involves not felling more trees or catching more fish than can be replaced by normal reproduction.

Plants at work

- Green plants use chlorophyll to trap light energy for photosynthesis.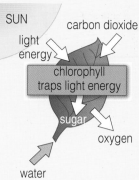

- During photosynthesis, green plants use this energy to convert carbon dioxide and water into sugar and oxygen:

  carbon dioxide + water $\xrightarrow[\text{chlorophyll}]{\text{light energy}}$ sugar + oxygen

- The new material that plants produce by photosynthesis is called biomass.

- Plants release oxygen for animal respiration and use up waste carbon dioxide.

- Plants also use oxygen for their own respiration.

- Plants also need nutrients from the soil, such as nitrates, for healthy growth.

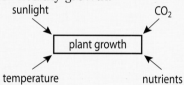

  Extra nutrients are sometimes added to the soil in the form of fertilisers.

- Root hairs absorb water and nutrients from the soil.

- Green plants are the producers that are the first link in a food chain.

- The rate of photosynthesis is affected by light, carbon dioxide and temperature.

- Green plants affect the amounts of carbon dioxide and oxygen in the atmosphere.

- **Flowers** are made up of sepals, petals, stamens and carpels.

- The anthers make pollen grains and the ovary makes ovules.

- Pollination is the transfer of pollen from the anthers to the stigma.

- Fertilisation happens when a pollen nucleus joins with an ovule nucleus.

- After fertilisation, the ovary changes into a fruit and the ovule grows into a seed.
  Under the right conditions the seed can grow into a new plant.

Questions

1 Every year, 250 tonnes of lead from fishermen's weights gets into the environment.
It is thought that birds like the mute swan eat the lead weights when feeding.
a) How do you think the lead gets into the blood of the swan?
Swans in town areas are more affected by this type of poisoning than those in the country.
b) Why do you think this is?
c) How could this pollution be reduced without banning fishing altogether?

2 The following data were collected from a river:

pike	1
trout	10
water fleas	500
algae	10 000

a) Draw a pyramid of numbers (not to scale) for the river.
b) Which living thing would you remove if you wanted to increase the number of trout in the river?
c) Give one other effect of removing this living thing from the river.

3 Some DDT was sprayed on a lake to control mosquitoes.
Look at the table showing the amounts of DDT in a food chain.

cormorant	26.5 ppm
pike	1.3 ppm
minnow	0.2 ppm
algae	0.05 ppm
water	0.000 05 ppm

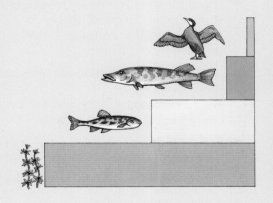

Explain how the cormorant has 500 000 times more DDT in its body than there is in the water.

4 The Royal Society for the Protection of Birds has said that more than 40 bird species are threatened by intensive farming. Birds in decline on farmland include the skylark, barn owl, lapwing and golden eagle.
a) List the ways in which you think farming can reduce bird numbers.
b) What steps do you think could be taken to improve this situation?

5 Plan an investigation to find out how clean your local river is.
What evidence of pollution would you look for?
What chemicals would you test for, and how?
How could you use 'indicator animals' to tell you how clean the river is?

6 Decomposers, like fungi, are very useful in the environment.
Explain why plants and animals depend upon them so much.

Energy

Without energy nothing can ever happen!

All living things need energy to stay alive and to move. You get your energy from your food.

Factories and transport need the energy that comes from fuels. And we need energy to heat our homes.

Go with energy

▶ Julie is playing with her group:

In the picture there are 8 forms of **energy** labelled.

a Write down the names of these 8 forms of energy.

Nuclear energy is not shown here. Add it to your list.

b What is nuclear energy?

Some energy is called **potential** energy.

c Write down 2 examples of potential energy from the picture.

▶ What kind of energy has

d a stretched elastic band?
e a book on a shelf?
f a moving car?

Light energy (radiant energy) from the spotlights

When the drummer lifts her hands, she gives them **gravitational** potential energy

The lights and people are hot with **thermal** energy (heat)

Sound energy comes from the group

When the guitar string is stretched, it has **strain** potential energy

The people have movement energy (**kinetic** energy)

Electrical energy is needed for the lights and instruments

The people have **chemical** energy stored, from the food they have eaten

Energy diagrams

Here is an **Energy Transfer Diagram** for a torch:

g Copy and complete this diagram.

h Look at the numbers in the diagram. How many joules are transferred to light up the room?

i What is the *efficiency* of the torch?

. . . . energy stored in the . . . .
100 J

. . . . energy in the wires

. . . . energy lighting up the room

. . . . energy heating up the torch and room
95 J

▶ A lot of energy is wasted in a car. For every 100 J of chemical energy in the petrol, only 25 J are transferred to kinetic energy. The rest just heats up the engine and the air.

j Draw an Energy Transfer Diagram for this, to scale.

This is what happens in energy transfers.
Although there is the same amount of energy afterwards, not all of it is useful.

This is summed up in the 2 laws of energy:

Law 1 The total amount of energy in the universe stays the same. It is 'conserved'. Energy cannot be created or destroyed.	**Law 2** In energy transfers, the energy spreads out, to more and more places. As it spreads, it becomes less useful to us.

Making electricity

One way to make electricity is to use the energy of falling water.
Your teacher can show you this:

The falling water turns a turbine, and this turns a dynamo.

This is like a **hydro-electric power station**, where the water is stored behind a dam.

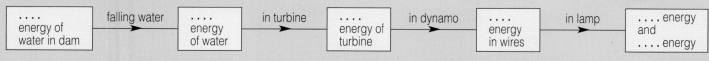

k What form of energy does the water in the dam have? (Hint: it is high in the mountains.)

l Copy and complete the energy flow-chart for this:

. . . . energy of water in dam	falling water →	. . . . energy of water	in turbine →	. . . . energy of turbine	in dynamo →	. . . . energy in wires	in lamp →	. . . . energy and . . . . energy

m How could you make electricity from energy in the *wind*?

▶ Another way to make electricity is to burn a fuel, which boils water to make steam.
The steam then turns a turbine, and this turns a dynamo (a generator):

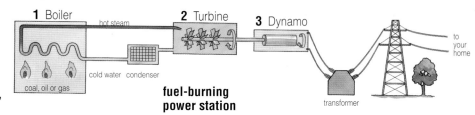

fuel-burning power station

n Draw a flow-chart for this power station, like the one in question **l** above.

▶ Fuel-burning power stations cause pollution.
They give out sulphur dioxide and carbon dioxide gases.

o The sulphur dioxide dissolves in the rain to cause **acid rain**.
What effect does acid rain have on lakes, forests and buildings?

p Carbon dioxide 'traps' the Sun's energy and keeps the Earth warm.
This is called the **greenhouse effect**.
However too much carbon dioxide would be a bad thing for the Earth. Why? What do you think could happen?

Trees killed by acid rain

---

1 Copy and complete:
a) Energy is measured in . . . .
b) The 9 forms of energy are:
c) Lifting a stone gives it . . . . energy.
d) In any energy change, the total amount of . . . . before the change is always . . . . to the total amount of . . . . afterwards.
e) After the change, not all of the . . . . is useful.
f) Sulphur dioxide from power stations can cause . . . . rain, and carbon dioxide may warm up the Earth too much, because of the . . . . effect.

2 What are the energy transformations in
a) a Bunsen burner?   b) a television?
c) a yo-yo?   d) a hair-dryer?
e) a clockwork toy?   f) an apple tree?

3 In a nuclear power station, nuclear energy heats water to make steam. Draw a flow-chart for it, like the one shown above.

4 In one second a lamp transfers 100 J, but only 4 J is light energy.
a) Draw an Energy Transfer Diagram for it.
b) What is the efficiency of the lamp?

Things to do

26b Energy from the Sun

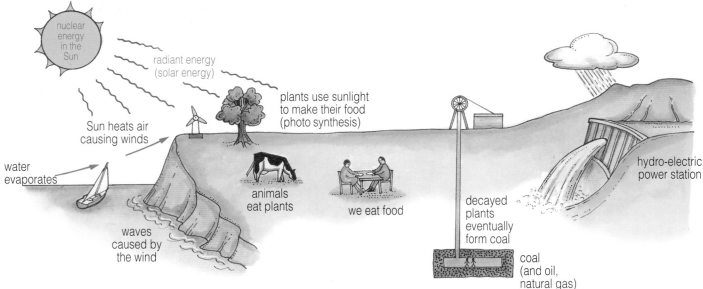

▶ We get most of our energy from the Sun.
Use the diagram to help you to answer these questions:

a In plants, what is the name of the process that transfers solar energy to chemical energy (in food)?

b When you drink a glass of milk, it gives you energy. How did the energy get into the milk?

Here are some food-energy chains that are in the wrong order. Write each one in the correct order.
c humans, Sun, sheep, grass
d ladybird, rose, greenfly, Sun
e dead leaves, tree, Sun, blackbird, woodlouse

f Explain how water from the sea gets to the dam for this hydro-electric power station:

A hydro-electric power station

▶ Coal, oil and natural gas are called **fossil fuels**.
g Explain how i) coal, and
ii) oil and natural gas,
were formed. (Your teacher may give you a Help Sheet.)

h How can you heat a house using solar energy?
Draw a sketch to show how.

Plant and animal materials are called **biomass**.
Biomass can give us energy as food, and in other ways too.
For example, methane gas can be made from rotting rubbish or cow dung. Wood is used as the main fuel in many parts of the world:

Energy resources

▶ Look at the pie-chart and answer these questions.

i What was the biggest resource of energy in 1996**?**
j What was its percentage**?**

k Some fuels are **renewable**. What does this mean**?**
l Which 2 of these resources are renewable**?**

m There are 5 other renewable sources of energy. Write down as many as you can.
n Why do you think these 5 sources are not shown**?**

o What is a **non-renewable** resource**?**
p Which of the resources in the pie-chart are non-renewable**?**
q Which of them are fossil fuels**?**

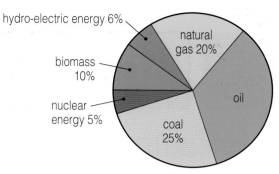

World energy resources in 1996

▶ The time-chart shows how long the 3 fossil fuels are likely to last:

r How old will you be when the oil runs out**?**
s Predict what you think the pie-chart will look like when you are 60.

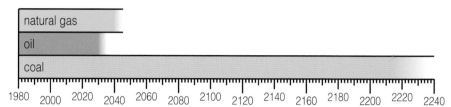

World trade in energy

The graph shows the energy sold commercially each year:

t Which of these resources is not shown in 1970**?**
u Why is biomass not shown at all**?**

v What happened to world demand during these 30 years**?**
w Estimate the world energy demand in 2010.

x Discuss what the graph will look like when you are 60. Can you predict its shape**?**

y Draw a pie-chart for the year 2000.

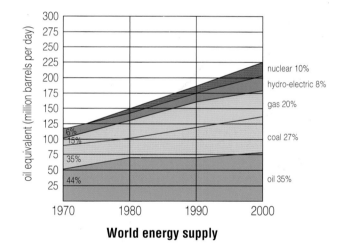

World energy supply

Reading the meters

Your teacher will give you a Help Sheet on which you can record how much energy you use in your home.

---

1 Copy and complete:
a) Most of our energy comes from the . . . .
b) The Sun's . . . . is passed to plants and . . . . by a food-energy chain.
c) Coal, ... and . . . . are fossil . . . .
d) Coal and . . . . and . . . . and uranium are non- . . . . sources of energy.
e) The 7 renewable sources of energy are:

2 Do a flow-chart to show how energy in a coal-mine makes a cup of tea for you.

3 Make a table showing how people could save non-renewable fuels. For example:

Action to be taken	How it saves fuel
turn off the lights	uses less electricity

Things to do

23

Warming up with energy

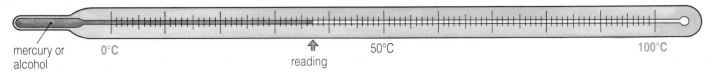

mercury or alcohol   0°C   ⬆ reading   50°C   100°C

a   What do you measure with a **thermometer?**

b   What is the reading on this thermometer**?**
(This is the temperature of a human body.)

c   What happens to water at   i) 0°C**?**   ii) 100°C**?**

d   Explain how you think a thermometer works.

Heat (energy) and temperature

Thermal energy (heat) is ***not*** the same thing as temperature.
To understand this, let's compare these 2 things:

A white-hot spark

The tiny sparks are at a very high temperature, but
contain little energy because they are very small.

Each atom in the spark is **vibrating**.
Because it is very hot they are vibrating a lot.
But there are not many of them, so the total amount
of energy is small.

This idea about atoms is called the **Kinetic Theory**.

A bath-full of warm water

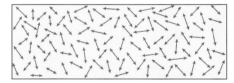

The water is at a lower temperature, but
it contains more energy.
This is because it contains more **atoms**.

Each atom is vibrating at a low temperature,
but there are many of them.
There is a lot of thermal energy (heat).

Warming up water

Plan an investigation to see what happens when you give
the same amount of energy to different amounts of water.

- How will you make sure that you give the ***same***
amount of energy each time**?**

- Show your plan to your teacher, and then do it.

- Explain what happens, using these words:
energy   atoms   vibrating   temperature

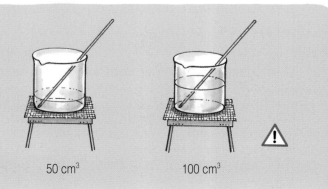

50 cm³   100 cm³

Energy on the move

Energy always travels **from** hot things **to** cold things.
There are 3 ways that the energy can be transferred:

Conduction

The metal handle gets too hot to hold.
The energy has been **conducted** through the metal.

The metal is a good **conductor**.
The wooden spoon is an **insulator**.

Convection

The air over the heater is warm.
The hot air is rising upwards, in **convection** currents.

You get similar convection currents when you heat a beaker of water.

Radiation

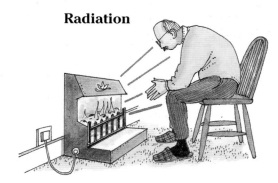

Radiant energy is travelling through the air, just like solar energy from the Sun.

The rays can travel through space, at the speed of light. They are also called **infra-red** rays.

▶ Here is a picture of a Bunsen burner heating up some gauze:

e After a while, the base feels warm at the point A. Why is this**?**

f If you put your hand at point B, it is hot. Why is this**?**

g If you put your hand near the red-hot gauze, at point C, it feels warm. Why is this**?**

▶ Here is a 'model' to help us see the difference between these 3 ways.
Three ways of getting a book to the back of the class:

1 Conduction: you can pass a book from person to person – just as the energy is passed from atom to atom.

2 Convection: you can carry the book to the back of the class – just as hot air moves in convection, taking the energy with it.

3 Radiation: a book can be thrown to the back of the class – rather like the way energy is radiated from a hot object.

---

1 Copy and complete:
a) When an object is heated, the energy makes the . . . . vibrate more. The hotter the object, the more the . . . . vibrate.
b) Energy travels from hot objects to . . . . objects by . . . . , or . . . . , or . . . .

2 Explain why a white-hot spark falling into a bath of water does not make the water hot.

3 Explain how an electric fire heats up a room.

Things to do

Conduction

▶ What would you feel if you stirred some hot soup with a metal spoon and with a wooden spoon? Can you explain this?

Energy on the move

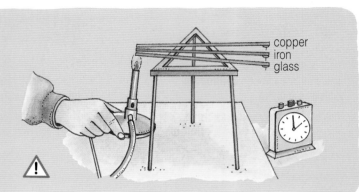

copper
iron
glass

- Set up 3 rods as shown, of copper, iron and glass:
- Use vaseline to fix a drawing-pin at the end of each rod.
- Then heat the ends of the rods equally, with a Bunsen burner.

- What happens? How long does it take for the first and second pins to fall off?

a Which way was energy flowing in the rods?

b Does the energy flow at the same rate through all the rods? Explain your answer.

c Which of these 3 materials would be best for making a pan? Explain your answer.

▶ The diagram shows how we can explain conduction, using the idea of atoms:

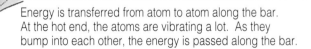

Energy is transferred from atom to atom along the bar. At the hot end, the atoms are vibrating a lot. As they bump into each other, the energy is passed along the bar.

▶ As you saw, copper is a good **conductor**.
In fact, **all metals are good conductors**.
Glass is an **insulator**.
Air is a very good insulator. We use this to keep us warm:

Birds fluff up their feathers in winter, to trap more air. The air is a good insulator and keeps them warm.

An anorak has a lot of trapped air. This slows down the transfer of thermal energy from your body.

Insulation in the loft of your house keeps you warm, and saves money. The material contains a lot of air.

Keeping warm

Your teacher will give you some materials that could be used for clothes, or to insulate your house.

Your job is to find out which of these materials is the best insulator.

- You could use a thermometer, or you could use a temperature sensor connected to a computer.
  What other equipment will you use?

- How will you make it a fair test?

- How will you record your results?

- Show your plan to your teacher, and then do it.

- Which material is best? **Why** do you think it is best?

⚠️
hot water

temperature
sensor

Saving energy at home

Here are 2 houses:

One of them has been carefully insulated.

d Which house has **not** been insulated?

e What is the total heating bill for this house?

f Imagine you lived in this house.
Which parts would you insulate first?

g What is the total heating bill for the insulated house?

h All these places have been insulated:
walls, roof, floor, doors, windows.
- Put them in order of the money saved.
- Next to each one, write the amount of money saved.

i Draw an Energy Transfer Diagram for each house.

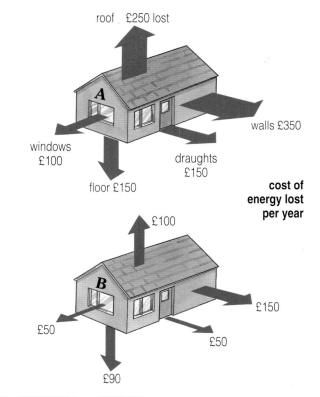

roof £250 lost

A

windows
£100

walls £350

draughts
£150

floor £150

**cost of
energy lost
per year**

£100

B

£50

£150

£50

£90

Things to do

1 Copy and complete:
a) All metals are good . . . .
    Copper is a very good . . . .
b) Glass is an . . . .
    Air is a very good . . . .
c) Thermal energy passes through the
    bottom of a pan by . . . .
    The energy is passed from each
    vibrating atom to the next . . . .

2 Make lists of where a) conductors and
b) insulators are used in your home.

3 Write a letter to a pupil in your last
school explaining what conduction is.

4 A double-glazed window has 2 sheets
of glass, with air between.
Plan an investigation to see if double-
glazing helps to insulate.
(Hint: you could use a beaker inside a
bigger beaker.)

5 Explain this statement: "All the energy
used in heating our homes is wasted."

Convection and radiation

Convection

Have you ever noticed that flames always go upwards?
This is because hot air is lighter than colder air.
The hot air rises.

hot air rises

a Where is the hottest part of the room – the floor or
the ceiling? Why?

b Why does smoke go up a chimney?

- Fill a beaker with cold water.
- Very gently, place a crystal of purple dye
  at the bottom and near the side:
- Put a *small* flame under the crystal.
- What happens? Explain what you see.

The water moves in a **convection current**.
This carries the energy round the beaker.

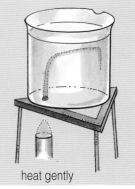
heat gently

▶ You get the same thing in a room.
The room is heated by the convection currents
moving round:

c Why does a hot fire sometimes give you a cold
draught on your feet?

On a sunny day, hot air currents can rise from the
ground. Glider pilots can use them to lift their wings.

The Sun can cause very large convection currents,
which we feel as **winds**.

▶ Use what you know about convection currents to
explain what is happening in these photos:

Radiation

This sun-bather is getting hot:
Her body is *absorbing* energy.

d Where is the energy coming from?

e Could the energy have reached her by
conduction or convection? Explain
your answer.

This energy is called **solar energy** or **radiant energy**.
The rays include **infra-red rays** and **ultra-violet rays**.

f How can you use solar energy to cook food?

▶ Our bodies also *emit* (give out) radiation.
We *radiate* energy.
This is shown on the thermogram:

g Which part of the man is giving out
   i) the most energy?
   ii) the least energy?

h Use the key to estimate the temperature of his cheek.

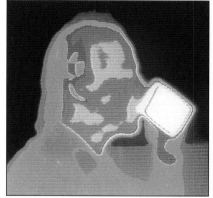

☐	above 38°C
	35°C
	32°C
	29°C
	26°C
■	below 23°C

Melanie and Chris are discussing the colour of cars.

Melanie says, "I think black cars get hotter in the Sun."
Chris says, "Silver is brighter – I think a silver car will
get hotter."

Plan an investigation to see who is right.

* How will you make it a fair test?
* How many readings will you take?
* How will you show your results?

Show your plan to your teacher before you do the investigation.

---

1 Copy and complete:
a) Thermal energy (heat) can be carried
   through a liquid by a . . . . current. The
   hot liquid . . . . and the . . . . liquid falls.
b) . . . . currents also flow in air.
c) . . . . rays travel from the Sun through
   empty space. This energy is called
   . . . . energy or . . . . energy.
d) A black object absorbs more . . . . than
   a silver one.
e) A silver surface . . . . the rays like a
   mirror. This is used in a . . . . cooker.

2 Explain why:
a) Food cooks faster at the top of an oven.
b) Fire-fighters enter smoke-filled rooms by
   crawling.
c) Houses in hot countries are often white.
d) There is shiny metal behind the bar of an
   electric fire.

3 A potato is being cooked in boiling water.
Explain, as fully as you can, how energy gets
from the gas flame or hot-plate into the
middle of the potato.

Things to do

Physics at Work

A down-hill skier

Look at this photo of a down-hill skier:

a What kind of energy does he have at the top of the hill**?**

b What kind of energy is it changed into, as he moves down-hill**?**

c There is some friction between his skis and the snow. What can you say about the temperature of the skis as he slides down**?**

d What other friction force does he feel**?** Why is he crouching**?**

e What has happened to all the energy when the race is finished**?**

An **elephant** sometimes gets too hot.

f It has big ears. Explain how this helps it to cool down.

g Explain carefully why it some- times uses its trunk to spray water over its back. How many reasons can you think of**?**

This **marathon runner** has just finished a race.

h Why is she wearing a shiny plastic cover**?**

The **brakes** on this racing car are glowing red-hot.

i Why is this**?**

j What happens to this heat energy**?**

The diagram shows a **rocket-balloon**:

k When the balloon is blown up, what kind of energy does it have**?**

l Where did this energy come from**?**

m When the air is released,
  • what happens to the balloon**?**
  • what happens to the energy**?**

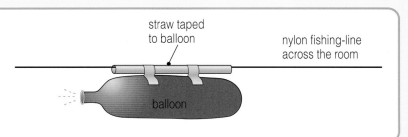

straw taped to balloon

nylon fishing-line across the room

balloon

An ordinary filament **light bulb** is only about 5% efficient. So for every 100 joules of electrical energy, only 5 joules are transformed to light energy.

n   What happens to the other 95 J?

An energy-saving bulb is also shown:
For every 100 J of electrical energy you get 25 J of light energy.

o   What is its efficiency?

p   Draw an Energy Transfer Diagram for each kind of bulb, to scale.

The diagram shows a side view of a **solar panel**. It is using solar energy to heat water for a house.

q   Which way is water flowing in the pipe?

r   Why is the hot water outlet at the *top* of the tank?

s   Explain how energy is transferred through the wall of the pipe to the water inside the tank. Use the idea of particles (atoms or molecules) in your explanation.

t   Why is there a black surface in front of the pipe and a shiny surface behind it?

u   Explain, step by step, how energy is transferred from the Sun to the hot water tap.

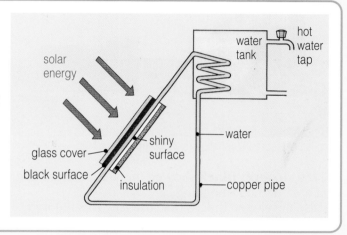

v   Why are chicks covered with fluffy feathers?

w   What happens if they get covered in oil?

Petrol consumption
The table shows some data for a car travelling on a level motorway.

x   Explain what the table is about.

y   Plot a graph of the data.

z   Explain what the graph tells you. Can you explain the shape?

speed (mph)	20	30	40	50	60	70
(km/h)	32	48	64	80	97	113
petrol used (cm³/km)	60	65	73	86	110	156

The cut-away diagram shows the *inside* of a 'thermos' **vacuum flask**, for keeping tea warm.

A   How does this design stop heat transfer by conduction?

B   How does this design stop heat transfer by convection?

Energy

Ideas about Energy

Ideas about energy started to become important when engineers like **Thomas Newcomen** (in 1705) and **James Watt** (in 1764) tried to improve steam engines.

A replica of George Stephenson's **'Locomotion'** of 1825

In 1760, **Joseph Black** showed that temperature and heat are not the same thing.
He also developed the 'caloric' theory. This theory said that heat was a kind of invisible liquid, that flowed out of hot objects and soaked into cold objects.
At first this seemed to be a good theory, because it explained most experiments. But it couldn't explain everything – it couldn't explain why your hands get warm when you rub them together quickly.
Nevertheless, scientists kept to this 'caloric' theory as the best theory they had.

In 1798, **Count Rumford** was in charge of drilling the holes in cannons. While a gun was being drilled, he noticed that it got very hot (by friction).
By drilling for a long time and taking measurements, he showed that the gun continued to heat up, long after it should have run out of 'caloric liquid'.
As he wrote: *'It appears to me to be extremely difficult to form any distinct idea of heat, except it be **motion**.'*

James Joule was born in Salford, Lancashire in 1818. As a teenager he was taught by **John Dalton** (who had suggested the idea of atoms in 1803).
In 1837, Joule began a series of precise experiments on energy.
In his electrical experiments he looked at the heating effect of a current in a wire. He found that the heating depends on the *square* of the current. So twice the current gives four times as much heat.

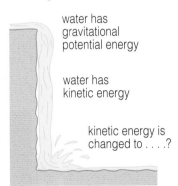

In his most famous experiment, he built a pulley system so that falling weights turned some paddles that were in a pan of water. As the weights fell, the turning paddles heated up the water (by friction), and Joule measured the change in temperature.

Joule predicted that the water at the bottom of a waterfall would be slightly warmer than the water at the top.
In 1847 he married Amelia, and they went on honeymoon to the Alps. Joule spent a lot of his honeymoon measuring the temperatures at the top and bottom of waterfalls.

water has gravitational potential energy

water has kinetic energy

kinetic energy is changed to . . . .?

From all his experiments, Joule got evidence to convince other scientists that energy is 'conserved'.
This is the famous **Law of Conservation of Energy**:
Energy can be changed from one form to another, but it cannot be created or destroyed. The total amount of energy stays the same.

Later it became clear that heat is really the movement energy of atoms and molecules (see page 24).

Questions

1 Why do you think ideas about energy started to be important to people making steam engines?

2 What was the problem with the 'caloric' theory?

3 What happens to the heating effect in a wire if the current increases
   a) to 3 times as much?
   b) to 10 times as much?

4 From the description above, try to sketch a diagram of Joule's 'paddle-wheel in a pan' apparatus.

5 Use the diagram to explain why you would expect the water to be slightly warmer at the bottom of a waterfall.

6 Explain how 'heat is really the movement energy of atoms'.

Revision Summary

Energy

- Energy can exist in several different forms, including: thermal energy (heat), light, sound, electrical, nuclear, chemical energy, etc.

  Movement energy is called kinetic energy.

  Gravitational potential energy is stored in an object that has been lifted up.
  Elastic (or 'strain') potential energy is stored in a stretched catapult.

- Fuels store energy. They give out the energy when they burn with oxygen.

  Coal, oil and natural gas are fossil fuels.
  Coal was formed over millions of years when dead plants were buried and squeezed by layers of rock. Oil and natural gas were made in a similar way from dead sea animals.

  These are **non-renewable** sources of energy (they get used up).
  Uranium is another non-renewable resource.

- We can also get energy from sunlight (solar energy), wind, waves, hydro-electric dams, and biomass (e.g. wood from trees). We can also get energy from tides and geothermal stations.
  These sources are **renewable**.

- Most of our energy comes (indirectly) from the Sun. Solar heating causes winds, waves and rain.

- Electricity can be generated (made) from
  – non-renewable fuels (see the diagram below), or
  – renewable resources (e.g. a wind-generator).

- The laws of energy:
  1. The amount of energy before a transfer is always equal to the amount of energy after the transfer. The total amount of energy stays the same. We say the energy is 'conserved'.
  2. In energy transfers, the energy spreads out and becomes less useful to us.

- 1 kilojoule = 1000 joules.

- If the temperature of an object rises, its atoms vibrate more.
  The thermal energy (or heat) is the total energy of all the vibrating atoms in the object.

- To get a job done, energy must be transferred from one place to another.
  Energy can be transferred by electricity, by sound, by light, and by thermal (heat) transfer.

  Heat energy can be transferred by
  – conduction (through solids, liquids and gases),
  – convection (when liquids or gases move),
  – radiation (even through space).

Conduction from a hot object to a cold object:

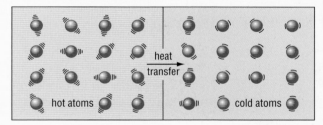

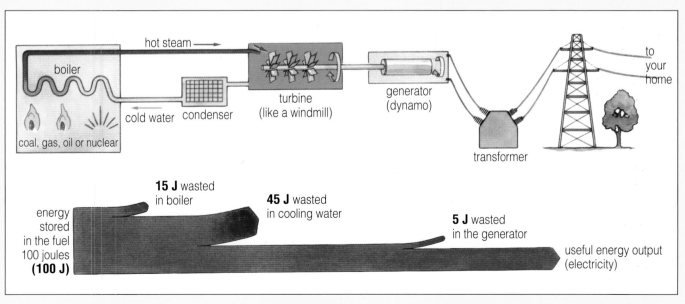

Questions

1 The diagram shows some of the energy transfers that take place in a hair-dryer during one second:

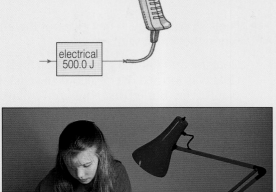

a) Not all the energy transfers are shown in the diagram. Explain how you can tell this.
b) Draw an Energy Transfer Diagram of this, and label it.
c) What happens eventually to all the energy?

2 When you switch on a light, it is the result of a long chain of events. These are listed, but in the wrong order. Write them down in the correct order.

A plants change to coal over millions of years
B the Sun produces energy
C water is heated, to make steam
D the plants die
E plants take in solar energy
F the energy is radiated, and travels to the Earth
G coal is burnt in oxygen (in air)
H steam makes a turbine turn
I the generator produces electricity
J electricity heats up the lamp and it shines
K electricity travels through wires to your home
L the turbine turns a generator

3 Jo has 2 mugs. They are the same except that one is black and one is white. They were filled with hot coffee and allowed to cool. Jo took their temperatures every 2 minutes, as shown in the table:

a) Plot a graph (of temperature against time) for each mug, on the same axes. Draw the lines of 'best fit'.
b) Which result do you think is wrong?
c) What is the temperature of the black mug after 3 minutes?
d) What is the difference in temperature after 9 minutes?
e) What conclusion can you draw from the graphs?

Time (min)	Black mug (°C)	White mug (°C)
0	90	90
2	68	78
4	55	67
6	45	58
8	37	52
10	31	43
12	26	37

4 Theo has 2 insulated pans of water at 20°C. He gets 2 identical blocks of iron, both at 100°C, and puts one in pan A and one in pan B. He measures the 'final' temperature that the water rises to, and puts his results in the table:

a) Explain carefully why the rise in temperature is less for pan B.
b) What is the final temperature of (i) the iron block in pan A? (ii) the iron block in pan B?
c) The 2 iron blocks were identical. Which one transferred more heat energy to the water? Explain your reasoning.
d) Explain the difference in the iron atoms when they were hot and when they were cold.

	Temperature of the water at the start (°C)	Temperature of the block at the start (°C)	Volume of water (cm³)	'Final' temperature of the water (°C)
A	20	100	500	35
B	20	100	1000	28

Elements, mixtures and compounds

27

Everything around you is an element, a mixture or a compound.
You are a combination of elements, mixtures and compounds.
The elements are the building blocks.
There are 92 natural ones. How many can you name?

In this topic you will be looking at lots of elements.
Some will be in mixtures .... Some will be in compounds ....

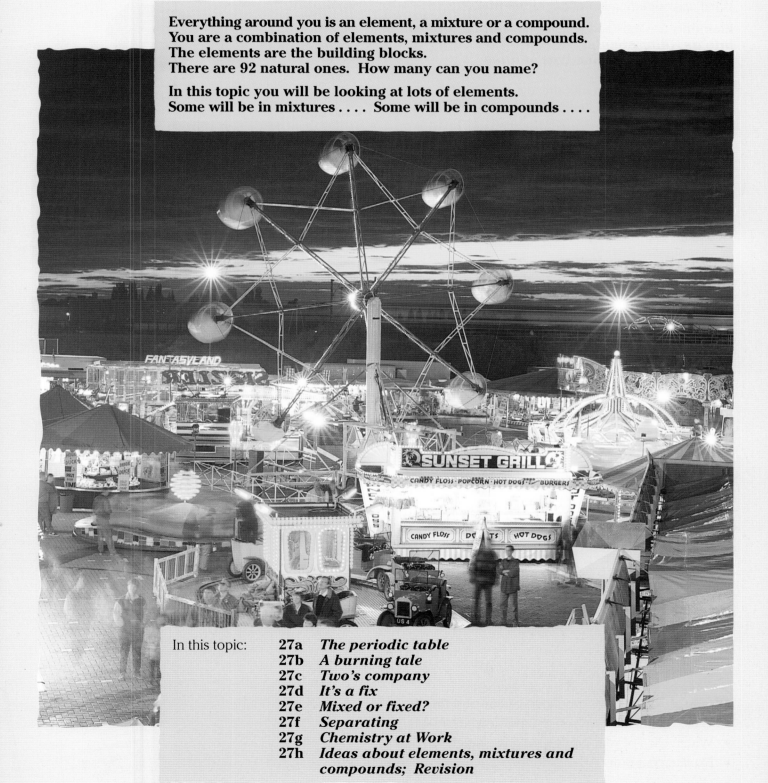

The periodic table

What do you remember about **elements?**

Elements are substances which *cannot be broken down into anything simpler*.
An element has *only one type of atom*.

The elements here are sodium, gold, copper and chlorine. Can you identify each one?

You've met lots of elements already.
Which of the elements in the box:

a rusts?

b has the symbol H?

c has the symbol S?

d has the symbol Cu?

e turns blue with starch?

f is about 21% of the air?

g What does *classifying* mean?

Elements
copper
iron
hydrogen
iodine
oxygen
sulphur

Scientists classify the elements in the **periodic table**.
But how are the elements arranged?
Let's look for patterns.

How are books classified in your school library?

Grouping elements

Look at this information about elements.

Element	Melting point in °C	Boiling point in °C	Appearance	Reaction with cold water	Other information
sodium	98	890	silver-grey solid	reacts violently	conducts heat and electricity
silver	960	2212	shiny silver solid	no reaction	conducts heat and electricity
helium	−270	−269	colourless gas	no reaction	very unreactive, doesn't conduct
lithium	181	1330	silver-grey solid	reacts very quickly	conducts heat and electricity
copper	1083	2595	shiny pink-brown solid	no reaction	conducts heat and electricity
chlorine	−101	−34	green-yellow gas	dissolves	reactive, doesn't conduct
argon	−189	−186	colourless gas	no reaction	very unreactive, doesn't conduct
fluorine	−220	−188	pale yellow gas	dissolves	very reactive, doesn't conduct
gold	1063	2966	shiny gold solid	no reaction	conducts heat and electricity
potassium	63	765	silver-grey solid	reacts very violently	conducts heat and electricity
neon	−250	−246	colourless gas	no reaction	very unreactive, doesn't conduct
bromine	−7	58	red-brown liquid	dissolves	reactive, doesn't conduct

Make a data card for each element.
Use your cards to match up similar elements.
You can move the cards around to get the best match.

• Which elements have you grouped together? Why?

• Within each of your groups, put the elements in order.

• Explain your order.

DATA CARD

Element _____
Appearance _____

Melting point _____
Boiling point _____
Reactivity _____

Mendeleev was a Russian scientist. In 1869 he made
a pattern of elements. He put the elements in **groups**.
This pattern is called the **periodic table**.

Your teacher will show you a copy of the **periodic table**.
The columns of elements are called **groups**.
The rows of elements are called **periods**.
Are **your** groups the same as those in the periodic table?

h Which elements are in the same group as chlorine?

i Name 2 elements in the same period as chlorine.

j Where are the **metals** in the periodic table?

k Within each group, where are the **most reactive** metals?

Your teacher may show you some metals reacting.
How do sodium and magnesium react with water?

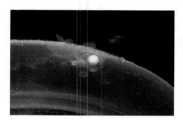

sodium and cold water   magnesium and cold water   magnesium and steam

l Which is more reactive, sodium or magnesium?

▶ Look at a copy of the full periodic table.

m Write the symbol and name of the most reactive metal.
(You can use your answers to **j**, **k** and **l**, to help you answer this.)

Video highlights

The Spotlight Video Company needs your help.
The company wants to make a new video.
It will be about elements and the periodic table.

- The video will be for 13-year-old pupils.
- It should be about 5 minutes long.
- It should be interesting and exciting. (It **might** be funny!)
- It should explain about elements and the periodic table.

Your group should write a script for the video.
What will be seen on the screen? Explain what filming will be
needed.
Who would you like to present your video? Money is no object!

1 Copy and complete:
a) Elements have only one type of . . . .
b) Elements are classified in the . . . . table.
c) The columns of elements are called . . . .
d) The rows of elements are called . . . .

2 Name 2 elements in each case which
are: a) solids b) liquids c) gases.

3 Choose one group of elements.
Use books to find out about the group.
Make a wall poster about the elements.

Things to do

A burning tale

500 B.C.

The Greeks thought that the universe was made from 4 elements: fire, water, air and earth.
They believed **everything** was made of these elements.

So what happens when something burns?

The fire is released.

The water and air escape

The earth or ashes are left behind.

EARTH AIR·FIRE WATER

For over 2000 years people thought these were good ideas.
Then in the 1600s some scientists began to think about it again.
They thought that burning depended on the air.
But they believed the air was one single substance.

Robert Boyle heated some tin in a sealed flask.
When the seal was broken, the tin weighed more than before heating.
Boyle thought the particles of fire had lodged between the particles of tin.

Georg Stahl (1660–1734) was a German scientist. He developed another idea. It was called the phlogiston theory (from the Greek phlox=flame).

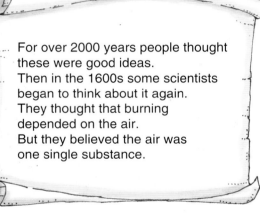

Every substance that burns has 2 parts — ash and PHLOGISTON.

When something burns the PHLOGISTON escapes. The ash is left behind.

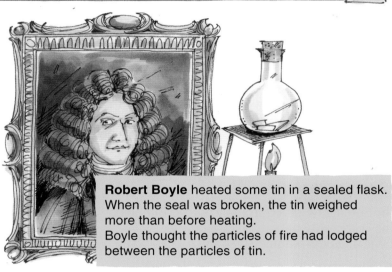

But this burnt charcoal has only left a little ash.

That's because it contains so much PHLOGISTON!

In the early 1700s, the phlogiston theory was thought to be a great idea. But it didn't explain everything. Many materials like Boyle's tin, **gained** weight after heating. They should have been **losing** phlogiston. The theory must be wrong.

Antoine Lavoisier was a French scientist. He worked with his wife. Together they worked on the problem of burning. They knew the phlogiston theory wasn't quite right.

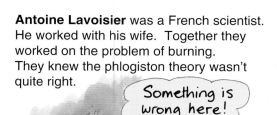

Something is wrong here!

Lavoisier heated sulphur. He found that the sulphur gained weight when it burnt. He thought the air was combining with the sulphur. But it needed a visit from **Joseph Priestley** in 1774 to help Lavoisier to understand.

This is the piece of apparatus Lavoisier used for his early burning experiments. How do you think it works?

Joseph Priestley worked in England. He heated mercury in air. He made a red substance. When he heated the red substance he got a new gas.

Priestley went to France to tell Lavoisier about the gas. Lavoisier repeated and improved Priestley's experiments. He soon understood the results. Air must be more than one gas. One gas is needed for burning. This is oxygen.

This gas lets things burn very brightly in it.

When a substance burns it combines with oxygen in the air.

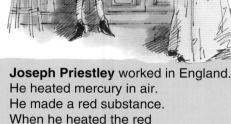

MERCURY

Things to do

1 Read about Robert Boyle's experiment.
a) Suppose Boyle had reweighed his heated flask **before** breaking the seal. What do you think he would have found?
b) Why did the flask weigh more **after** the seal was broken?

2 Supporters of the phlogiston theory argued strongly with those who disagreed. Write a cartoon strip to show an argument between 2 scientists in the 1700s. One scientist believes the phlogiston theory, the other does not.

3 Lavoisier was working during the French Revolution. Find out what life was like in France at this time. What problems would scientists have had?

4 Lavoisier was sentenced to death after the French Revolution. He had become a hated tax collector for the government. Revolutionaries wanted him dead. The judge said "The Republic has no need of men of science." Do you think your country has "no need of scientists?" Explain your views.

5 Lavoisier found that only some of the air was used up when mercury was heated in air.
a) Design some apparatus which he could have used to show this.
b) What percentage of the air is oxygen?
c) Oxygen is a very useful gas. How is pure oxygen separated from the air?

Two's company

Legoland

Lego can make lots of different things.
The pieces are building blocks.

A few **elements** can make lots of **compounds**.
The elements are the building blocks.

In Book 8 you learnt about elements and compounds.

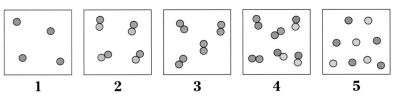

Elements have only one type of atom.
Compounds have two or more
different atoms joined together.

a Which boxes contain the elements?

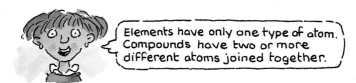

1   **2**   **3**   **4**   **5**

▶ Here are some formulas for compounds. See if you can work out their names.

b MgO   **d** HCl   **f** CO_2
c $CuCl_2$ **e** FeS   **g** H_2O

▶ Look around the room.
h Write down some of the compounds you can see.
i Write down some of the elements you can see.

Most elements are not found on their own. They are in compounds.

Some common compounds

Making a new compound (1)

Take a piece of clean copper foil.
Hold it in tongs.
Heat it in a medium Bunsen flame for about 3 minutes.
Take it out of the flame.
Leave it to cool on a heat-resistant mat.

⚠ heat
eye protection

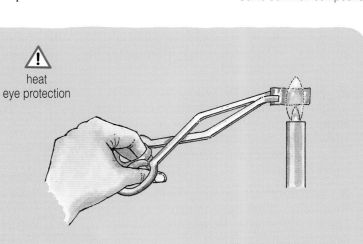

j Write down everything you see.
k Is there a reaction?
l Copy and complete this word equation:

copper + oxygen ⟶ ....
        (from air)

Making a new compound (2)

Follow the instructions opposite to make a new compound:

m   Write down everything you see.

n   How do you know there is a reaction?

The symbol equation is:
$CuO + H_2SO_4 \longrightarrow CuSO_4 + H_2O$

o   Copy and complete the word equation:
. . . . + sulphuric acid $\longrightarrow$ copper sulphate + ...

Half fill a test-tube with dilute sulphuric acid.
Add one spatula measure of copper oxide.
Stir the liquid.
Leave the tube in your
rack for 5 minutes.

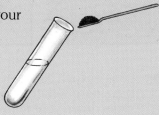

acid
eye protection

Making a new compound (3)

Follow the instructions opposite to make a new compound:

p   Write down everything you see.

q   How do you know there is a reaction?

r   Copy and complete the word equation:
. . . . + copper sulphate $\longrightarrow$ zinc sulphate + ...

s   Copy and complete the symbol equation:
$Zn + ... \longrightarrow ZnSO_4 + ...$

t   Do you think copper will react with zinc sulphate?
Explain your answer. Test out your prediction.

Half fill a test-tube with copper sulphate solution.
Put a piece of zinc into the tube.
Stir the liquid.
Leave the tube in your
rack for 5 minutes.

eye protection

Breaking compounds

When elements join together they make compounds.
It is not easy to get the elements back.

Look at this sample of copper sulphate crystals:
Copper sulphate has the formula $CuSO_4$.
It contains copper, sulphur and oxygen. How could you get the
copper out? Discuss this in your group. Write down your ideas.
Your teacher may let you try some of them.

1   Copy and complete:
a)   . . . . have only one type of atom.
b)   . . . . have 2 or more different atoms
      joined together.
c)   Magnesium can react with oxygen in the
      air. The word equation is:
      . . . . + ... $\longrightarrow$ . . . .
d)   The formula of . . . . is MgO.

2   Draw a table like this:

Element	Compound

Put these in the correct column:
chlorine   glass   gold
sugar   iron oxide   sulphur
carbon   copper sulphate

3   Look at Ann's science homework.

> I lit a spill. I put it into a tube
> of hydrogen gas. The gas
> reacted with oxygen in the air.
> I saw a flash. I heard a 'pop'
> sound. I made some water
> in the tube.

From Ann's work:
a)   Write the names of 2 elements.
b)   Write the name of 1 compound.
c)   Was there a reaction?
      How do you know?
d)   Write a word equation.

Things to do

It's a fix

▶ Look at each statement below.
Is it a description of an element? Is it possible to tell?
Write down your ideas. Use a code for each answer: ✓ for *element*
? for *not possible to tell*
✗ for *non-element*.

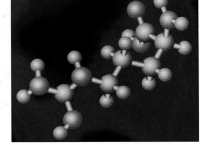

a made of only one type of atom
b is called water
c looks shiny
d made of atoms
e gives off carbon dioxide when heated

f made of molecules
g has the symbol Sn
h has the symbol O_2
i has the formula CO
j has the formula FeS

▶ Discuss the ideas with others in your group. Do you all agree?

Researching compounds

Use books or ROMs to find out which elements make up these compounds:

k PVC   l paper   m candle wax   n Teflon

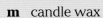

How much of each?

Compounds are made when elements join together.
But **how much** of each element?

Magnesium reacts with oxygen in the air.
But how much of each reacts?

Look at the diagram. This apparatus could help you find out.

magnesium + oxygen ⟶ magnesium oxide

In this experiment you need to know how much magnesium you start with. You then need to know how much magnesium oxide you make.
How do you think you can do this using the apparatus drawn?
Discuss this in your group.

Your teacher will give you an instruction sheet.
Read through all the instructions before you start.
This is a difficult experiment. Your results will tell your teacher how well you have done it!

⚠️ Do not look directly at burning magnesium

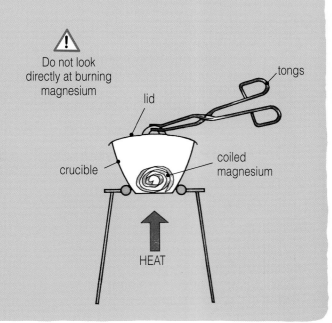

tongs
lid
crucible
coiled magnesium
HEAT

How much of each? – The results

Each group should have a result. Your teacher will collect these from all the groups.
Copy the class results into a table like this one:

Group	Mass of magnesium at start in grams	Mass of magnesium oxide at end in grams
A		
B		
C		
D		

Draw a graph of the results.

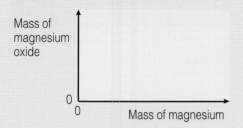

What do you notice? Can you see a pattern in your results?

Magnesium reacts with oxygen. The masses of each element which combine are in **proportion**.
A fixed amount of magnesium always combines with a fixed amount of oxygen. The compound has **fixed composition**.
The compound always has the formula MgO.

▶ Copy and complete the table. The first one has been done for you.

Name	Formula	Number of each type of atom	
aluminium chloride	$AlCl_3$	1 aluminium	3 chlorine
magnesium oxide	MgO		
sodium fluoride	NaF		
	Al_2O_3		
	H_2O		
		1 carbon	4 chlorine

Things to do

1 Copy and complete:
Compounds have . . . . composition. They have a fixed formula. The . . . . for carbon dioxide is CO_2. It has . . . . carbon atom and . . . . oxygen atoms.

2 Draw a room where you live. You can draw people and furniture in your room. Label 10 objects in the room. Say what they are made from. Say whether they are elements or compounds.

3 Luke made a graph of some class results.

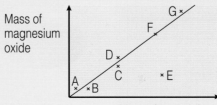

a) Which group had a strange result? What do you think went wrong?
b) Which 2 groups started with the same amount of magnesium?

Mixed or fixed?

In a compound, two or more elements join together.
But how much do you remember about **mixtures**?

▶ Look at these ideas about mixtures and compounds.

One substance only

Made of 2 or more substances

Composition can vary

Easy to separate into elements

Fixed composition

Difficult to separate into elements. A reaction is needed.

Draw a table like this:
Write each idea in the correct column.
(You should have 3 in each.)

Mixture	Compound

Lots of natural substances are mixtures.
Some are mixtures of elements. Some are mixtures of compounds.
Often the mixtures must be separated before we can use them.

I'm not keen on the local water. Are you?

a How could you improve the water?

I ♥ SCIENCE

You should have separated Your air!

b Which gas is in Lisa's balloon?

I'm having a few problems with the car!

CRUDE OIL

c How could you get the petrol?

▶ Look at these photos. They are about mixtures.
Can you explain the separations?

g How can you get the cream from the milk?

This is a hot country.
You can get salt from sea-water.

d How is the salt separated from the sea?

Salt is sodium chloride NaCl.

e Will it be easy to get chlorine from salt? Explain your answer.

This is a filter coffee maker.

f How does it work?

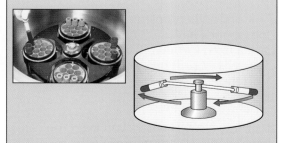

This is a centrifuge. It is used to separate blood cells from plasma.

h How do you think it works?

Separating dyes

In this experiment you will use **chromatography** to separate dyes in inks. Inks are often a mixture of dyes. You can try this with felt-tip pen or fountain pen inks.

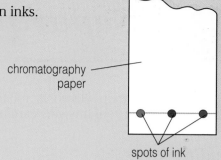

chromatography paper

spots of ink

- Cut a piece of chromatography paper to fit inside a beaker. Draw a faint pencil line about 1 cm above the bottom of the paper.

- Carefully use a felt-tip pen or a teat-pipette to spot some ink on the line. Put the spot about 1 cm away from the edge. Make the spot about 2 or 3 mm in diameter.

- Leaving 1 cm spaces, put spots of other inks on the line.

- Carefully put about 0.5 cm depth of water in your beaker. Try not to wet the sides of the beaker.

- Now put your chromatography paper in the beaker as shown in the diagram. Wrap the top of the paper round a pencil to keep it upright in the water.

- Let the water soak up the paper. Take the paper out when the water is nearly at the top of the paper.

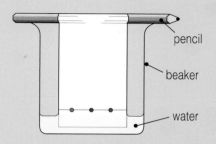

pencil

beaker

water

i Why must the ink spots be above the level of water at the start?

j Why do you think the different dyes separate during chromatography?

k How could you improve this experiment to get a better separation?

Make a table to show your results:

Colour of ink	Number of dyes in ink	Colour of dyes in ink

---

1 Copy and complete.
Choose a word from the box:

> mixture   easy
> hard   compound

a) A . . . . has fixed composition.
b) In a . . . . the elements or compounds do not combine.
c) It is . . . . to separate a compound into its elements.
d) Usually a mixture is . . . . to separate.

2 Look at the properties of A, B and C.
How would you separate a mixture of them?

Substance	Dissolves in cold water?	Dissolves in hot water?
A	✗	✓
B	✗	✗
C	✓	✓

3 Why can we use this to strain tea but not coffee?

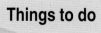

4 Chromatography can show which dyes are in different coloured inks.

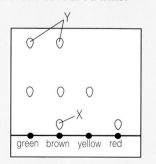

green   brown   yellow   red

a) Which 2 inks contain only one dye?
b) Which ink contains 3 dyes?
c) Which colour would the spot X be?
d) Predict which colour the spots labelled Y would be.

Things to do

45

Separating

27f

How much do you know about elements, mixtures and compounds? Try out these exercises.
Make sure you write down your answers carefully. There's lots to do here!

Spot the difference

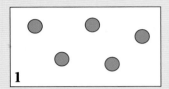

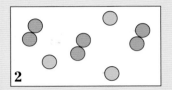

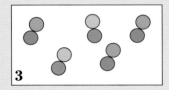

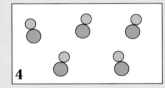

Which of these do you think is:

a an element?

b a mixture of elements?

c a compound?

d a mixture of compounds?

Colour me in

Get a copy of the periodic table.
Think about the elements you know.
Colour the metals in blue.
Colour the non-metals in red.

Find the element

Make up your own word search for elements.
Write the names of the elements horizontally (across) or vertically (down).
Hide at least 6 elements in the middle of other letters.
Keep a record of your answers.
Let someone else in your group try the word search

Look for clues

Here are 2 elements, one mixture of them and one compound of them.

e Name the non-metal element.

f Which is the mixture of iron and sulphur?

g Which is the compound?

h How could you get iron from the mixture?

Now 2 more difficult questions:

i How could you get sulphur from the mixture? You must use a different method to **h**!

j What is the compound called?

Try a reaction

⚠ eye protection

Fill a test-tube a third full with dilute acid.
Add a 1 cm piece of magnesium ribbon.
Write down what you see.

Can you remember the Reactivity Series?

Think about the zebra in Book 8.

k Which metals react faster than magnesium with acid?

l Which metals are not so reactive with acid?

Copy and complete the word equations.
(Think first. Do they react?)

m magnesium + copper sulphate ⟶

n magnesium + sodium chloride ⟶

A complete wreck

Read this extract from the *Dove Times*.

Experts were worried last night. A strange mixture was found on Dove Beach. A local man thinks it is from the ship *The Red Lady*. It was wrecked a few months ago down the coast. It was made of iron. It carried a cargo of salt and limestone. But sand from the beach may be in the mixture too.

Plan an investigation to get the pure substances from the mixture.
Try to get pure iron, salt and sand.
Show your plan to your teacher.
If it is safe, you can carry out your investigation.

Needing water

The crew from *The Red Lady* might be in trouble!
In order to survive, they need pure water.
The apparatus opposite will help!

o Copy the diagram. Label the apparatus.

p What is the process called?

q Explain the process. Use the words: evaporate, condense.

r What does the thermometer do?

s How do you know the water is pure?

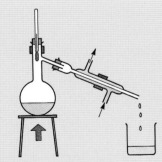

This apparatus gets pure water from sea-water.

1 Copy and complete. Use the words in the box:

elements	metals	compounds
reactive	unreactive	non-metals

a) Pure substances are . . . . or . . . .
b) Elements can be . . . . or . . . .
c) Some metals are . . . . e.g. Mg.
d) Some metals are . . . . e.g. Cu.

2 Imagine you have discovered a new element. Describe 4 tests you could do to see if it is a metal or a non-metal.

3 Predict if a reaction will take place:
a) copper + magnesium oxide
b) zinc + potassium chloride
c) zinc + copper sulphate.
Write word equations for the reactions.
(You could try symbol equations too.)

Things to do

Chemistry at Work

Elements and compounds

Sulphur

Sulphur is used in the first step in making sulphuric acid. Molten sulphur is sprayed into a furnace and burned in a blast of hot air.

a Which gas in the air does the sulphur react with**?**

b Write a word equation to show what happens when sulphur burns in air.

c Why do the gases given off from a factory making sulphuric acid have to be carefully monitored**?**

Look at the table below showing the uses of sulphuric acid:

Uses of sulphuric acid	Percentage used (%)
Making new chemicals	25.7
Paints and pigments	21.6
Detergents and soaps	13.3
Fertilisers	11.2
Plastics	7.0
Fibres	5.3
Dyes	2.8
Other uses	

d Work out the percentage of sulphuric acid that should be under the heading 'Other uses' in the table above.

e Use a computer to display the uses of sulphuric acid in a pie-chart.

Magnesium

Magnesium is used in fireworks and flares.

f What is the colour of the flame produced when magnesium burns**?**

g Write a word equation for magnesium burning.

h The makers of fireworks want magnesium to burn more quickly than a piece of magnesium ribbon. What can they do to the magnesium to make this happen**?**

Helium and oxygen

Did you know that helium is used by deep-sea divers?
It is mixed with oxygen gas for divers to breathe in.
This is safer than breathing in normal air which
contains nitrogen. The nitrogen can dissolve in a
diver's blood and can form a bubble as the diver
rises to the surface. This can kill the diver.

i Which gas do you think is more soluble in blood,
nitrogen or helium? Why do you think this?

j What do divers call it when a bubble of gas is
formed in their circulatory system?

k What happens to the voice of a diver breathing in
a mixture of oxygen and helium?

l Find out about and explain another use of helium.

Alloys

An alloy is a *mixture of metals*.
Alloys are made to improve the properties of a metal.
For example, steel is an alloy of iron.
It has traces of carbon mixed with the iron, but can
also have other metals added.
Tungsten mixed in makes the steel very hard and
is used to make cutting tools.
Cobalt and nickel are added to make stainless steel,
which does not rust.

m Which type of steel would you use to make
the sharp edge of a lathe in your technology
department?

n Name some objects that are made from stainless
steel.

o Why do you think cars aren't made from stainless steel?

p The atoms of a pure metal are all the same size
and packed closely together in layers.
Explain why adding atoms of a different size
might make it more difficult to bend the metal.

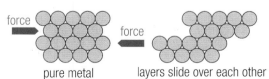

force → pure metal   ← force layers slide over each other easily in a pure metal

q Find out about the alloys used to make aeroplanes
or the alloys used to make coins.

Ideas about elements, mixtures & compounds

The famous Greek philosopher **Aristotle** had a theory about the basic building blocks of all substances.
He believed that everything was made up from different combinations of:

- earth,
- fire, and
- air,
- water.

These ideas were put forward around 350 BC, but were not developed much further for centuries.
Nobody could come up with any better way to explain the different properties of materials.

The alchemists

It wasn't until about 775 AD that Aristotle's ideas were eventually refined. An Islamic **alchemist** called **Jabir Ibn Haiyan** accepted the Greek ideas. He liked the theory but needed to modify it to explain his own observations and experiments.
The alchemists were very interested in gold. One of their aims was to turn other metals into gold. In their efforts to achieve this, they carried out thousands of experiments. The Islamic alchemists translated the works of the ancient Greeks and used their ideas to guide their experiments.
They were the first to see the important link between theory and experiment. In fact, Jabir is sometimes called the **Father of Chemistry**.
According to Greek theory, minerals and metals are mixtures of earth (on the way to becoming fire) and water (on the way to becoming air). The 'earthy' bit dominates in minerals, and the 'watery' bit dominates in metals.

Jabir changed the idea slightly.
He said that deep underground the 'earthy' bits are changed into sulphur (a brittle, yellow non-metal).
The 'watery' bits are changed into mercury (the silvery, liquid metal you've seen in thermometers).
Then the sulphur and the mercury combine to form one of 6 metals that they knew about.
These were iron, lead, copper, tin, silver, and, of course, gold. The metals were different because they contained different amounts of sulphur and mercury.
The sulphur and mercury might also be impure in some metals.

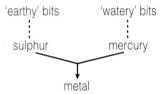

Jabir described gold as the perfect combination of pure sulphur and mercury. With his theory, it now made sense to think that you could treat one metal and convert it into another.
If you came up with the perfect combination, you hit the jackpot and made gold!

The theory inspired alchemists for hundreds of years to carry on the search for the way to change a cheap metal, such as lead, into gold.
But they never did succeed!

Questions

1 What did the Greeks believe about the way matter is made up?

2 The Greeks also had ideas about disease and illness, based on their ideas about matter.
Imagine you are an ancient Greek doctor.
Your patient has a very high fever.
Explain to them what you think is wrong and suggest a treatment.

3 Why do you think that Jabir is called the **Father of Chemistry**?

4 Explain why Jabir might have had his theory about metals, after looking at a piece of gold.

5 Why did the alchemists never manage to change lead into gold?

6 Jabir made many important discoveries.
Do some research and present a poster on Jabir's contribution to chemistry.
(You will find other references about him under the name Geber. This was how his name was translated when European scientists discovered his work centuries later.)

Revision Summary

Elements

- Everything is made from very small particles called atoms.
  An element contains only one type of atom.
  Elements are simple substances. They cannot be broken down into anything simpler.

- Each element has a symbol,
  e.g. carbon is **C**, magnesium is **Mg**, iron is **Fe**.

- All the elements can be arranged in the periodic table.
  The columns of elements in the table are groups.
  The rows are periods.

- All the elements in a group have similar properties.
  They often react in the same way.

- There are 2 main types of element: metals and non-metals.
  Examples of metals are: copper, magnesium, tin, sodium.
  Examples of non-metals are: oxygen, hydrogen, carbon, sulphur.

- Metals are usually hard, shiny solids.
  They often have high melting points.
  They are good conductors of heat and good conductors of electricity.
  A few metals are magnetic, e.g. iron.

- Non-metals are usually gases or solids with low melting points. Most are poor conductors of heat and electricity. They are insulators.
  The solids are often brittle (they break easily).

- Metals are found on the left-hand side of the periodic table.
  Non-metals are found on the right-hand side.

Compounds and mixtures

- Each element contains only one type of atom. Compounds have 2 or more different atoms joined together.

- When atoms join together they make molecules.

molecules of the element nitrogen, N_2 molecules of the compound water, H_2O

- Elements combine to make compounds.
  This happens in a chemical reaction.
  We can show a chemical reaction by a word equation:
  e.g. magnesium + oxygen → magnesium oxide

- A compound has a fixed composition.
  Each compound has its own formula,
  e.g. magnesium oxide is always MgO.

- A mixture contains more than one substance.
  It does not have a fixed composition.
  The parts that make up the mixture are not combined, e.g. air is a mixture of nitrogen, oxygen, carbon dioxide and other substances.

- Usually we can separate a mixture into pure substances. Methods we can use are:
  - filtration
    (to separate an insoluble solid from a liquid)
  - distillation
    (to separate pure liquids from solutions)
  - chromatography
    (to separate mixtures of colours).

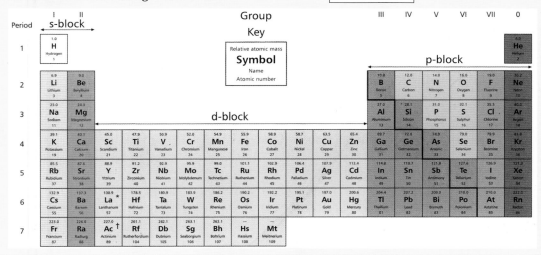

Questions

1

In the outline of the periodic table, the numbers represent elements.
Give the **numbers** of:
a) 3 elements in the same period
b) 3 elements in the same group
c) 2 metals with similar properties
d) 2 non-metals with similar properties
e) the most reactive metal.

2 Name an element in each case which:
a) is a gas at room temperature and made of molecules
b) is always present in sulphides
c) is a non-metal and a liquid at room temperature
d) has the symbol N
e) is a more reactive metal than sodium
f) is present in all the molecules opposite.

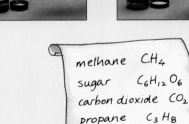

methane CH_4
sugar $C_6H_{12}O_6$
carbon dioxide CO_2
propane C_3H_8
ethanol C_2H_5OH

3 Copy and complete these word equations:
a) magnesium + sulphur $\longrightarrow$ _____ _____
b) zinc + iron sulphate $\longrightarrow$ _____ _____ + _____
c) magnesium + _____ oxide $\longrightarrow$ _____ _____ + copper
d) zinc oxide + sulphuric acid $\longrightarrow$ _____ _____ + water

Can you write symbol equations too?

4 How can you get pure sulphur and pure salt from a mixture of them?
What apparatus would you need? What would you do?
Use diagrams to help you to explain.

5 a) Name the compound made when iron reacts with chlorine.
b) Give 2 differences between iron metal and compounds containing iron.
c) Which is more reactive, iron or magnesium?
Write about 2 experiments you could do to find out.
What apparatus would you use?
What measurements would you make?
What results would you expect?

Salt and Sulphur on your chips?

6 This is a chromatogram of black ink:
Explain how the chromatogram is made.

The active body

Top sportsmen and sportswomen train hard to develop their strength and stamina.
They also need balance, quick reactions, agility and speed. These are important to all of us, however fit we are.

In this topic you will look at the important systems that make up your active body.

28a The shape you're in

"I may be bony, but where would you be without me?"

What keeps you in shape? In a word – **bones**.
But not all animals have bones.

a   Can you name 3 animals that don't have any bones at all?

Larger animals need lots of bones to keep them in shape.
They need a **skeleton**.

b   Write down some ways in which your skeleton helps you.

▶   Your teacher can give you a Help Sheet to find the bones
in your body.
But you don't have to find them all – there are over 200!
Without your skeleton, you would feel really let down!

Protection racket

The bones of your skeleton protect important organs in your body.

c   Which part of your skeleton protects your brain?
d   Which organs are protected by your ribs?

A great supporting act

Your main supporting bones are shaped like tubes.

- Balance a straw between 2 clamp stands.
- Measure the length of your straw.
- Hang a weight holder from the middle of your straw.
- Carefully add slotted weights until the straw collapses.
- Record the weight needed to bend the straw.
- Now repeat the test with half-length and quarter-length straws.

How does the length of the straw change its strength?

Joints

▶ Try walking without bending your knees, keeping your legs quite straight.
It's not very easy is it?
So how do you think we move our bones?
Bones can move at **joints**.

Look at these different types of joints:

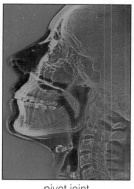
pivot joint

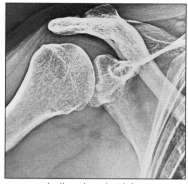
ball and socket joint

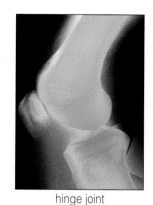
hinge joint

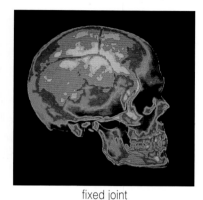
fixed joint

Where do you think they are found in your body?
What type of movement can you make at these joints?

▶ Copy and complete this table with your answers:

Type of joint	Where found	Type of movement
pivot	neck	nodding or turning
ball and socket		
hinge		
fixed		

Things to do

1 Copy and complete:
The . . . . in your skeleton protect many important . . . . in your body.
Bones also allow . . . . to occur at joints.
Your elbow is an example of a . . . . joint and your shoulder is an example of a . . . . and . . . . joint. Many bones are shaped like a tube. This is a good shape to . . . . your body.

2 Use your Help Sheet to find:
a) the largest bone in your body, and
b) the smallest, bone in your body.
On your Help Sheet:
c) label as many bones as you can, and
d) shade in red the bones that protect important organs.

3 Find out as much as you can about what these do:
a) **tendons** b) **ligaments** c) **cartilage**.

4 X-rays can penetrate through skin and soft tissue but not so easily through bones. X-rays can help doctors to find out if bones are broken.
a) Which bones are fractured in this X-ray?
b) How do you think the patient will be treated to repair the broken bones?
c) When an X-ray is taken of the gut, the patient drinks a liquid that will not let X-rays through. Why do you think this is?

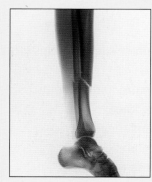

Muscles and movement

Are you as muscular as the woman in the photograph?
Probably not. But you still have over 350 muscles that do
important jobs.

a How do you think the body-builder has developed such
   powerful muscles?

Your muscles provide the force needed to move bones at **joints**.

▶ Feel your calf muscle at the back of your leg.
   Now lift your heel but keep your toes on the floor.
   Can you feel your muscle pulling?

No pushing!

Muscles cannot **push** – they can only **pull**.

Push up against the underside of the bench with the front of your hand.

b What does your **biceps muscle** feel like?

When it pulls it gets shorter and fatter – we say that it **contracts**.

Now push down with the back of your hand against the bench-top.

c What does your **triceps muscle** feel like?

Your triceps contracts to pull your arm straight.

When a muscle is not contracting, it returns to normal size.
We say that it **relaxes**.

Muscles like your biceps and triceps work in pairs.
When one contracts the other relaxes.
We say that they are **antagonistic**.

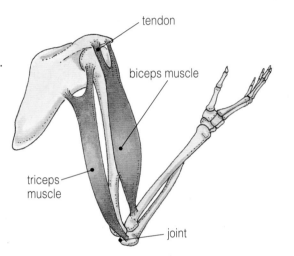

tendon

biceps muscle

triceps
muscle

joint

▶ Copy and fill in the table to show which muscle contracts and which relaxes:

	Biceps muscle	Triceps muscle
Pushing up with the front of your hand		
Pushing down with the back of your hand		

Muscles at work

The pictures show how a sprinter's leg muscles work
at the start of a race.

▶ Look carefully at each picture and find out:

d Which muscle **bends** the knee.

e Which muscle **straightens** the knee.

f Which muscle **bends** the ankle.

g Which muscle **straightens** the ankle.

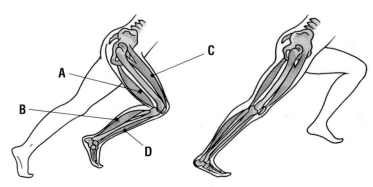

A

B

C

D

Mighty movers

You can test your finger strength in this investigation.

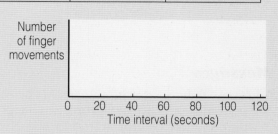
rubber band

clamp stand

- Arrange the clamp stand as shown.
- Place your hand flat on the table.
- Put your middle finger through the rubber band.
- Now move your finger down to touch the table.
- Count the number of these finger movements you can do continuously for 2 minutes.
  Be sure to touch the table each time and keep your hand flat.
- Record the number of finger movements for each 20-second period in a table like this:

Time interval (seconds)	0–20	20–40	40–60	60–80	80–100	100–120
Number of finger movements						

h Plot a line-graph with axes like this:

i What sort of pattern was there to your results?

j Try to explain any pattern that you observed.

Number of finger movements

0   20   40   60   80   100   120
Time interval (seconds)

---

1 Copy and complete:
Your . . . . provide the force to move . . . . at joints.
A muscle cannot . . . . ; it can only . . . .
When a muscle pulls it gets . . . . and fat.
We say that it . . . .
When a muscle is not contracting we say that it . . . .

2 Plan an investigation to find out whether exercise or diet is more important in increasing muscle size.

3 Make a model of an arm using your Help Sheet.
Glue the sheet onto cardboard and cut out the shapes of the bones. Join them together with a paper fastener. Use elastic bands for the muscles.
How much weight will your model support? Try to evaluate how much your model works like the real thing.

Things to do

Moving parts

What happens if you accidently touch a hot iron?
If you have any sense, you move away!

a How quickly do you move away?

b Why do you think that you move away quickly?

c How do you think that this happens?

You pull your hand away so quickly because messages are sent around your nervous system at high speed. These tell you what is happening and what to do. This is an automatic action because you do it without thinking.

An **automatic** action like this is called a **reflex**.

Messages

You know that muscles move parts of your body.
But your muscles have to be **told** when and how to work.
Your muscles are controlled by messages that travel along **nerves**.

▶ Look at the diagram:

d What is it that detects the heat of the iron?

e Our skin is a **sense organ**.
Do you know any other sense organs in your body?

f What do you think happens when the messages reach the brain and spinal cord?

g What happens when the messages reach the muscle?

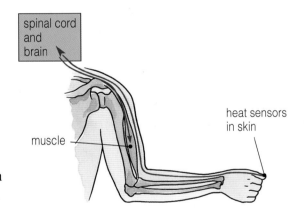

spinal cord and brain

heat sensors in skin

muscle

Reducing the friction

Your bones move a lot at **synovial joints**.
At these joints, there are tough **ligaments**.
The ends of the bones have a layer of **cartilage**.
Synovial fluid covers the surface of the cartilage.

▶ Look at this diagram of the hip joint:

Which part of this synovial joint do you think:

h holds the bones together?

i reduces friction?

j holds the synovial fluid in place?

k acts as a shock absorber?

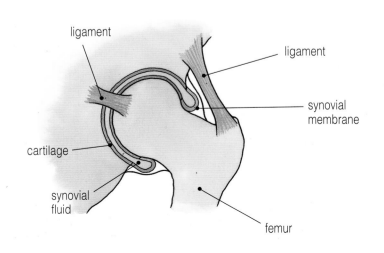

ligament

ligament

synovial membrane

cartilage

synovial fluid

femur

There's a catch

How fast are your reactions?
Do you think they speed up with practice?

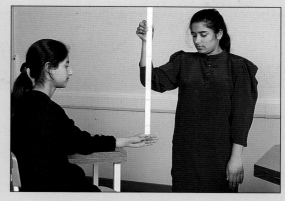

You can measure your reaction time with a falling ruler, as shown in the photograph:

- First add a time scale to the ruler.
  Your teacher will give you a Help Sheet for this.

- Then place your arm on the bench as shown:
  Your partner holds the ruler with the zero next to your little finger, but **not** touching it.
  When your partner lets go of the ruler, try to catch it as quickly as possible.
  Read the scale next to your little finger.
  This shows how long you took.

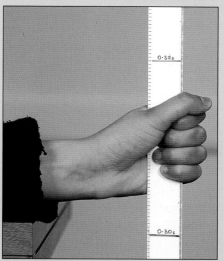

- Now repeat this test 10 times.
  You can record your times in a table like this:

Trial	Time (seconds)	
	Ruler not touching hand	Ruler touching hand
1		
2		

- Now do it another 10 times, but with the ruler now just **touching** your hand.

l What happened to your reaction time with practice?

m Was your reaction time quicker with or without the ruler touching your hand?
Why do you think this is?

n Which of your sense organs were you using?

o Can you change the test so that you use only your hearing?

---

1 Copy and complete:
Sense . . . . in our bodies sends messages at . . . . speed through our . . . .
The messages get our . . . . to move our bodies.
When our nerves work in this way it is called a . . . . action.
Our reflexes are automatic. They work very . . . . and often . . . . us from harm.

2 a) What is meant by your reaction time?
b) Name 3 sports in which you think that reaction time is:
i) important   ii) not important.
c) If you were a tennis player, how could you try to improve your reaction time?

3 Which animals have quick reflexes?
Give some examples of situations where animals need quick reactions in nature.

4 How do you think each of the following can affect a person's reaction time:
a) tiredness? b) coffee (caffeine)?
c) alcohol? d) practice?

Things to do

Who's sensitive?

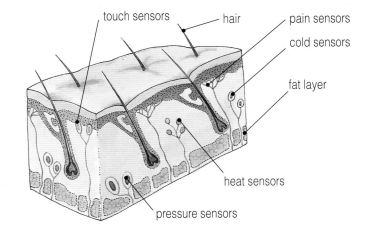

Your skin covers the whole of the outside of your body.
There's about 2 square metres of it.
It acts as a **barrier** between your insides and the air outside.
Write down how you think your skin helps you.

Skin structure

▶ Look at the picture of part of your skin magnified:

touch sensors   hair   pain sensors
cold sensors
fat layer
heat sensors
pressure sensors

a What sort of things is your skin sensitive to?
What can it feel?

b What do you think the hairs are for?

c Why do you think the fat layer is important?

Test the water

Put one hand into a bowl of iced water and the other into a bowl of warm water.
Keep them there for 1 minute.
Now put both hands into a bowl of water at room temperature.

d What did each hand **feel** like when you took it out of the first bowl?

e What did each hand **look** like when you took it out of the first bowl?

f How did each hand **feel** when you put it into the second bowl?
Try to explain your observations.

Raising a sweat

Andy has just had a hard game of squash.
He looks sweaty and his face is flushed.

g Why do you think that he sweats after he exercises?

He looks flushed because more blood gets to the surface of his skin.

h Why do you think this happens?

i Andy gets changed and goes out into the cold winter weather.
How do you think his skin changes?

j Why do you think this happens?

Get the point?

Your skin contains lots of tiny **touch sensors**.
Which parts of your hand and arm are most sensitive to touch?

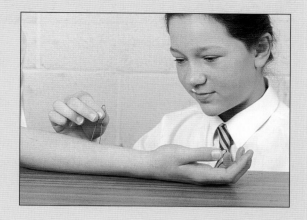

- Bend a hair-pin until the points are 5 mm apart.
- Blindfold your partner.
- Gently touch your partner's fore-arm with either 1 or 2 points of the hair-pin.
  Your partner has to say whether they can feel 1 point or 2 points.
- Now repeat this 5 times choosing either 1 point or 2 points each time.
- Record the number of correct choices with a tick in a table like the one below.
- Repeat, this time touching the back of your partner's hand and then their fingertip.
- Now bend the hair-pin to 2 cm apart and repeat the whole exercise again.

Part of body	Hair-pin 5 mm apart	Hair-pin 2 cm apart
Fore-arm		
Back of hand		
Fingertip		

k Which part of your skin do you think was:
- most sensitive?
- least sensitive?

l What does this tell you about the number of touch sensors in each part?

m Plan an investigation to find out which part of your hand and arm is most sensitive to temperature.
Show your plan to your teacher, and then try it out.

1

	A	B	C	D	E	F	G	H	I	J	K	L	M

	N	O	P	Q	R	S	T	U	V	W	X	Y	Z

Blind people are able to read by using **Braille**. Each letter of the alphabet is shown by a pattern of 6 dots.
Can you work out what this says?

2 a) What are the 5 senses?
b) If you were riding on a bus, which of these 5 senses would let you know that you were moving?

3 Copy and complete:
Your skin acts as a barrier. It prevents the loss of . . . . by evaporation. It also stops harmful . . . . from entering your body. The hairs and the . . . . layer insulate the skin and reduce the amount of . . . . lost. Sensors in your skin are sensitive to . . . ., pressure and . . . .

4 Find out as much as you can about the following:
a) skin grafts
b) a chemical in the skin called **melanin**
c) finger-prints.

Things to do

Keeping in control

Keeping warm

▶ Look at the thermal image photograph:
It shows which areas of the body give out most energy.

a Which parts of your body lose energy most easily?

b How does the mountaineer in the photograph cut down this heat energy loss?

Air is a good **insulator**.

c How is the mountaineer's clothing designed to trap air?

d The best types of sleeping bag are made out of duck-down. Why do you think that this is better than synthetic fibres?

Body size and cooling

Do small animals lose heat energy more quickly than large animals?

- Half fill a 250 cm³ beaker and a 100 cm³ beaker with hot water.
- Place a temperature sensor in each beaker.
- Record the temperature of each beaker and start logging.
- Record the temperature of each beaker every 2 minutes over the next 20 minutes.
- Plot your results on graph paper.

e How does the graph show that one beaker cools faster than the other?

f Measure the graph to show how much each beaker cools in 15 minutes.

g Why do you think one beaker lost energy more quickly?

h How could you improve this experiment to make it more accurate?

i Who do you think would lose heat energy more quickly in cold weather, a baby or an adult?

computer

interface

250 cm³ beaker   100 cm³ beaker   stop-clock

Which do you think gives better insulation: fur or feathers?
Plan an investigation and use temperature sensors to find out.

Keeping your cool

On hot days a lot of heat energy escapes from your body by **sweating**.
As the sweat dries, it takes heat energy from your skin.

▶ Look carefully at the graph:

j At what temperature is the amount of sweat and urine the same?

k If the temperature rises, what happens to the amount of sweat produced? Explain the reason for this.

l If the temperature rises, what happens to the amount of urine produced? Explain the reason for this.

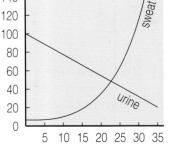

Quantity of urine/sweat produced (cm³/h)

sweat

urine

5 10 15 20 25 30 35
Outside temperature (°C)

Controlling body water

The amount of water in your body is controlled by your **kidneys**.
If you have any extra water in your body, your blood takes it to your kidneys.
The kidneys take the extra water out of the blood to make **urine**.

m Where in your body are your kidneys**?**

n Where do you think your urine is stored before it leaves your body**?**

o How does your urine get from your kidneys to your **bladder?**

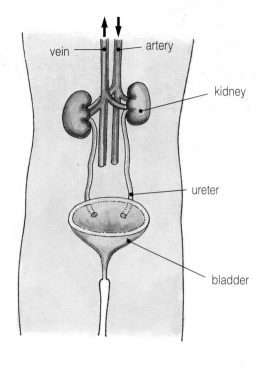

Our kidneys also filter chemical waste out of our bodies.
Most of this waste is in the form of **urea**.

▶ Look at the table:

	Blood concentration (g/l)	Urine concentration (g/l)
Water	900	950
Protein	70	0
Glucose	0.3	0
Urea	3.0	20

p Explain the difference in the amounts of urea in the blood and in the urine.

q Explain the differences in i) the amounts of glucose
and ii) the amounts of protein.

r What could cause the volume of water in the urine to   i)   increase**?**
ii) decrease**?**

---

1 Copy and complete:
Our average body temperature is . . . .°C. On hot days we lose . . . . and so keep our body temperature . . . . Also more . . . . gets to the surface of our . . . . to lose heat energy.
Small animals cool . . . . more quickly than larger animals. Our . . . . control the amount of water in our . . . . They also get rid of . . . . chemicals like urea.

2 A **dialysis machine** is used to treat patients with kidneys that are not working properly. Copy this simple diagram and use it to explain how chemical waste, like urea, is removed from a patient's blood.

3 When our body temperature falls below 35°C, we get **hypothermia**.
Which types of people do you think are most at risk from hypothermia?
Explain how the following are important in preventing hypothermia:
a) type of clothing   b) a hot meal   c) heating.

4 Find out what you can about **Donor Cards**.
Write some points   a) in favour of, and
b) against, the use of Donor Cards.

Things to do

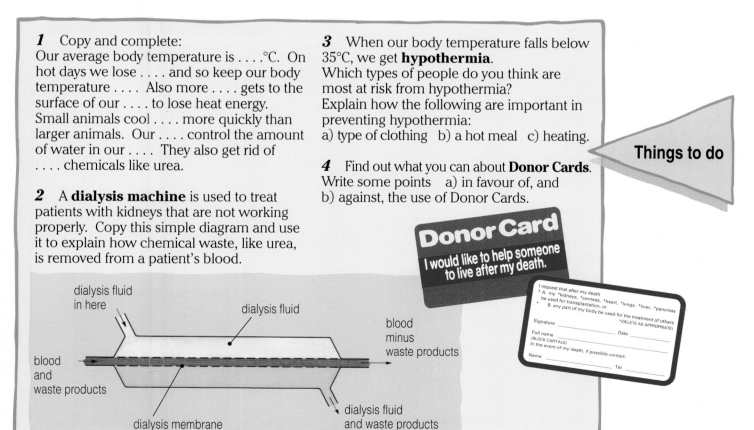

Biology at Work

28f

Sports injuries

In some sports a person runs the risk of being injured.

a   What parts of the body have the most common injuries**?**

Sprains occur in ligaments.

b   What do ligaments join together**?**

c   What do you think happens to a ligament when a sprain occurs**?**

d   How would you treat a sportsperson with a sprain**?**

If ligaments tear badly, then a dislocation can occur at a joint.

e   What is a dislocation**?**

f   What is meant by a pulled muscle**?**

Fractures are broken bones.
In which sports could the following fractures occur:

g   fracture of the radius (the lower arm)**?**
h   fracture of the collar bone**?**
i   fracture of the ankle**?**

j   Why do you think many injuries occur *early* on in a sports season**?**

a dislocated shoulder

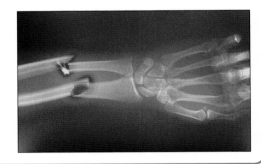

Arthritis and artificial hips

As we get older our joints don't work as smoothly.
Friction at a joint can cause pain.

k   Which fluid cuts down friction at a joint**?**

l   Which tissue acts as a shock absorber at a joint**?**

Osteoarthritis affects older people.

m   Use the diagram to explain how osteoarthritis occurs.

Rheumatoid arthritis is an inherited condition.

n   Find out how rheumatoid arthritis can affect a joint.

Arthritis can make it very painful for people to walk.
Some people have operations to replace their hip joints
with artificial ones like the one in the picture:

o   Why is the hip joint a 'ball-and-socket' joint**?**

An artificial hip joint must have the same properties
as the natural one.

p   Write down what you think these properties are.

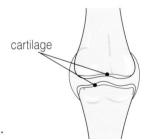

cartilage

cartilage breaks down and lumps form where the bones meet

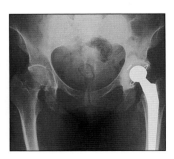

Blood pressure

When the heart pumps it produces a pressure in your arteries.
We call this **blood pressure**.
Your blood pressure rises if you do anything to make your
heart beat faster or if your arteries become narrower.

q What might cause your heart to beat faster**?**

r What could cause your arteries to narrow**?**

A stroke victim
'learning' to walk
again

Constant high blood pressure is harmful.
It puts a strain on the heart and makes it work harder.
It can also cause an artery to burst.
If this happens in the brain it can cause a **stroke**.

s Why would a stroke cause damage to the brain**?**

t What sort of effects can a stroke have on a
person's body**?**

If an artery bursts in the heart it can cause a
coronary heart attack.

u Why would this cause damage to the heart muscle**?**

v What sort of things could increase the chances of
getting coronary heart disease (hint colon: think of diet,
exercise and lifestyle).

w Find out how a **coronary artery by-pass** can relieve
patients of the symptoms of coronary heart disease (**CHD**).

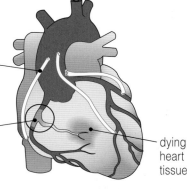

by-pass vessel

blocked coronary
artery – the tissue
it normally supplies
with blood dies

dying
heart
tissue

The right exercise

People can exercise to reduce the effects of CHD.
But the exercise must be *appropriate* to a person's age,
weight and lifestyle.

If you are fit, you will have a ***low heart rate*** and ***quick
recovery time*** after exercise.

Draw a bar-chart of the heart rates of the 5 people in
the table:

x Explain why the heart rates are different for each
person.

People	Heartbeats per minute
Fit teenager at rest	65
Fit teenager, exercising	170
Unfit teenager, exercising	190
Fit adult at rest	70
Unfit adult, exercising	200

Draw line-graphs of the recovery rates for
the fit and unfit teenagers after exercise.

y Compare the recovery rates of the two teenagers
after exercise.

z Use your graphs to explain what sort of people
have fast recovery rates.

	Heart rate per minute						
	0	1	2	3	4	5	6
Unfit teenager	190	160	135	115	103	95	88
Fit teenager	170	120	90	80	72	65	65

The active body

In 1543, **Andreas Versalius** published a book called *On the Fabric of the Human Body*. It contained accurate and detailed accounts of the organs and structure of the human body. It had superb illustrations based upon dissections that Versalius had carried out. It was the first detailed book on **anatomy**.

William Harvey was an English physician who used this anatomical knowledge, and respect for detail, to make a unique discovery of the circulation of blood around the body. In 1628, he published his book *On the Motions of the Heart and Blood*.
In it Harvey explained that blood moves around the body in a circle, from the left side of the heart in arteries and then back to the right side in veins.

He also suggested that there are thousands of tiny blood capillaries connecting arteries to veins. But he was never able to observe these connections between arteries and veins as microscopes hadn't been invented.

Harvey based a lot of his ideas upon **detailed observations** and clever experiments, using **deductive reasoning**.

One of these experiments is shown in the diagram and demonstrates the flow of blood towards the heart in veins. It shows that when the arm is lightly tied with a bandage, the veins show up with small swellings where the valves are. Blood can be pushed past these points towards the heart but it cannot be pushed back.

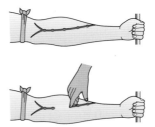

Harvey also took **quantitative measurements** in his investigations, for instance, he measured the output of the heart and was able to calculate the amount of blood in the circulatory system in any given time. Harvey was the first person to study the **physiology** of the human body, that is, how the body works. Around this time there was a great deal of interest in anatomy and physiology: scientific societies were established, schools were founded and books published.

Towards the end of the seventeenth century, the Italian physiologist **Marcello Malpighi** was to prove Harvey right when he observed and described capillaries. They did indeed form the link between arteries and veins and were thin enough for substances to be exchanged between the blood and the cells.

Questions

1 What do we mean by the study of a) anatomy and b) physiology?

2 Why do you think a person needs to study anatomy before he or she can understand physiology?

3 Draw a simple diagram to show Harvey's ideas about the circulation of blood in the human body. Use the following words: veins, arteries, right and left sides of the heart and capillaries.

4 Try to explain what is meant by the following phrases in the account: a) detailed observations b) deductive reasoning c) quantitative measurements.

5 Try out Harvey's experiment on veins with a friend. Make sure that you have your teacher's permission and do not tie the bandage too tight.

6 Choose one of the scientists and find out more details about his life.

7 Scientists work in many different ways. Use the account above to list as many ways as you can.

Revision Summary

The active body

- Oxygen is used in your cells to release energy from food during respiration.

  oxygen + glucose   carbon dioxide + water + energy

- During respiration, glucose is broken down into carbon dioxide and water.

- The lungs, diaphragm and ribs and their muscles are all involved in breathing.

- Air gets to the air sacs of your lungs through the wind-pipe and air passages.

- Oxygen passes through the air sacs into the blood capillaries.
  Carbon dioxide passes the opposite way, from the blood capillaries into the air sacs.

- Tobacco smoke contains harmful chemicals including tar, nicotine and carbon monoxide that can damage your lungs and cause diseases such as lung cancer, bronchitis and heart disease.

- Your air passages have cells with cilia (hairs) which move mucus up to your nose. Mucus helps us by trapping dust and a number of microbes. Smoking prevents the cilia from working and so a person's lungs become congested with mucus. This causes 'smoker's cough'.

- Your heart needs to work efficiently in order to pump blood to the lungs and other parts of the body and return it to the heart.

- Your blood transports the oxygen, dissolved food, carbon dioxide and other waste chemicals around your body.

- Food and oxygen pass out of the blood capillaries into the cells. Carbon dioxide and other waste chemicals pass in the opposite direction.

- Your skeleton supports and protects your body and allows you to move.

- Your muscles provide the force needed to move bones at joints.

- When one muscle in a pair contracts, the other one relaxes. We say that they are antagonistic, e.g. your biceps and triceps muscles.

Food and digestion

- A healthy diet has a variety of foods, each in the right amount.

- A balanced diet contains carbohydrates, proteins, fats, minerals, vitamins, fibre and water.

- Different foods are rich sources of some of these, e.g. fish is rich in protein, and cereals have lots of carbohydrate and fibre.

- Carbohydrates and fats are used as fuel during respiration to release energy.

- We should balance our energy intake (the amount of energy in our food) with our energy output (the amount of energy our body uses up in a day).

- Proteins are needed for growth. We use them to make new cells and to repair damaged tissue.

- We need small amounts of vitamin A, vitamin B group, vitamin C, iron and calcium to stay healthy.

- We must digest our food before our bodies can use it.
  Digestion means breaking down large, insoluble molecules into small, soluble molecules.

- Enzymes can digest large food molecules, like starch, proteins and fats.

- The gut is a tube along which our food passes.

- Food has to be digested if it is to pass through the gut wall into the blood and transported to other parts of the body.

- Some material cannot be digested and is egested from the gut as waste.

- Malnutrition can involve either having too little or too much of certain foods.

Questions

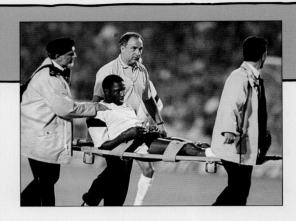

1 Many sports injuries affect muscles and bones.
Use a first aid book to find out as much as you can about:
a) fractures b) torn muscles c) dislocations.
Which sports do you think are more likely to cause each type of injury?

2 Devise a programme of exercise to develop:
a) the biceps,
b) the triceps, and
c) the pectoral muscles.

3 a) What joins muscles to bones?
b) What joins bones to bones?
c) What cuts down friction at a joint?
d) What is arthritis?

4 A young child runs out into the road from between 2 parked cars.
A car driver reacts very quickly by slamming on the brakes.
The car screeches to a halt. Luckily the child is unhurt.
Explain, as fully as you can, the way in which the driver's nervous system worked.

5 Can you explain the following?
a) On a cold day, birds like thrushes fluff their feathers up.
b) Several thin layers of clothing keep you warmer than one thick layer.
c) In hot weather, you make small amounts of concentrated urine.

6 How does your body   a) gain water?   b) lose water?
How does your body control the amount of water loss   c) on a hot day?
and   d) on a cold day?

7 Why do you think that small animals lose heat energy more easily than large animals?
Small animals, like mice and shrews, have to spend a lot of time eating. Why do you think this is?

Sight and Sound

29

We use our eyes and ears all the time.

We need them to make sense of the world around us.

Light waves and sound waves are useful to us in many other ways as well, as you will see and hear . . .

Reflection and refraction

29a

▶ Kate is looking into a **plane** mirror.
A ray of light from the lamp is *reflected* from the mirror:

a Which is the incident ray? Which is the reflected ray?

b If the angle of incidence is 20°, how big is the angle of reflection?

c Explain why Kate sees the lamp.

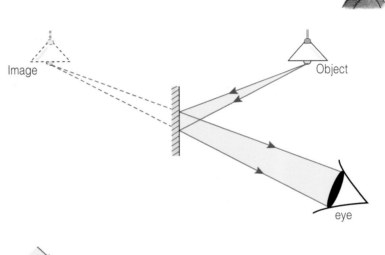

▶ Kate sees an **image** of the lamp. It is called a *virtual* image – you cannot touch a virtual image.

d Write down the word IMAGE as it would look when seen in a mirror.

▶ Here is another diagram of Kate looking at the lamp:

It shows 2 rays from the lamp going into Kate's eye.
When Kate looks at the mirror, she sees the image **behind** the mirror.
The image is *where the rays appear to come from*.

e If the lamp is 2 metres from the mirror, where exactly does Kate see the image?

▶ This diagram shows a beam of light being *scattered* from a piece of paper:

f Why can't you see an image in a sheet of paper?

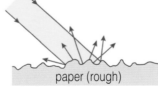
paper (rough)

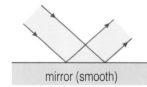
mirror (smooth)

MIRROR ЯOЯЯIM

Your teacher may give you a Help Sheet with these diagrams:

Tina likes to go to pop concerts, but often she can't see over the crowd.
How can she use mirrors to see the band?

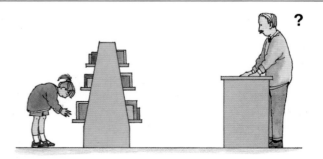

Mr Brown wants to see all the shelves in his shop, in case of shop-lifters.
How can he use a mirror (or 2 mirrors) to see his shelves?

Refraction

▶ The diagram shows a ray of light going into a glass block:

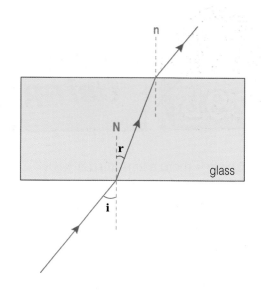

g What happens to the ray when it enters the glass?
This is called **refraction**.
On the diagram you can see a blue dotted line labelled **N**.
This is called the **Normal** line.

h Is the light ray bent away from or towards the normal?

i Which is bigger – the angle of incidence (**i**) or the angle of refraction (**r**)?

Light travels very fast in air – at 300 000 km per second!
In glass it travels more slowly. As the light is slowed down,
it is refracted towards the normal.

j What happens to the light ray as it leaves the glass?

Lenses

▶ The diagram shows 2 lenses:

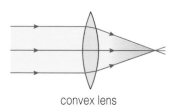
convex lens

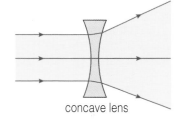
concave lens

k One of them is a **converging** lens and one is a **diverging** lens. Which is which?

Investigating lenses

Your teacher will give you 3 convex lenses (thick, medium, and thin).

• Use each lens as a magnifying glass to look at your finger:

• Which lens magnifies the most? Which least? Is there a pattern?

• What happens if you use 2 lenses together?

• Use them to look at a photo in this book. What do you see?

1 Copy and complete:
a) When light is reflected, the angle of . . . . is . . . . to the angle of . . . .
b) The distance from an object to a plane mirror is . . . . to the distance from the . . . . to the mirror.
c) When light goes into glass, it is . . . . towards the normal line.
When light comes out of glass, it is refracted . . . . from the normal.
d) In a convex lens, the . . . . come closer together. It is a . . . . lens.
e) A concave lens is a . . . . lens.
f) A fat convex lens is a strong . . . . glass.

2 Think about all the ways that mirrors are used – in homes, shops, and cars. Make a list of all the uses that you can think of, in 2 columns: (1) plane mirrors, (2) curved mirrors.

3 Dave's imagic trick. (Try it!)
The diagram shows Amy
looking at a cup:
She cannot see the coin
lying in the cup.
Dave pours some water into the
cup. Now Amy can see the coin!
Why? Can you explain it by drawing
a ray diagram?

Things to do

Using light

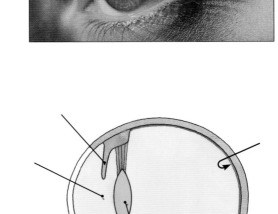

▶ Where is there a lens in your body?
Is it convex or concave?
Does it converge or diverge rays of light?

▶ Sketch a simple diagram of an eye, like the one shown
(or your teacher may give you a Help Sheet).
Then add these labels in the right places:

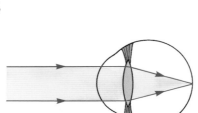

lens   retina   iris   pupil   cornea

a You are using your eyes to see this page.
Explain, step by step, how the light travels from the
window until it is focussed on your retina.
You can start like this:

Light from the window shines on the book, and then…

b What happens to the pupil in your eye if you look at a
bright light?

Focussing your eyes

The lens in your eye can change shape. When you look at
near objects it gets fatter. For far objects it gets thinner.
The muscles in your eye make the lens go fatter or thinner,
until the image is sharp:

Looking at a near object, your lens is **fat**.

If you can't see a near object clearly, you are long-sighted.
(You may need spectacles with con<u>vex</u> lenses.)

Looking at a far object, your lens is **thin**.

If you can't see a distant object clearly, you are short-sighted.
(You may need spectacles with con<u>cave</u> lenses.)

Eye tests

Plan, and carry out, an investigation to find out the distances
at which you can read letters of different sizes.

• How will you make it a fair test?

• Is it the same for the left eye, the right eye, and both eyes?

• Plot a graph of the **distance from your eye** against the
size of the letter. What do you find?

• Is your graph the same as other people's?

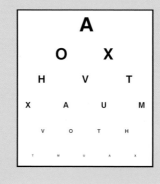

A	4 mm
O X	3 mm
H V T	2 mm
X A U M	1.5 mm
V O T H	1 mm
T M U A X	0.6 mm

size of letters

The camera

In a camera, a lens is used to make an image on the film:

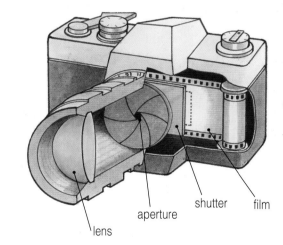

Use a convex lens to focus the light rays from a lamp, like in a camera:

- What do you notice about the image?
- Move the lamp to different distances from the screen. Each time, focus the image. Measure the distances shown on the diagram, and record them in a table.
- What pattern do you find?

- In a camera, how do you focus on
  - near objects?
  - far objects?

- Does your eye focus on objects in this way?

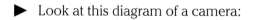

▶ Look at this diagram of a camera:

c Which part of the camera is like your retina?

The **aperture** can be changed to let in more or less light.

open   closed

d Which part of your eye is like this?

e When should the camera use a small aperture?

f In what other way can a camera change the amount of light going to the film?

g The camera and your eye both use a lens. In what ways are the lenses i) similar? and ii) different?

h Explain carefully how your eye and a camera use different ways to focus the image.

---

1 Copy and complete:
a) My eye lens is a . . . . lens. It . . . . the rays of light.
b) To focus on near and far objects, my eye . . . . changes shape. To focus on . . . . objects, it is fatter.
c) A long-sighted person cannot focus on . . . . objects. A short-sighted person cannot focus on . . . . objects.
d) The . . . . in a camera and in my eye are inverted (upside-down).

2 Copy and complete:
a) A camera uses a . . . . lens.
b) To focus a camera on near objects, the lens is moved . . . . from the film.
c) The . . . . in a camera is like the iris in my eye.

3 Draw up a table or a poster which shows all the ways in which a camera and your eye are i) similar, and
ii) different.

Things to do

A world of colour

▶ Which is your favourite colour?
What does it remind you of?

a How many colours are there in a rainbow?

b How can you remember their names?

Making a spectrum

You can make a **spectrum** using a prism:

c When the light enters the prism it is
refracted. Is it refracted towards the
normal or away from the normal?

The white light is **dispersed** by the prism, to
make a spectrum.
This shows that white light is really a mixture
of seven colours.

d Write down the full names of the 7 colours,
in order.

e Red light has the longest wavelength.
Which colour has the shortest?

The light is refracted because it travels slower
in the glass than in the air.
Different colours travel at different speeds, and
so are refracted by different amounts.

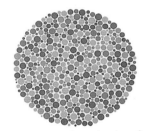

Can you see a red number here?
If you can't, you may be colour-blind.

f Which colour do you think travels slowest
in glass?

Filters

What do you see when you look through a piece of red
plastic or red glass?
A red **filter** will only let through red light:
It **absorbs** all the other colours:

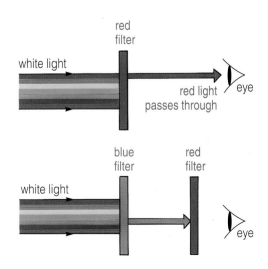

g Which colour passes through a green filter?

h Which colours are absorbed by a green filter?

i Use this diagram to explain what you see when you
look through a blue filter and a red filter together:

j Where have you seen filters used?

Seeing coloured objects

k The paper in this book looks white.
Write down which colours you think are being reflected from it.

l Use the diagram to explain what happens when white light shines on green paper:

m Explain what is happening when you look at this red ink.

Green things reflect green light and absorb the other colours. We see the green light.

Designing for the stage

Imagine you are the stage-designer for a pop group.
You have to design the band's clothes as well as the stage colours. The manager tells you that the stage lights will flash red or green or blue.
The picture shows someone's first attempt:

- Look at this picture in red light, in green light, and in blue light. (Or look through filters.)

- Draw up a table to show what colours a white, a red, a green and a blue object look like in white, red, green and blue lights.

- Then re-design the set and the clothes so that the band can be seen better.

Safety first

Plan an investigation to see which is the safest colour for you to wear when riding a bicycle, or walking on a road.

- How will you make it a fair test?

- How will you find out which is the safest colour for both day-time and night-time?

- Show your plan to your teacher and, if you have time, do it.

- How else can you improve your safety on the road?

---

1 Copy and complete:
a) White light is . . . . by a prism into a spectrum. The 7 colours are:
b) . . . . light has the longest wavelength.
c) The colour refracted the most is . . . .
d) A red filter lets . . . . light through, and . . . . all the other colours.
e) A blue T-shirt reflects . . . . light, and . . . . all the other colours.

2 What colour would a red book look:
a) in red light?   c) through a red filter?
b) in green light?   d) through a blue filter?

3 Which jobs may be dangerous or difficult if you are colour-blind?

4 Plan an investigation to see which colours are best for an easy-to-read disco poster.

Things to do

75

Musical sounds

▶ Touch the front of your throat while you say 'aaah'.
Can you feel it *vibrating*?

a Explain, step by step, how someone else can hear this sound.

b What is vibrating in   1) a guitar?
                                 2) a drum?
                                 3) the recorder in the photo?

Waves on a spring

You can use a 'slinky' spring to 'model' a sound wave.
When you vibrate the end, a wave of energy travels down the spring:

← wavelength →

→ energy   This kind of wave is called a **longitudinal** wave.

When you speak, the sound energy travels through the air. It is the **molecules** of air that vibrate:

The energy is transferred from molecule to molecule. They vibrate like the coils of the spring.

c Why can't sound travel through a vacuum?

An oscilloscope

You can use a **c**athode **r**ay **o**scilloscope (**CRO**) to
investigate sound waves.

The sound energy enters the microphone. The energy is
transferred to electrical energy, which goes to the oscilloscope.
A graph of the wave is shown on the screen:

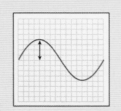

What happens if you   1) turn the Y-shift knob?
                           2) turn the X-shift knob?
                           3) switch the time-base off and on?
                           4) change the Y-gain dial?

Loudness and amplitude

- Hum or whistle a quiet sound into the microphone.

- Then do the same sound but *louder*.
  How does the wave change?

- Sketch the 2 waves.

- How does the **amplitude** of a wave depend on
  the loudness of the sound?

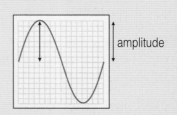

Which note is louder?

Pitch and frequency

- Hum or whistle a note with a low pitch, and then a high pitch. How does the wave change?

- Sketch the 2 waves.

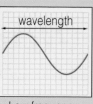

Low frequency

- Waves with a shorter wavelength have a higher *frequency*. The molecules are vibrating more often. Frequency is measured in **hertz** (**Hz**). A note of 300 Hz means it is vibrating 300 times in each second.

- How does the pitch of your notes depend on the frequency?

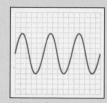

High frequency

Which note is high-pitched?

- Blow a dog-whistle. What do you notice? What is ultra-sound?

- Connect a signal-generator to a loudspeaker, to make sound waves of different frequencies. What is the highest note you can hear? Sketch its wave.

Musical instruments

- Make different sounds – aaah, ooo, eee – while you watch the screen.

- Play different musical instruments. Play the same note on each one, and sketch the waves.

- In what ways are the waves   1) the same?   2) different?

recorder

guitar

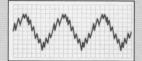

violin

1 Copy and complete:
a) A sound . . . . is caused by vibrations. It is a . . . . wave. The energy is transferred from molecule to . . . .
b) A loud sound has a large . . . .
c) A high-pitched sound has a high . . . .
d) Frequency is measured in . . . . (Hz).

2 Write down the names of 10 musical instruments that do not use electricity. For each one, say whether it is plucked, blown, bowed, hit or shaken.

3 Humming birds make a noise by beating their wings very quickly. Plan an investigation to find out the frequency at which their wings vibrate.

4 The diagrams below show 4 waves.
a) Which has the largest amplitude?
b) Which has the highest frequency?
c) Which was the quietest sound?
d) Which sound had the lowest pitch?
e) Which 2 have the same amplitude?
f) Which 2 have the same frequency?

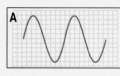

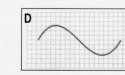

Things to do

Hear, hear

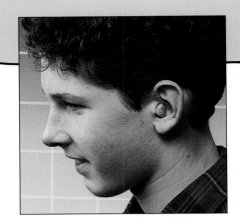

▶ Why do some people wear a hearing aid?
Do you know anyone who wears one?
What do you think is inside a hearing aid?

Your ear can easily be damaged. This causes deafness.
You looked at this in *Spotlight Science 7*.

a In what ways can your ear be damaged?
Write down as much as you can remember about this.

How loud?

If you stand too close to a loudspeaker in a disco, you could damage your hearing.
Does it matter ***where*** you stand? Plan an investigation to find out.

• What will you use to detect the sound?

• How will you keep a record of the different positions that you try?

• Predict what you think you will find.

• If you have time, try it.

Sound levels

The chart shows some data about loudness levels, which are measured in decibels (dB):

(The loudness levels are a rough guide, but actual values depend on the exact situation.)

b Continuous noise levels of 90 dB or more can damage your hearing.
Make a list of any of these situations in your life.

c The loudness shown for a rock concert depends on whether it is inside a hall or in the open-air.
Why do you think this is?

d The damage depends on the loudness level ***and*** the length of time you listen to it.
For how long is it safe to listen (without a break) to a personal stereo at 110 dB?

e Look at the list of exposure times.
There is a pattern. Describe the pattern you see.

f Professional rock musicians wear expensive ear-plugs. Why do you think they are each specially made to be close-fitting in the musician's ear?

Approx. loudness in decibels		Maximum safe exposure time
140	boom stereo in car, jet engine at 100 ft	—
130	rock concert indoors	—
120	rock concert outdoors, loud stereo in car	$7\frac{1}{2}$ mins
110	personal stereo full on; some cinemas	30 mins
100	personal stereo on 6/10 setting	2 hours
90	loud party, motorbike, train	8 hours
80	school canteen, traffic noise in car	
70		
60	conversation	
50		
40		
30	whispering	
20		
10		

Speed of sound

▶ Joanne sees a lightning flash on a hill which she knows is 1000 metres away. She hears the sound 3 seconds later.

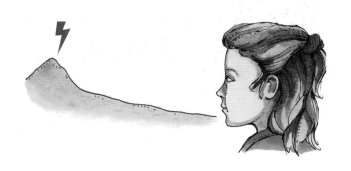

g Which travels faster, sound or light?

h Use the formula:

$$speed = \frac{distance\ travelled}{time\ taken}$$

to calculate the speed of sound in air.

▶ Sound can travel through solids, liquids and gases.

i What can you say about the particles in a solid compared with the particles in a gas?

j Can you use this idea to explain why sound travels faster in a solid than in a gas?

k Does sound travel faster in water or in air?

Echoes

Sailors can use **echoes** to find the depth of the sea:

▶ Suppose this ship sent out a sound wave, and got back an echo after 1 second.

l How long did it take for the sound to get down to the bottom?

m How far does the sound travel in this time? (The speed of sound in water is 1500 metres per second.)

n How deep is the sea?

o If the fish are 250 m deep, what would be their echo time?

p The boat then moves into very deep water. Explain why it is harder to detect the echo.

Reflecting a sound

Plan an experiment to see if the angle of incidence is equal to the angle of reflection for a sound wave.

1 Copy and complete:
a) Light travels . . . . than sound.
b) The formula for speed is:
c) Sound travels . . . . in iron than in water. It travels . . . . in water than in air.
d) When sound is reflected, you get an . . . . This is used in . . . . -sounding.
e) Ear damage depends on the . . . . level and the length of . . . . you listen to it.

2 Make a list of jobs you could not do if your hearing was damaged.

3 If you hear thunder 15 seconds after seeing lightning, how far away is the storm? (Speed of sound = 330 m/s)

4 Do you think background music in shops persuades people to buy more things? Plan an investigation to answer this.

5 School canteens are usually very noisy. How could you make yours quieter? Draw a plan of it and label all the improvements you would make if you were an architect.

Things to do

Physics at Work

Road safety

In the photo, the coat and the road-sign contain thousands of tiny shiny beads that act like mirrors.

a Explain why the man's coat looks brighter than his face.

b What does this say?

c Why is it written like this?

d How should the word STOP be written on a sign on the front of a police car?

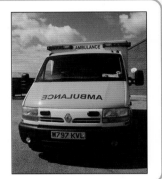

Use these 3 ray diagrams to explain,
in your own words,
and with examples,
the meanings of:

e transparent,

f translucent,

g opaque.

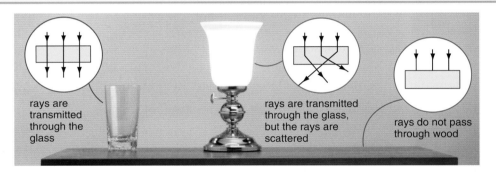

rays are transmitted through the glass

rays are transmitted through the glass, but the rays are scattered

rays do not pass through wood

Autocue

Politicians and newsreaders often use an autocue.
It lets them talk directly at the audience, so they don't have to look down at their notes, or memorise them.

h Use the diagram to explain why the speaker can see the words.

i Explain why the audience can't see the words.

j Look at the way the words are written on the projector.
Why is this?

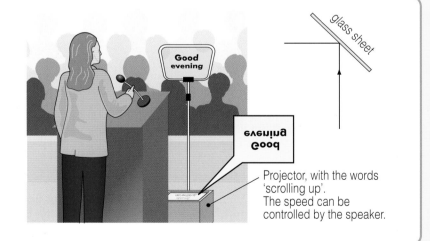

glass sheet

Good evening

Projector, with the words 'scrolling up'.
The speed can be controlled by the speaker.

Red + Green + Blue

The picture shows 3 spotlights shining on a screen:

k What colour do you get where the red + green overlap?

A **TV screen** has tiny spots of red, green and blue on it.

l What is happening when you see yellow on the TV screen?

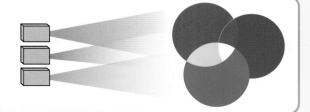

Curved mirrors

The photo shows a convex curved mirror (like the back of a spoon).

It is placed on a busy road opposite the exit of a house.

m What is the mirror for?

n Why is a convex mirror better than a plane mirror?

Astronauts

These astronauts can see each other, but they can't hear each other except on the radio.

What does this tell you about:
o light waves?
p sound waves?
q radio waves?

r How would this change if they stood together with their helmets touching?

Seeing double

If you look at the image of your face in a mirror, you can often see a faint second image of your face.

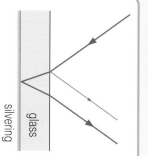

silvering
glass

Use the diagram to explain:

s Why do you see a second image?

t Why is it faint?

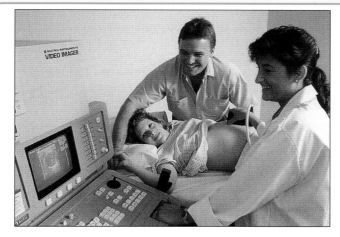

Whales can 'sing' messages to each other. They can hear each other a hundred miles away through the sea (but not through the air).
u Try to use particle theory (molecules) to explain why sound travels farther in water than in air.

Bats and **dolphins** use ultrasound to find food and 'see' in the dark.

v What is ultrasound?

w How do the bats and dolphins use it?

An ultrasonic **scanner** is used to look at a baby inside the mother's womb. It works like the echo-sounder on a ship.

x Explain how you think it works.

Geologists use **echo-sounding** to search for oil and gas.

y In the diagram, which microphone will receive the sound first?

z The speed of sound in rock is about 4000 m/s. If the sound arrives at the microphone after $\frac{1}{2}$ second, estimate the depth of the hard rock layer.

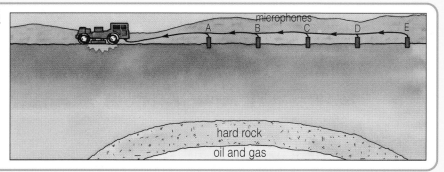

microphones
A B C D E
hard rock
oil and gas

Light and Sound

Ideas about Light

2500 years ago **Pythagoras** suggested that he saw an object because it gave out a stream of particles which travelled to his eyes, like a stream of tiny bullets. The particles were called '*corpuscles*'.

2200 years later, in 1666, **Isaac Newton** investigated white light passing through a prism. He showed that white light is made up of 7 colours (ROY G BIV).

About the same time, **Christiaan Huygens** suggested that light travels as a *wave*, not as corpuscles.

OR

waves spreading out like ripples on a pond ?

corpuscles shooting out like bullets ?

Newton wasn't sure. He tried to use both the wave theory and the corpuscular theory. Later in his life he seemed to favour the corpuscular theory.
For the next 150 years, Newton's followers used his name to oppose the wave theory, and most scientists believed the corpuscular theory.

Then in 1801 **Thomas Young** found convincing evidence for the wave theory. So for the next 100 years this theory was believed.

Then in 1905 **Albert Einstein** found good reasons to suggest that light travels as bundles of energy called *photons*, rather like corpuscles.

Today physicists believe that light can behave as both waves *and* particles. Sometimes it behaves more like a wave, sometimes more like a particle!

Ideas about Sound

One of the first experiments on sound was done by **Otto von Guericke** in 1654. He used an air pump to pump air out of a bottle. There was a clockwork bell inside the bottle, and its sound got weaker and weaker as the air was removed.

This shows that sound cannot travel through a vacuum. It needs a medium (a solid, liquid or gas) to pass on the vibrations.

Isaac Newton worked out a formula for the speed of sound in 1698.
The first person to measure the speed of sound accurately was **William Derham** in 1708. He watched and listened as a cannon was fired 19 km (12 miles) away.

Newton's work predicted that sound should travel faster in water than in air.
This was proved by an experiment on Lake Geneva in 1827. An under-water bell was rung at the same time as some gunpowder was lit. On another boat 14 km (9 miles) away, the flash was seen (at night) and the sound was heard through the water by a large ear trumpet dipping into the water.

Sound travels 4 times faster through water than through air. This is because the particles (molecules) of water are held closer together. They spring back together more quickly and pass on the sound pulses more quickly.

Questions

1 Explain how Newton's reputation was used in a non-scientific way to support the corpuscular theory.

2 a) Think about William Derham's experiment and explain in more detail what you think he did. What instruments would he need?
   b) With a distance of 19 km he found the sound took 56 seconds. What was the speed of sound?

3 a) Think about the Lake Geneva experiment, and sketch what you think the apparatus looked like on each boat.
   b) With a distance of 14 km the sound took 10 s. What was the speed of sound in water?

4 Choose one of the scientists and find out more details of his life.

Revision Summary

Light

- In air, light travels in a straight line, at a very high speed. In glass it travels more slowly.

- Light travels much faster than sound.

- If light rays are stopped by an object, then a shadow is formed.

- You can see this page because some light rays (from a window or a lamp) are scattered by the paper, and then travel to your eye.

- The law of reflection: the angle of incidence (i) always equals the angle of reflection (r).
- The image in a plane (flat) mirror is as far behind the mirror as the object is in front.

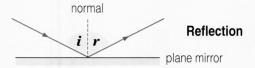

Reflection

- Refraction: when a light ray goes into glass it is refracted (bent) *towards* the normal line. This is because the light slows down in the glass. When light comes out of glass, it is refracted *away from* the normal line.

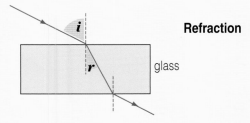

Refraction

- When white light goes into a prism, it is dispersed into the 7 colours of the spectrum (ROY G BIV).

Dispersion

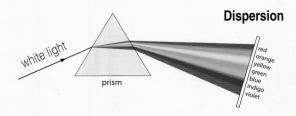

- A red filter will let through only red light (which we see). It absorbs all the other colours.

- A green object reflects green light (which we see). It absorbs all the other colours.

Sound

- Sound travels at about 330 metres per second (in air). Light travels much faster than this.

- Average speed = $\dfrac{\text{distance travelled}}{\text{time taken}}$

- All sounds are caused by vibrations.

- If a guitar string is vibrating, it sends out sound waves. These waves travel through the air to your ear. They transfer energy to your ear. The waves make your ear-drum vibrate and this sends messages to your brain.

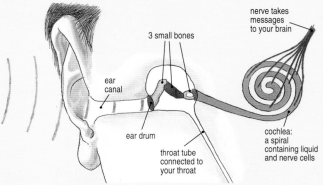

- Sound cannot travel through a vacuum. This is because there are no molecules to pass on the vibrations.

- To compare sound waves you can use a microphone and a CRO (oscilloscope).

- A loud sound has a large amplitude (a):

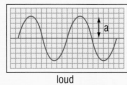

The loudness of a sound is measured in decibels (dB). Your ear is easily damaged by loud sounds.

- A high pitch sound has a high frequency:

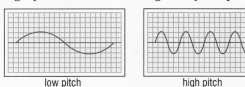

The frequency is measured in hertz (Hz).
The range of frequencies that can be heard varies from person to person (from about 20 Hz up to about 20 000 Hz).

Questions

1 Suppose you can choose from a variety of mirrors (plane and curved) and lenses (converging and diverging).
Work out a design for each of these:
a) a torch
b) a periscope to see at a football match
c) a periscope to see behind you in a car
d) a solar cooker
e) a spy camera to take photos round corners
f) an over-head projector for a teacher.

Draw a labelled diagram of each design. On each diagram, draw coloured lines to show what happens to the rays of light.

2 Natalya is only 3 years old. She can speak but she can't read yet, so it is hard to use the usual eye-test with her:
Design a test that could be used instead.

3 Some pupils were hypothesising about the effects of colour.

Anna said, "I think more people choose to eat green jelly than any other colour."
Jamie said, "I think that flies are more likely to land on yellow surfaces than white surfaces."

Choose one of these hypotheses, and plan an investigation to test it. Take care to make it a fair test.

4 The diagram shows the path of 2 rays of light from a fish to a fisherman:
a) Use the diagram to explain why the fisherman should not aim his spear directly where he sees the fish.
b) Why does water always appear shallower than it really is?

5 Kelly says, "There ought to be a law against playing music loudly." Do you agree with her?
Give your arguments for and against this idea.

6 The diagram shows a wave-form on an oscilloscope:
a) What is the time taken for 1 wave?
b) How many waves are there in 100 milliseconds?
c) How many waves will there be in 1 second?
   (1 second = 1000 milliseconds)
d) What is the frequency of the wave?
e) Would this be a high note or a low note?

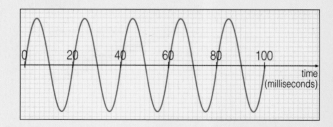

7 The time-keeper of a 100 m race stands at the finishing line. He starts his stop-watch when he hears the starter's pistol.

a) Will the time he measures be too long or too short?
b) By how much? (Speed of sound in air = 340 m/s)

Health

30

We all want to have happy, healthy and active lives.
But to do so, we need to take good care of our bodies.
We should eat the right foods and take regular exercise.
We should understand the dangers to our health of alcohol,
drugs and solvents.

In this topic you will also find out about disease and how
we can fight it.

Fit for life?

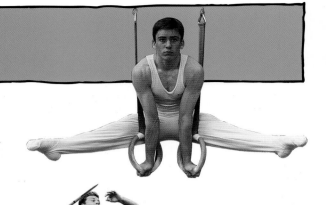

Are you fit**?**

▶ Write down some of your ideas about what it means to be fit.

Look at the people in the photos:
Each person must be fit to do their sport well.

S-factors

Four things make up fitness:

- **Strength** is the amount of force that your muscles can exert.

a Which exercises do you think could make you stronger**?**

b Which things that you do every day need strength**?**

c Which sports in the photographs need strong muscles**?**

- **Stamina** keeps you going during exercise.
  To develop your stamina, you need a strong heart and lungs.

d Which sports in the photographs need a lot of stamina**?**

e What sort of exercises do you think would improve your stamina**?**

f How can people's life-styles reduce their stamina**?**

- **Suppleness** lets you move freely and easily.
  If you are supple, you can bend, stretch and twist your body easily.

You often see people 'warming up' before they do sport.

g What exercises do they do**?**

h What might happen if they did not do these 'warm up' exercises**?**

i Which sports in the photographs need you to be supple**?**

- **Speed** is having quick reactions or how fast you travel over a distance.

j Which sports in the photographs need speed over a distance**?**

k Which sports in the photographs need quick reaction times**?**

l How can you improve both types of speed**?**

We're getting fitter!

More people are getting exercise from sport or fitness activities.
When you do different activities you need different amounts of your
S-factors.

▶ Look at the table.

Exercise	Strength	Stamina	Suppleness	Speed
Badminton	**	**	***	**
Climbing stairs	**	***	*	*
Cycling (hard)	***	****	**	*
Dancing (disco)	*	***	***	*
Football	***	***	***	***
Golf	*	*	**	*
Gymnastics	***	**	****	**
Hill walking	**	***	*	*
Jogging	**	****	**	*
Swimming	****	****	****	**
Tennis	**	***	***	***
Weight-training	****	*	*	*

*no real effect **good effect ***very good effect ****excellent effect

m Which exercises do you think are best for i) strength?
ii) stamina? iii) suppleness? iv) speed?

n Which exercise do you think is i) best and ii) worst
for your all round fitness?

o Karen is 14. She isn't sporty. What exercises can you suggest
to keep her fit?

Fitness programme

Think up a fitness programme that a year 9 pupil could do in
10 minutes a day. Make a leaflet of your programme.
It should:

- include all four S-factors (strength, stamina, suppleness, speed).
- not involve any special equipment like weights.
- not be too difficult.
- not need a large space to do it in.

You should not try the programme out unless it has been checked by your teacher.
And remember, if you feel any strain during exercise, stop and rest.

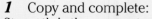
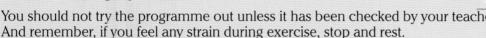

Things to do

1 Copy and complete:
Strength is the amount of . . . . that your . . . .
can exert . . . . . keeps you going when
you exercise hard. If you can bend, twist
and stretch your body easily, then you are
. . . . Speed can mean being fast over a . . . .
or having quick . . . . You need all 4 of these
. . . . to be fit.

2 Think up a fitness programme for
someone who does a) netball b) rowing
c) sprinting.

3 Use the table above to suggest suitable
exercises for these people:
a) a 45-year-old man who has recovered
from a heart attack.
b) a 27-year-old mother who had her first
baby 10 weeks ago.
c) a 50-year-old woman who has never
played sport.

4 Choose one sport that you enjoy and
design a poster to encourage people to take
part in it.

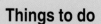

30b Are you healthy?

What do you think we mean when we say that someone is **healthy?**

▶ Write down some of your ideas about health.

A scientist once described health as:
'the state of complete physical, mental and social well-being'.

a Under the headings 'physical', 'mental' and 'social', make a table of the different things that can affect a person's health.

A healthy diet

In the last lesson we saw how important it is to exercise to be healthy. But you also need the right sort of food to enable you to exercise.

b Write down the foods that make up a **balanced diet**. Remember that you need *enough* of each of these foods.

c Which of these foods are *energy* foods and which are *growth* foods?

You need to balance your **energy input** with your **energy output**.

d What happens if your energy input is greater than your energy output?

e What happens if your energy output is greater than your energy input?

A healthy lifestyle

Sometimes people do things that have a bad effect upon their health.

f For each of the following habits, explain the bad effects that they can have upon a person's health:

> **smoking cigarettes**   **drinking alcohol**   **eating fatty foods**
>
> **solvent abuse**   **taking harmful drugs**   **not exercising**

We will be looking at some of these harmful habits in the next few lessons.

A social life

To have a healthy lifestyle, it is important to meet other people, make friends and just have fun!

Sport is an obvious way of meeting other people, but there are plenty of other ways in which you can make contact with other people, exchange ideas and have a positive outlook on life.

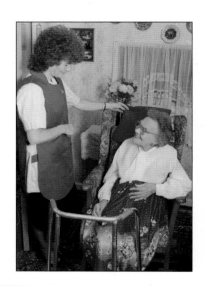

g Discuss with a friend and write down your ideas about how some of the following can help to give you a healthy outlook on life:

> **starting a rock group**   **baby-sitting**   **going to a dance**
>
> **environmental work**   **care of the elderly**   **a part-time job**
>
> **helping at a junior school**   **choir or orchestra**   **church groups**

Lots of clots

For healthy growth you need a balanced diet.
You especially need protein and vitamins for growth.

When you were a baby you got your protein from milk.
The enzyme **rennin** is made in the stomachs of young animals.
It makes milk solid, so that it stays in the stomach longer.
It can then be digested.

Plan an investigation into how quickly rennin clots milk.
Think about the factors that might affect how quickly rennin works.
Choose one factor and investigate its effect.

- How will you make it a *fair test?*
- How will you decide when the milk has clotted?
- How will you record your results?

Show your plan to your teacher before you try it out.

Health and disease

As we have seen, you don't have to have a disease to be unhealthy.
But lack of health can be caused by disease.

Some diseases are caused by **germs**, such as bacteria, viruses and fungi.

h Find out the names of 3 diseases that are caused by bacteria.
i Find out the names of 3 diseases that are caused by viruses.
j Find out the names of 2 diseases that are caused by fungi.

Some diseases are **not** caused by germs (**microbes**).
Diabetes, arthritis, cancers, cystic fibrosis and motor neuron disease
are **not** caused by microbes.

Find out about these diseases from books, ROMs and the internet.

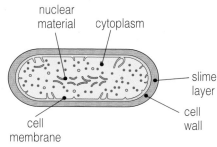

The basic structure of a bacterium.

Things to do

1 Here is a table which shows Liam's height since he was born:

Age (years)	birth	2	3	4	5	6	7	8	9	10	11	12	13	14	15	16	17	18
Height (cm)	50	85	95	103	110	115	120	125	130	135	140	145	150	160	170	173	174	175

a) Plot a line-graph to show how Liam's height has changed.
b) Explain the shape of the graph.
c) During which years was Liam growing fastest?

2 Copy and complete:
Health can be described as 'the state of complete physical, ... and . . . . well-being.'
A . . . . diet combines the correct types of foods in the right . . . . This should include . . . . and fats for energy and proteins which are needed for . . . . and the repair of cells. Too much intake of fatty foods can lead to problems in the . . . . system. Certain nutrients such as . . . . and . . . . are needed in small amounts in the diet, but if they are absent, they can result in . . . . diseases.

3 a) Make a list of habits that can have a bad effect upon the health of a person.
b) What particular advice would you give to i) teenagers ii) 30 year olds and iii) pensioners, about how to maintain a healthy lifestyle.

4 There has been a lot of coverage in the press about athletes and performance-enhancing drugs. Use books, ROMs and the internet to write about i) whether this is right or wrong ii) how these drugs improve performance and iii) the bad effects that these drugs can have on an athlete's body.

Hormones also control your growth.

30c A drink problem

Alcohol is a **drug**.
In Britain drinking alcohol is **socially acceptable** but people can become **addicted** to it.

a Write down what you think the highlighted words mean.

Most drugs affect the brain and nervous system.
Alcohol is a **depressant** drug.

b What effect do you think alcohol has on the way your body works?

Alcohol is made by **fermentation**.

c Can you remember what happens during this process?

d Alcohol is sipped and swallowed. But where do you think it goes after that?
Your teacher may give you a Help Sheet which shows how alcohol can affect your body.

Units of alcohol

All these drinks contain **1 unit** of alcohol:

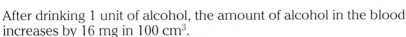

After drinking 1 unit of alcohol, the amount of alcohol in the blood increases by 16 mg in 100 cm³.

▶ Match **e** to **j** with the correct units of alcohol in the pictures.

e The legal limit for driving.

f No obvious effects, but your reactions are slower.

g Speech is slurred, seeing double, feeling emotional, may be tearful or looking for a fight.

h Talkative, your judgement is not so reliable.

i Possible loss of consciousness.

j Feeling more cheerful.

1 unit

12 units

2 units

16 units

3 units

5 units

Dave goes downhill

When Dave started work for a local firm he soon got to know the other lads. He had the odd drink with them at lunchtime even though it made him feel a bit sleepy.

With the money he made, Dave could afford to go down the pub in the evenings as well. Some nights he would stay out so late that he found it difficult to get up for work next morning.

One afternoon Dave made a mistake that could have caused a serious accident at work. As he had been warned about being late many times, this was the last straw – he was sacked!

Out of work and with nothing to do, Dave now needed a drink even more. He became bad-tempered and started to borrow money from friends for a drink.

k What do you think was the cause of: i) Dave's mistake at work? ii) Dave being late for work?

▶ Look at the graph:

l How many units of alcohol are removed from the blood every hour?

m Dave goes home at 11 p.m. after drinking 10 pints of beer. How long does it take for all the alcohol to get out of his blood?

n At what time would he be below the legal limit for driving?

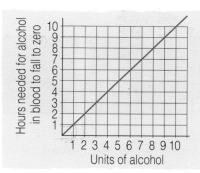

What people say about drinking

I can take or leave alcohol. If there's none around then I'm happy with soft drinks.

I have a good drink with the lads after a rugby match.

My dad was down the pub every night and I'm just like him.

I have a drink at parties. It makes me less shy about talking to people.

I like a drink after work – it helps me to unwind.

I always have a glass of wine with a good meal.

I get lonely on my own. A drink cheers me up a bit.

All my crowd drinks. At weekends we get mental.

In your groups discuss:
- Why you think each person drinks.
- Which people you think are at low risk from alcohol.
- Which people you think could become problem drinkers.

Either Choose to be one of the characters and act out a discussion about the dangers of heavy drinking.

or Choose a character and write a story to show how heavy drinking can cause difficulties in the family.

1 Copy and complete:
Alcohol is a . . . . because it affects your . . . . system by . . . . down your reactions. For this reason, people should not drink if they are to . . . . machines or . . . . a car. A pint of beer contains . . . . units of alcohol. The legal limit for driving is . . . . People who drink too much can become . . . . to alcohol.

2 When Louise was 13 she took a friend home at lunchtime. They helped themselves to drinks from her parents' drinks cabinet. Write an ending to the story.

3 What do you think should be done to get rid of the problems caused by alcohol? How successful do you think these would be:
a) pubs opening for longer or shorter times?
b) raising or lowering the age at which it is legal to buy alcohol?
c) making alcoholic drinks more expensive?

Things to do

Linda and Carl

What does the word **drug** mean to you?

Here are some pictures of different drugs.
► Use them to help you write about what a drug is.

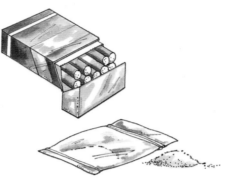

a How can a drug get into your body?

b Why can it affect *all* of your body?

c How do you think a drug can save lives?

d How many drugs do you know of?
Make a list of them.

e Did you include any of these in your list:
aspirin, coffee, alcohol, cigarettes, insulin, aerosols?
Why do you think that these can be drugs?

Disco girl killed by one tablet of new drug

An 18-year-old girl has died after taking a single tablet of a new designer drug. A court heard yesterday how Linda took the pill to give her energy at an all-night disco. She collapsed on the dance floor and was rushed to hospital screaming in pain. She suffered 2 heart attacks and died from lack of oxygen to the brain 2 days later. Her parents were at her bedside.

The judge branded the drug barons who supply drugs like ecstasy "scum and filth". He imposed 6-month sentences on 3 young people who admitted pushing the drug.

In your groups discuss:

• Why Linda took the drug in the first place.

• How she got hold of the drug.

• What action should be taken, and by who?

In your groups: Talk about situations where teenagers may be offered drugs. What reasons might influence them to accept or refuse?

and Write a script for a short scene showing the dangers of taking drugs. Choose a role and try to speak and act as if you are the person.
Your teacher might choose your group to act your scene to the class.

or Write one or two paragraphs saying why you think teenagers start to take drugs.
Say what your views on drug-taking are.

Solvent abuse

What do you think is meant by **solvent abuse?**

▶ Use your ideas and some of these facts to write a few lines about it.

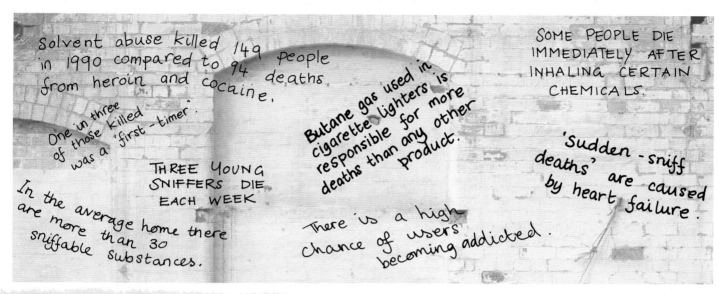

Solvent abuse killed 149 people in 1990 compared to 94 deaths from heroin and cocaine.

One in three of those killed was a 'first-timer'.

THREE YOUNG SNIFFERS DIE EACH WEEK

In the average home there are more than 30 sniffable substances.

Butane gas used in cigarette lighters is responsible for more deaths than any other product.

There is a high chance of users becoming addicted.

SOME PEOPLE DIE IMMEDIATELY AFTER INHALING CERTAIN CHEMICALS.

'Sudden-sniff deaths' are caused by heart failure.

Lingering death of glue-sniffer Carl

A 21-year-old man was found hanged in a garage after 10 years of glue-sniffing.

When he was 11, Carl and some older friends went to a nearby building site and experimented with glue. He said "It was a laugh at the time and all the gang tried it."

His sniffing really started after he moved house and started at secondary school. His mother also had a new baby so he didn't get so much attention. Carl started to truant from school and discovered a gang of sniffers. At 14 he was taken into care – he felt rejected by his family. He shop-lifted to get glue and got into trouble with the police. By 18 he was often aggressive. He drifted from hostels to bedsits and often slept rough. What money he had was used to get more glue.

Carl aged 11 with friends

f Why do you think Carl started to sniff glue**?**

g What events in his life might have made him continue the habit**?**

h Why do you think that Carl truanted from school**?**

i How do you think people like Carl could be helped**?**

1 Copy and complete:
A drug is a . . . . that affects the . . . . system. Some . . . . save . . . . but others can kill if you take an . . . . Some people can't stop taking some drugs because they are . . . . Solvents are . . . . available and can attract . . . . people and those too . . . . to afford other drugs.

2 Explain how each of the following might make a few young people start to take a drug:
a) curiosity b) friends c) self-pity.
What type of person might be influenced most easily?

3 Two teenagers are found by a teacher, in an old house, inhaling solvent.
What happens next? What should the teacher do in the best interests of the teenagers and the school? Write the rest of the story.

4 Design a leaflet which shows some of the signs and symptoms of solvent abuse that shopkeepers could keep by the till.

Things to do

Microbes and disease

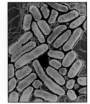

Do you know why people get ill**?**

▶ Make a list of some of the things that you think make people ill.

Your skin acts as a barrier to microbes.

a Can you remember the main types of microbes**?**

Bacteria and viruses are a common cause of disease.

b Make a list of some diseases caused by these microbes.

The **symptoms** of a disease are the body's response to waste chemicals made by the microbes.

c Write down some symptoms that you know of.

Points of entry

Look at these ways in which diseases can be spread:

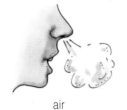

air   food   touch   water   animals

d For each method shown in the picture, write down:
i) A disease that can be spread in this way (your teacher can give you a Help Sheet).
ii) How its spread can be prevented.

e Can you think of any other ways in which diseases can be spread**?**

▶ Use your Help Sheet of diseases to find out the answers to the following questions.

f What type of microbe causes i) tuberculosis**?** ii) measles**?** iii) athlete's foot**?**

g What are the symptoms of i) polio**?** ii) mumps**?** iii) the common cold**?**

h How are i) malaria ii) rubella, and iii) athlete's foot spread**?**

Seldomill Health Authority
Memo to: *Analysts*   **From:** *Mike Robe*

The children at Sick Lee High School have been going down with severe stomach upsets. I think that the disease may be linked to places where they eat their lunch. These are the school canteen, the Greasy Cod Chip Shop, Sid's Snack Bar and Betty's Bakery.
Please plan an investigation to find out the source of infection. Write me a report about your plan, the tests you intend to use, and how you will show your results.

Please hurry!

Antibiotics: useful drugs

Your doctor might give you an **antibiotic** to help you fight a disease.
The first antibiotic was discovered by Alexander Fleming.

Just like Fleming!

- Using sterile forceps, place a sterile paper disc into each of:

  A – disinfectant   **B** – alcohol   **C** – crystal violet
  D – washing-up liquid

- Leave to soak for 5 minutes.

- You will be given an agar plate which has harmless bacteria growing on it.

- Divide the underneath of an agar plate into 6 sections and label them **A** to **F**.

- Remove the discs with sterile forceps and shake off any excess liquid.

- Place each disc on the correct part of the agar plate.

- Your teacher will give you a **penicillin** and a **streptomycin** disc for sectors **E** and **F**.

- Sellotape the lid to the base so it cannot come off.

- Incubate your plate for 48 hours at 25°C. Then examine the growth of bacteria.

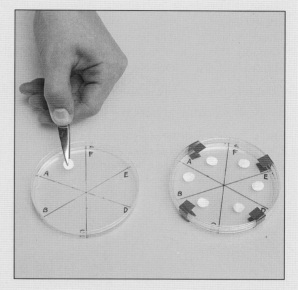

i Which chemical had most effect upon the growth of the bacteria?

j How were you able to measure this effect?

k How could you use this test to find out the best concentration of an antibiotic to use?

---

1 Copy and complete:
Bacteria and . . . . are the main microbes that cause disease. The . . . . of a disease are caused by chemicals made by the microbes. A drug that fights the disease inside your body is called an . . . . Alexander . . . . discovered one of the first antibiotics.

2 Name 4 ways in which diseases can be spread.
For each way say how you think the disease can be prevented.

3 Drugs that kill microbes inside the body are called **antibiotics**.
Find out what **antiseptics** and **disinfectants** are and how they help to fight disease.

4 How do you think the following can help to spread disease:
a) flies?
b) hypodermic needles?
c) kitchen cloths?

Things to do

Self-defence

How is it that our bodies are able to fight off disease?
If you catch a disease like measles, you don't get it again –
you become **immune**.

Why do you think this happens? Write down your ideas.

Fighting off the enemy

Do you remember from Book 8 how white blood cells defend your body?

All germs (that's bacteria and viruses) have chemicals on their surfaces.
These chemicals are called **antigens**.
When you catch a disease like measles, the white blood cells in your
body make chemicals called **antibodies**.
These antibodies attach themselves to the antigens on the surface of
the germs.
They cause the germs to clump together and make them harmless.
Now another type of white blood cell, let's call them 'killer cells', are
able to 'eat' the 'stuck-together' germs.

After any disease, the antibodies stay in your blood, making you immune.

a   So how can you become immune to some diseases and not others?

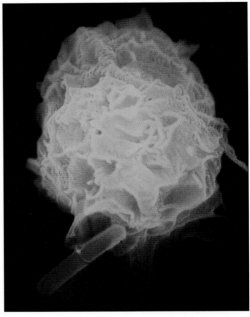

A white blood cell attacking an *E.coli bacterium*

Each germ has antigens of a particular shape. So you produce antibodies
that match the shape of each antigen. This is why you have to catch the
disease before you become immune to it.

1. Bacteria enter your body through a cut in your skin.

2. Your body makes antibodies to fight the invaders.

3. The bacteria are destroyed by the antibodies.

4. Antibodies stand by ready to fight off any future attack. The body is **immune**.

▶ Study the cartoons and use the information to write a brief explanation
of what happens when harmful bacteria invade your body.

You can also become immune to a disease by **vaccination**.
A vaccine is a weak form of the disease microbe.

b   Explain how you think vaccination works.
c   Your body can make millions of *different* antibodies.
Why do you think this is?
You can find out more about vaccination on page 102.

d   Find out how **antiseptics** kill germs outside your body.

Disinfectants are strong chemicals that kill germs on floors and
work surfaces.

e   Why are **disinfectants** not used to kill germs on or in our bodies?

A toddler being vaccinated

Mr Clean

Bob is the caretaker at the high school.
He's got a problem.
The label has come off his big bottle of disinfectant.
So he doesn't know how much to add to water before use.
If he adds too little, it won't kill the germs.
If he adds too much, it'll be expensive.
Help Bob out by finding the **smallest** amount of disinfectant that will kill the germs.

(Hint: You could use agar plates and paper discs with different concentrations of disinfectant on them.)

Your teacher will give you an agar plate with harmless bacteria growing on it.

How much disinfectant will you add?

How will you make it a *fair test*?

How long will you leave it to work?

How will you record your results?

Ask your teacher to check your plan, then try it out.

Things to do

1 Copy and complete:
If you catch a disease and you don't get it again, you are . . . . to it.
Your body makes chemicals called . . . .
They stick the germs together and make them . . . .
The . . . . stay in your blood to give you immunity to the disease. A . . . . is a weak form of the disease microbe. It can be . . . . into your body or taken by mouth. It gives you . . . . to a disease.

2 Find out whether the following are true or false.
a) Tetanus is caused by germs getting into an open wound.
b) A pregnant woman cannot pass on rubella to her unborn child.
c) Smallpox vaccine is no longer given because the disease has been wiped out.
d) There is a low risk of whooping cough vaccine causing brain damage to some babies.

3 Why is it important that the following places are free from germs?
a) Swimming pools.
b) School kitchens.
c) Doctor's surgeries.

4 Try to find out what diseases people can be vaccinated against.
Which vaccines have you been given?

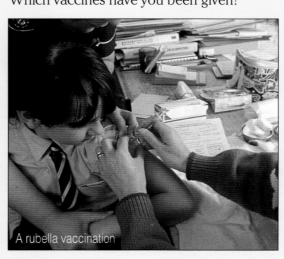
A rubella vaccination

The spread of disease

1600

Can you remember what microbes are?

400 years ago nobody had heard of microbes.

They didn't even know where other living things came from.

Look, this meat is full of maggots!

Yes, the meat has created the maggots.

We now know that food rots because of microbes.
In the old days, most people thought rotting food *made* the microbes.

The mutton gravy has changed into new life.

John Needham believed in this **spontaneous creation**. He thought that when an animal died parts of it formed new creatures.

BOILED

Lazzaro Spallanzani showed that food does not go bad if the microbes are killed. He killed the microbes by sealing the food and then boiling it.

In 1854 **Louis Pasteur** isolated microbes and added them to sterilised soup – they multiplied.

It's off!

He was able to show that it was microbes that made wine and milk decay.

There is a vital **force** in all living things. When they die it produces microbes.

Felix Pouchet still believed in spontaneous creation. He came to opposite conclusions to Louis Pasteur.

I boiled the broth in each flask.

The microbes can't get into this flask. They get stuck in the neck.

BROTH BROTH

Pasteur's experiments were more reliable than Pouchet's. He proved that microbes caused diseases such as anthrax.

In the nineteenth century, hospitals were not very clean places. Microbes spread easily and wounds often became infected.

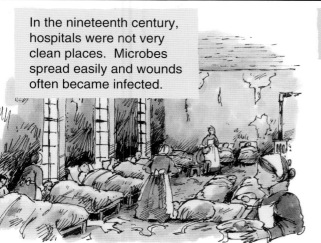

Women giving birth in hospitals sometimes died of fever afterwards. **Dr Ignaz Semmelweiss** noticed that doctors never washed their hands between patients.

Our doctors are carrying the infection on their hands.

They must wash their hands in disinfectant between patients.

Disinfect

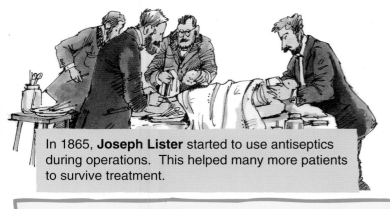

In 1865, **Joseph Lister** started to use antiseptics during operations. This helped many more patients to survive treatment.

Modern operating theatres are kept as free from microbes as possible.

1 Write down what you can remember about the 3 main types of microbes.

2 What happens if a bottle of milk is left open to the air?
Give your answer as if you agreed with John Needham and Felix Pouchet.

3
a) How was Louis Pasteur able to kill microbes in milk?
b) What do we call this process today?
c) Name 4 other ways in which microbes in food can be killed.

4
a) How did Semmelweiss discover that disease was spread in hospitals?
b) How was he able to reduce this spread of disease?

5 Look at the operating theatre in Lister's time.
a) What conditions can you see that reduce the spread of infection?
b) What things do not reduce this spread?
Now look at the modern-day operating theatre.
c) What precautions have been made in it to prevent the spread of infection?

Things to do

Biology at Work

Undernutrition

Undernutrition or starvation often occurs in under-developed countries.

a Why do you think this is**?**
b What do you think are the symptoms of undernutrition**?**

c During periods of starvation, which stored foods does the body use for energy**?**

When energy intake is lower than it should be, the body uses up protein as an energy source.
d What ***should*** this protein normally be used for in the body**?**
e What effect will the use of protein as an energy source have on muscles and other tissues**?**
f What do you think aid programmes to famine-hit countries aim to do**?**

Tropical crops, such as cassava (a root crop) and sweet potato, have a high energy content but are low in protein.
g Why would these crops alone be insufficient to relieve famine**?**

Enough wheat and rice is grown to feed everyone in the world.
h Use the following clues to explain why there is hunger in the world:
   • wars   • transport   • drought   • food mountains   • pests.

Overnutrition

In rich, industrialised countries, like Britain and the USA, more people suffer from overnutrition than from undernutrition.
i Why do you think this is**?**

Overnutrition results in a person becoming too fat or **obese**.
j Can you think of 3 causes of obesity**?**

Obesity can cause a person a number of problems.
k Explain how being obese can result in the following:
   i)   coronary heart disease
   ii) high blood pressure
   iii) varicose veins
   iv) breathlessness.

Look at the graph:

l What is the normal weight for a person who is 5 ft 11 in**?**

m How would you describe a 5 ft 7 in person who is 50 kg**?**

n How would you describe a 5 ft 9 in person who is 130 kg**?**

o What actions could an obese person take in order to lose weight**?**

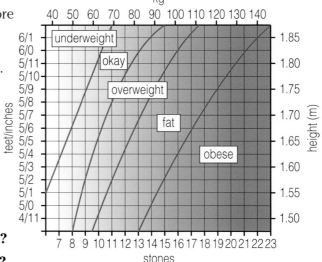

Average height to weight ratios

Infectious disease

p Name 3 groups of microbes that can cause infectious disease.

q Give 3 ways in which these microbes can be spread from one person to another.

The early stage of a disease is called the **incubation period**.

r What is happening to the disease microbe inside the body during this time?

Disease microbes can do damage to tissues and release **toxins** which cause the **symptoms** of a disease.

s Give some examples of common disease symptoms.

Look at the graph:

t What symptom of the disease is shown on the graph?

u How long was the incubation period?

v What caused the fever and how long did it last?

Antibiotics are used to relieve disease symptoms, but many microbes are becoming resistant to their action.

w How do you think a microbe can develop resistance to a particular antibiotic?

In Scotland, in 1997, a new strain of *E.coli* 0157 caused an outbreak of food poisoning that affected 500 people and killed 20.

Look at the newspaper report:

x How do you think the disease was spread?

y Why did the existing antibiotics prove useless?

z Find out about other diseases which are increasing due to increased resistance to antibiotics.

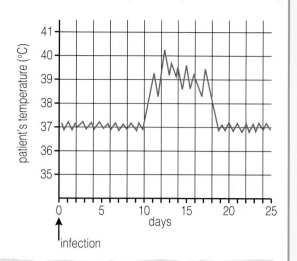

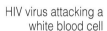
infection

Death toll rises in food bug outbreak

Five people have died of food poisoning in Britain's worst case of *E-coli bacteria* contamination.

A hospital has been closed to all GP-arranged admissions except suspected cases of the *E.coli 0157* food poisoning outbreak.

The butcher's shop thought to be the source of the outbreak announced yesterday that is was temporarily closing.

Seven members of staff linked to the food poisoning outbreak in Scotland are infected.

Thirty-two adults and a child were being treated yesterday in the hospital, where the Lanarkshire Infectious Disease Unit is based. The number giving cause for concern rose from ten to 15 over the weekend, and the number showing symptoms rose from 189 to 209.

Acquired immune deficiency syndrome (AIDS)

AIDS is caused by HIV virus which attacks the body's immune system.

HIV attacks the white blood cells that protect us.

A How could HIV be detected in a person?

HIV is only transmitted if the blood or semen (fluid which contains the sperms) of an infected person enters the blood stream of another person.

B How might this occur by the following:

  i) the transfusion of infected blood?

  ii) drug addicts sharing needles?

  iii) sexual activity with many partners?

  iv) In each case above, suggest how the spread of HIV can be prevented.

There is no cure for AIDS and as yet no vaccine for HIV. AIDS has spread very quickly in parts of Africa.

C Why do you think this is?

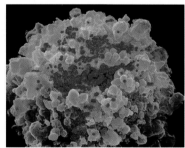
HIV virus attacking a white blood cell

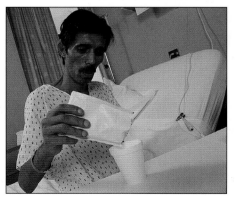
A patient suffering from AIDS

Health

Jenner vaccinating his son

Vaccination

In the eighteenth century, a farmer called **Benjamin Jesty** noticed that people who had caught cowpox did not get smallpox. Smallpox is a far more dangerous disease than cowpox. He scratched the skin of each member of his family and put some cowpox material on the wound. This prevented them from getting smallpox when there was a major outbreak of the disease in 1774.

In 1776, **Edward Jenner**, a physician in Gloucestershire, carried out a medical experiment.
It is reported in this newspaper article:

THE GLOUCESTER TIMES

BOY SURVIVES SMALLPOX

1776

DOCTOR EDWARD JENNER has carried out a reckless experiment on a young boy.

He scratched some liquid from a smallpox blister into the arm of 12-year-old James Phipps. Smallpox is responsible for many deaths every year. How is it that the parents gave their consent? It seems to be a miracle that the boy has survived.

Doctor Jenner puts it down to "Scientific observation"! Apparently he has noticed that milkmaids never catch smallpox.

Although they often catch cowpox, a mild disease. He told our reporter, "I took some pus from a cowpox blister and scratched it into the arm of young James. He later developed cowpox, but soon recovered. Later I inoculated him with smallpox, but he did not show signs of the disease – I believe that he is now immune to it."

Where will all this experimenting end?

Will we all start growing horns as a result of the new cowpox inoculation?!!

---

1 How do you think cowpox is different from smallpox?

2 How do you think that cowpox is caught?

3 What do you think gave Jenner the idea of inoculating against smallpox?

4 Explain why you think James did not catch smallpox.

5 Try to explain the reporter's attitude to Jenner's experiment.

In the nineteenth century, **Louis Pasteur** showed that he could heat anthrax bacteria and make it safe. When he then injected the vaccine into sheep, it gave them immunity to anthrax.

Mothers queue up to have their children vaccinated against polio in the mid 1950s

6 How do you think that heating the anthrax bacteria made them safe?

7 Why do you think that injecting the 'safe' anthrax bacteria gave the sheep immunity?
(Hint: try to use the words 'antigens' and 'antibodies' in your answer.)

Poliomyelitis ('polio' for short) is a virus that destroys nerve cells. It can damage the spinal cord causing the victim to become paralysed.

In 1953, **Jonas Salk** made a vaccine that prevented polio. It was so successful that polio has now disappeared from developed countries.

8 Use books, ROMs and the internet to find out more about the work of Jonas Salk and how he developed the anti-polio vaccine.

Revision Summary

Health

- Being healthy involves having a balanced diet, taking suitable exercise, having a healthy lifestyle and being free from disease.

- Microbes include bacteria and viruses, some of which can cause disease.

- The body has natural barriers to infection, such as the skin.

- The production of antibodies and specialised cells in the blood are part of the body's defence system.

- Antibodies can protect you from disease by giving your body immunity.

- Antibodies can pass through the placenta to the fetus and through breast milk to the baby.

- Vaccines contain chemicals and cells which stimulate the body's defences.

- Antibiotics and other medicines can also help you fight disease.

- Not all diseases caused by microbes can be treated easily by drugs, e.g. some bacteria have become resistant to the effects of many antibiotics.

- Eating too much or too little of certain foods can affect your health.

- Exercise is important for healthy living. A person should take exercise that is appropriate to their age and body needs.

- Alcohol abuse can affect a person's health, lifestyle and family.

- Abuse of solvents and other drugs can affect your health.

Cells

- Animals and plants are made up of cells. Lots of cells grouped together make up a tissue. Different tissues make up organs, e.g. the heart is made up of muscle, nervous and connective tissues. Organs make up organisms, e.g. you have lungs, a heart, a brain, kidneys, a liver, etc.

- Cells are made up of: a membrane which keeps the cell together and controls what passes in and out of the cell; the cytoplasm (where the chemical reactions of the cell take place); and the nucleus (which controls the cell and contains instructions to make more cells).

- Plant cells have a thick cell wall to support the cell. Plant cells have chloroplasts to trap light energy for photosynthesis.

- Some cells have changed their shape to do different jobs, for example: Palisade cells in the leaf contain lots of chloroplasts to absorb light. Root hair cells are long and thin, with a large surface area to absorb water and nutrients. Cells lining your air passages have cilia (hairs) to move mucus up to your nose. Sperm cells have tails to swim to the egg and fertilise it. Egg cells have a food store to feed the fertilised egg.

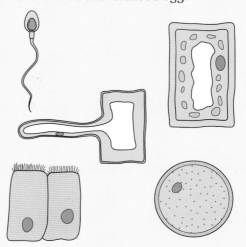

- Cells make new cells by dividing. When new cells are made, growth occurs and there is an increase in size.

- At fertilisation there is a joining together of male and female cells. In humans, a sperm joins with an egg. In flowering plants, a pollen cell joins with an ovule cell.

- These sex cells enable information to be transferred from one generation to the next, so we inherit characteristics from our parents.

Questions

1 Ask your parents and grandparents some questions about their lifestyle.
   a) What sports and activities did they do when they were your age?
   b) Did they do them in school?
   c) How many sports and activities did they do outside school?
   d) What facilities did they have?
   e) How much time did they spend watching television or playing board games?
   What are your conclusions?
   Do you think they were fitter and more active than you are?

2 Suppose that you have a young kitten or puppy. Plan an investigation to measure its growth.
   How will you measure its growth (try 2 ways)?
   How often will you take measurements?
   How long do you think this investigation will take?
   How will you display your results?

3 Choose a topic, either alcohol abuse or solvent abuse.
   Make a leaflet about it, to go in a doctor's surgery.
   Write about the danger to health and how it can affect your body.
   If possible use drawings and photos from newspapers in your leaflet.

4 *Drug and solvent abuse costs the country millions of pounds every year.*
   Use the following headings to help you to explain this sentence: a) medical treatment b) burglary and theft c) catching the drug pushers.
   What actions do you think would reduce drug abuse?

5 Look at the picture. It shows some of the antibodies that Martin has in his blood.
   a) Does Martin's blood contain antibodies to fight polio?
   b) Is he immune to polio?
   c) Can he catch polio?
   d) Does Martin have the antibodies in his blood to fight measles?
   e) Is he immune to measles?

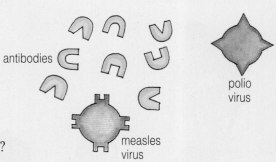

antibodies

polio virus

measles virus

6 Do some research and find out what operations were like in the nineteenth century.
   Draw a diagram or describe what you think the conditions were like.
   What are modern operating theatres like today?
   Draw a diagram or do some writing to show how conditions have improved.

7 Do you think that snooker is a sport?
   Write down any reasons that you can think of to support your answer.
   Now do the same for ice-skating, chess, and ballroom dancing.

Using forces

31

Your life is full of forces.
Everything that you do needs a force – a push or a pull.

You use forces to move around, and to transfer energy.

In this topic, we'll look at forces as they move, as they turn, and as they exert a pressure.

Then we'll look at the force of gravity, and how it affects our Solar System.

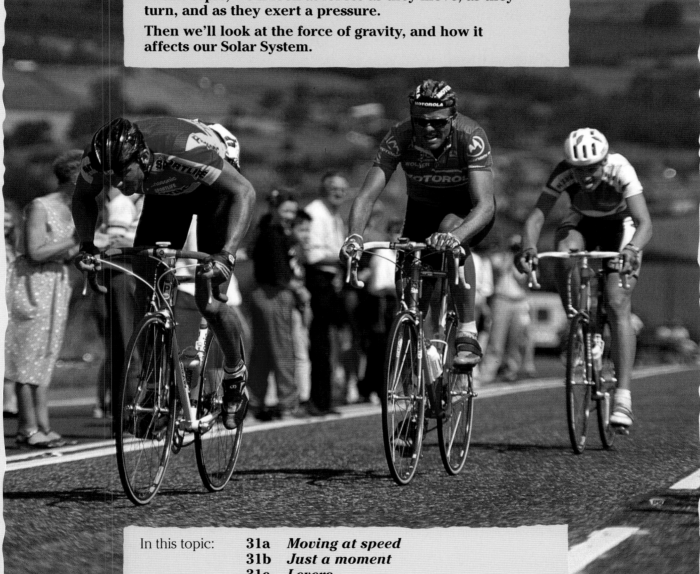

Moving at speed

31a

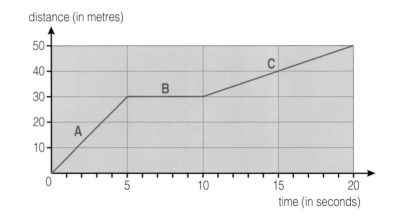

a If you wanted to measure the speed of a bicycle, what 2 things would you have to measure?

b Write down the formula for calculating speed.

c A cyclist travels 50 m in 10 seconds. What is her average speed?

d Copy out this table and then complete it:

> **average speed** = $\dfrac{\text{distance travelled}\ \text{(in metres)}}{\text{time taken}\ \text{(in seconds)}}$

	Distance travelled	Time taken	Average speed
an ant	20 cm	10 s	
a jogger		100 s	2 m/s
a car	100 m		20 m/s
a plane	2000 km	2 h	

e A cyclist can go at constant speed, or *accelerate*, or *decelerate*. Explain what these 2 bold words mean.

Distance – time graphs

Theo went for a short ride on his bike.
Here is a graph of his journey:

f How far did he go in the first 5 seconds?

g What was his speed during part A?

h How long did he stop for?

i What was his speed during part C?

distance (in metres)

(graph: distance vs. time (in seconds), with sections A, B and C)

Balanced and unbalanced forces

If an object is standing still, then a force is needed to start it moving. If it is already moving, then a force is needed to make it accelerate, or decelerate, or change direction.

In the diagram, object **A** has a force on it, and so it will start to move and accelerate.

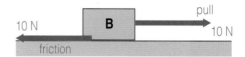

Object **B** has 2 forces on it. One of them is friction.

The 2 forces are equal and opposite. They are **balanced**, so there is **no resultant force** and the object stays as it is.

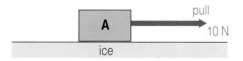

In diagram **C**, the 2 forces are not balanced:

j What is the resultant force on **C**?
Which way does the object move?

k Using a scale of 1 cm for 1 newton, draw an object with a force of 10 N pulling on it. Draw a friction force of 4 N. What is the resultant force?

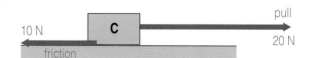

Safety matters

When a driver has to brake, it takes time for him to react. In that fraction of a second, the car can travel many metres. This is called the **thinking distance**.

You measured your reaction time earlier (page 59). For most people, when they are not expecting to brake, the reaction time is 0.7 second!

No seat belts! Testing cars with dummies

l Suppose you were driving at 20 m/s (this is 45 mph).
If your reaction time is 0.7 s, how far would you travel before you started to press the brake?

m How would this thinking distance be affected if the driver was tired?
What else could affect this thinking distance?

▶ The **braking distance** is the distance the car will travel *after* the brake is pressed.

n At 20 m/s (45 mph) on a dry road, with good brakes, the braking distance is 31 m. What is the **total stopping distance**?

o On a wet road, the braking distance is *twice* as much. **Why** is it longer? What is the total stopping distance then?

p What other things would affect the braking distance?

Shortest stopping distances, *on a dry road, with good brakes*

At 13 m/s *(30 mph)*

Thinking distance	Braking distance	Total stopping distance
9 m	14 m	23 m

At 22 m/s *(50 mph)*

Thinking distance	Braking distance	Total stopping distance
15 m	38 m	53 m

At 30 m/s *(70 mph)*

Thinking distance	Braking distance	Total stopping distance
21 m	75 m	96 m

The distances shown in car lengths are based on an average family car.

Finding your reaction time

- You can use the method of page 59 to find out how quickly you can react and reach a brake pedal with your foot:

- Find your reaction time when you are thinking of something else. For example, talking to someone.

- Imagine you are travelling at 20 m/s (45 mph) on a wet road. Use your reaction time to calculate the total stopping distance.

---

1 Copy and complete:
a) The formula for speed is:
b) The units for speed are m/s (. . . . per . . . .) or km/h (. . . . per . . . .) or m.p.h. (. . . . per . . . .).
c) When the forces on an object are equal and opposite, we say they are . . . .
d) If the forces are balanced, there is no . . . . force.

2 A girl jogs at 2 m/s.
a) How far would she go in 10 seconds?
b) How long would she take to go 400 m?

3 Copy and complete this table:

Name of runner	Distance (metres)	Time taken (seconds)	Speed (m/s)
Ayesha	60	10	
Ben		5	8
Chris	100		5
Donna	400		4

4 Suppose a driver can see only 25 m because it is misty. What should his maximum speed be?

Things to do

▶ The diagram shows 2 spanners:
Which spanner would you use to turn a very tight nut?
How can you make it even easier to turn the nut?

▶ Which is the best place to push on a door to open it –
at the hinge or at the door edge?

▶ Some water-taps are hard for old people or invalids to
turn. Design a better tap for an old person.

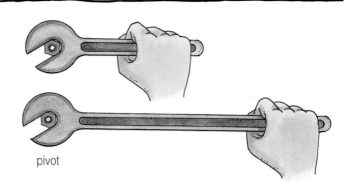

pivot

Hold a ruler at the very end, and put an object on it
(for example, a rubber):

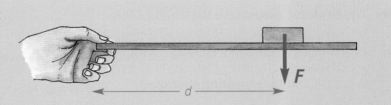

• Put the object at different positions on the ruler.
What do you notice?

• Try a heavier object, at different distances.

The turning effect depends on 2 things:
• the size of the force,
• the distance of the force from the pivot.

The turning effect of a force is called its **moment**.
The moment is calculated by:

Moment of the force = **force** × **distance from pivot**
(in newtons)   (in metres)

Moments are measured in units called **newton-metre (N m)**.

Example 1
A car-driver is tightening a nut.

She exerts a 10 N force, 20 cm
from the nut:

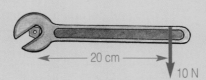

20 cm

10 N

How big is the turning effect?

Answer
Distance from pivot = 20 cm = 0.2 m

Moment = force × distance from pivot

= 10 N × 0.2 m

= 2 N m

a If the driver applies a force of 100 N,
40 cm from the pivot, what is the moment?

b A boy pushes a door with a force of 10 N,
60 cm from the hinge. What is the moment?

Moments in balance

Here is a see-saw:

The big girl has a moment which is turning in a clockwise direction.

c Which way is the small boy's moment turning?

d Why do you think that the small boy can balance the big girl?

When the see-saw is balanced, and not moving, it is 'in equilibrium'.

Then: | the **anti-clockwise moments** = the **clockwise moments** |

This is called **the principle of moments** (or **the law of levers**).

Testing the principle of moments

Your teacher can give you a Help Sheet for this.

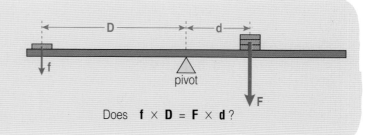

- You can use a ruler as a see-saw, and add weights:

- Work out the clockwise and anti-clockwise moments. What do you find?

Does $f \times D = F \times d$?

Example 2

A pole-vaulter is holding the pole:

His left hand acts as a pivot.
You can assume that the weight of the pole (50 N) acts at the centre of the pole, 1 m from the pivot.
How hard must his right hand push down?

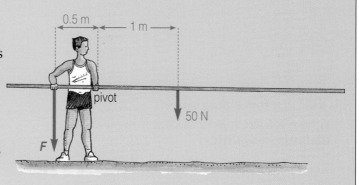

Answer

When balanced ('in equilibrium'):

anti-clockwise moments = clockwise moments

$$F \times 0.5 = 50 \times 1$$

$$F = \frac{50}{0.5} = \underline{100 \text{ newtons}}$$

---

1 Copy and complete:
a) The turning effect (or . . . .) of a force is equal to the force multiplied by the . . . . from the . . . . Its unit is . . . .
b) The principle of moments states that, when an object is balanced and not moving, the anti-clockwise . . . . are . . . . to the . . . . moments.

2 Explain why it is difficult to steer a bike by gripping the centre of the handle-bars.

3 The diagrams show metre rules balanced at their centres.
What is the weight of a) X? and b) Y?

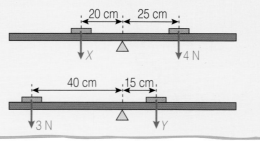

Things to do

Levers

In the last lesson you started to look at levers.
A lever is a simple **machine**. It helps us to
do work more easily.
Here is a lever being used to lift a big **load**:

The lever can turn about a pivot (or 'fulcrum').
The man is applying an **effort** force.

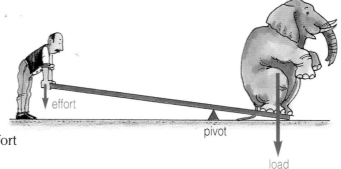

a Where would you move the pivot to make the effort even smaller?

b Which moves through a bigger distance – the man's hands or the elephant?

Example

A wheelbarrow with its load weighs 300 newtons.

The weight acts at a distance of 0.5 m from the centre of the wheel (the pivot).

What force is needed to lift the handles, which are 1.5 m from the centre of the wheel?

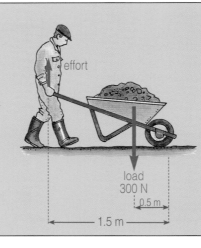

Answer

Use the principle of moments (p. 109).

When balanced ('in equilibrium'):

$$\text{clockwise moment} = \text{anti-clockwise moment}$$

$$\text{effort} \times 1.5 = 300 \times 0.5$$

$$\text{effort} = \underline{100 \text{ newtons}}$$

- Design a wheelbarrow that would need even less effort.

This lever is a **force-magnifier**.

c Where is there a lever in your body used as a **distance-magnifier?**

Here are some common machines using levers.
For each one you should be able to find the **pivot**, and
decide the positions of the **effort** force and the **load** force.
Your teacher will give you
a Help Sheet for this.

pliers

claw hammer

fishing rod

bottle opener

A balancing act

The gymnast is balanced on a beam:

Each part of her body is pulled down by gravity.

All the clockwise moments of the left-hand parts of her body are **balanced** by the anti-clockwise moments of the right-hand parts.

It's just as though all her weight is one force acting at one point **G**. G is called the **centre of gravity**.

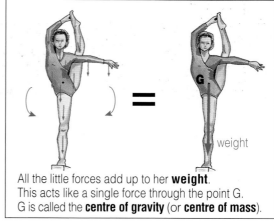

All the little forces add up to her **weight**. This acts like a single force through the point G. G is called the **centre of gravity** (or **centre of mass**).

d What would happen if her centre of gravity was not directly over her foot?

e Where is the centre of gravity of a metre rule?

Stability

If something is **stable**, it does not topple over. Use a box or match-box to investigate what makes an object stable.

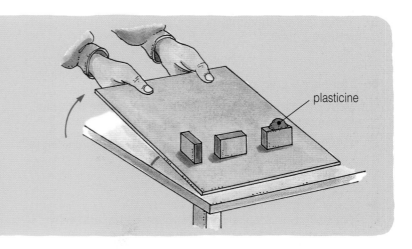

plasticine

• You can use plasticine to raise or lower the centre of gravity.

• To make the box more stable, should it have
  i) a high or a low centre of gravity?
  ii) a narrow or a wide base?

f Which is more stable: a racing-car or a double-decker bus?

g How are these 3 objects made stable?

Things to do

1 Copy and complete:
a) A lever can be a . . . .-magnifier or a . . . .-magnifier.
b) The centre of . . . . (centre of mass) is the point through which the whole . . . . of the object seems to act.
c) A stable object should have a . . . . centre of . . . . , and a . . . . base.

2 Which is more stable: a milk-bottle
a) full? or b) $\frac{1}{4}$-full of milk?
Draw diagrams of the bottles on a slope to explain your answer.

3 The diagram shows a tall crane with a counter-weight to balance the load.
a) Calculate the size of the counter-weight.
b) What can you say about the position of the centre of gravity?

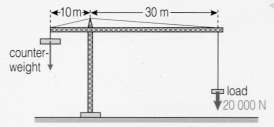

|←10 m→|←————— 30 m —————→|

counter-weight

load
20 000 N

Under pressure

▶ You can push a drawing-pin into the table:

But you can't push your thumb into the table, even though you use a bigger force.

Why do you think this is?

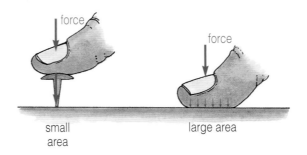

force

force

small area

large area

▶ The pin-point has a small area. All the force is concentrated in that area, to give a high **pressure**.

With your thumb, the same force is spread out over a larger area. The pressure is smaller.

a What is the real difference between a sharp knife and a blunt knife?

▶ Here is another example:

Why does the boy sink into the snow, while the skier stays on top?

What are snow-shoes? Why do eskimoes wear them?

▶ Look at the pictures shown below.
For each one, explain what is happening, and why.
Use these words in your answers:

high/low **pressure**   **force**   small/large **area**

1

This bag is always hurting me.

2

No problem, but my heels keep getting stuck.

Which is best for a muddy garden?

3

4

This chair is always leaving marks on the carpet.

Can you solve this problem for me?

To calculate the pressure you need to know 2 things:
* the force exerted (in newtons)
* the area it is spread over (in cm² or m²).

In fact:

$$\text{Pressure} = \frac{\text{force} \quad \text{(in newtons)}}{\text{area} \quad \text{(in cm}^2 \text{ or m}^2)}$$

If the area is in cm², then the unit of pressure is newtons per square centimetre (**N/cm²**).

If the area is in m², then the unit of pressure is newtons per square metre (**N/m²**).
This unit is also called a **pascal** (**Pa**). 1 Pa = 1 N/m².

Example

Nellie the elephant weighs 40 000 newtons.

She stands on one foot, of area 1000 cm².

What is the pressure on the ground?

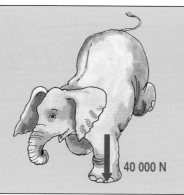

40 000 N

Answer

$$\text{Pressure} = \frac{\text{force}}{\text{area}}$$

$$= \frac{40\ 000\ \text{N}}{1000\ \text{cm}^2}$$

$$= 40\ \text{N/cm}^2$$

b Use the same method to calculate the pressure when a woman weighing 500 N stands on a stiletto heel of area 1 cm².

500 N

c Now compare these two pressures.
Which exerts the bigger pressure – the elephant or the shoe?
Which exerts the bigger force?

Shoe pressure

Plan a way to work out the pressure that you exert on the ground.

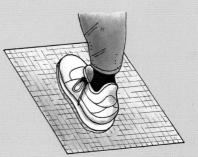

* Which 2 things do you have to measure?

* How can you do this?

* If you have time, do the investigation.

* Who makes the biggest and least pressures in your class?

---

1 Copy and complete:
a) The formula for pressure is:
b) Its units are . . . . per square centimetre (N/cm²) or . . . . per square metre (N/m², also called . . . .).

2 Explain the following:
a) It hurts to hold a heavy parcel by the string.
b) It is more comfortable to sit on a bed than on a fence.
c) Heavy lorries may have 8 rear wheels.

3 Design a beach-chair suitable for use on soft sand. Sketch your design.

4 What is the pressure when a force of 12 N pushes on an area of 2 square metres?

5 A man weighs 800 N. The total area of his 2 shoes is 400 cm².
a) What is the pressure on the ground?
b) He puts on some snow-shoes of total area 1600 cm². What is the pressure now?

6 This box weighs 100 N.
a) Calculate the area of each face.
b) Calculate the pressures when i) the red, ii) the yellow, and iii) the blue faces are on the ground.

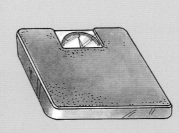

5 cm   10 cm   2 cm

Things to do

Pressure all around

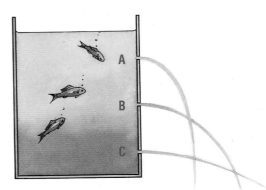

Pressure in liquids

▶ Why do you think deep-sea divers have to wear special clothes?
Why do submarines have to be strong?

Yes – it is because of the **pressure** on them.

▶ Water is surprisingly heavy. A tank of goldfish
probably weighs more than you do!

The weight of water presses down and exerts a pressure.
As a fish swims deeper, the pressure on it increases
more and more.

This tank has 3 holes in the side:

You can see that the water is spurting out under pressure.

Which jet of water is spurting out farthest?

Where is the pressure greatest – at A, B, or C?

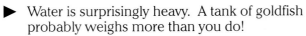

▶ Here is a side-view of a lake made by a dam:

The length of each arrow shows the size of the pressure.

a Where is the pressure least?

b Where is the pressure greatest?

c Why does the dam need to be thicker at
the bottom than at the top?

d Which forces are holding up the boat?
These forces are called the **upthrust**.

e The weight of the boat is 1000 N.
Where does this force act?

f The upthrust and the weight of the boat
are **balanced** forces. What does this mean?

g How big is the upthrust in this case?

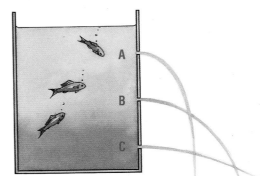

dam
wall

▶ The pressure of a liquid can be used to
work **hydraulic** machines:

What happens if you push in piston A?

Where is this used on a car?

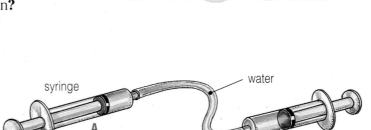

syringe   water

A   B

114

Pressure of air

Just as fish live at the bottom of a sea of water, we are living at the bottom of a 'sea' of air.
This air is called the **atmosphere**.

It exerts a pressure on us (just as the sea squeezes a fish).
This is called **atmospheric pressure**.

▶ If you blow up a balloon, you blow millions of tiny air **molecules** into it:

These molecules bounce around inside the balloon. Whenever a molecule hits the balloon, it gives the rubber a tiny push. Millions of these tiny pushes add up, to make the air pressure.

You are being punched on the nose billions of times each second by these tiny air molecules!

Can it be crushed?

Your teacher will show you an experiment with a metal can:

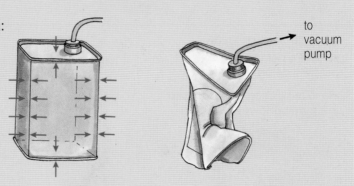

to vacuum pump

- At the start, the can has air inside and outside. The air molecules are bouncing on the inside and the outside.

- If a pump is used to take the air out of the can, what happens?

- Can you explain this? Try to use these words:
  molecules   air pressure

Sucking a straw

When you 'suck' on a straw, you use your lungs to lower the pressure inside the straw.

Explain why the liquid moves up, using these words:
molecules   air pressure

---

1 Copy and complete:
a) The pressure in a liquid is . . . . at the bottom than at the top.
b) A boat floats because the water pressure makes an . . . . force on it.
c) Air pressure is caused by billions of tiny . . . . bouncing around.

2 What happens to the air pressure as you go up a mountain? Why is this?

3 Explain why:
a) You can fill a bucket from a downstairs tap faster than from an upstairs tap.
b) Aeroplanes are often 'pressurised'.
c) Astronauts wear space-suits.

4 Alex says, "A vacuum cleaner works rather like a drinking straw."
Explain what you think he means, using the words: molecule, pressure.

Things to do

Ideas about gravity

350 B.C. **Aristotle** thought that heavy objects contained a substance called gravity.

He thought that light objects had a substance called levity.

For 2000 years, people believed this!

Then, in 1589, **Galileo** shocked people by actually doing experiments!

He is supposed to have used the leaning tower at Pisa:

They both have exactly the same acceleration.

In 1666, **Isaac Newton** was thinking about gravity:

Isaac calculated how much the Earth pulled on the Moon.
He found that the farther the distance, the weaker the force of gravity.
At twice the distance, the force is $\frac{1}{4}$.
At 3 times the distance, the force is $\frac{1}{9}$.

Newton took his ideas further . . .

If the Earth pulls on the Moon, then the Moon must pull on the Earth.

And the Sun must pull on the Earth

and on all the other planets.

Sir Isaac Newton
1642–1727

So the Solar System is held together by the force of GRAVITY!

Isaac worked out a formula:

This means that <u>every</u> object attracts <u>every</u> other object.

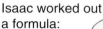

$$\text{Force} = G \times \frac{\text{mass 1} \times \text{mass 2}}{\text{distance squared}}$$

The force between 2 bottles on a shelf is only $\frac{1}{200\,000\,000}$ of a newton

– but the pull of the Earth on you is about 500 N – your **weight**.

He published his ideas in a famous book.

Principia Mathematica ~ 1686 ~

Newton's ideas seemed to work perfectly, until . . .

1916 **Albert Einstein** thought about the effect of gravity on space itself.

Let's think of space as like a rubber sheet.

A big mass like the Sun will 'warp' or bend the space near it.

Like this marble a space-ship will travel in a curve. BUT — so also will a ray of light.

So, light is affected by gravity. (An experiment proved it later.)

If the gravity of a star is very, very strong, it will pull so hard that the light from the star cannot escape . . . . . . it is a **black hole**!

---

1 Use the idea of gravity to explain:
a) Why is an astronaut lighter on the Moon than on the Earth?
b) What evidence is there that Saturn exerts a gravitational pull?
c) Which object has the greatest pull in our Solar System?
d) Why do the planets not travel in straight lines?

2 The diagram shows 4 cups on the Earth's surface. Copy the diagram and draw each cup half-filled with water. Which way is 'up'?

3 An astronaut on the Moon dropped a feather and a hammer at the same time. They hit the ground together. Why does this happen on the Moon but not on Earth?

Things to do

Rockets and satellites

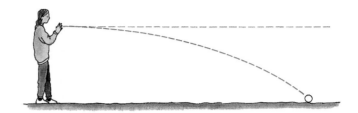

Anna throws a ball horizontally:
The ball moves in a curve.

a Why does the ball not move in a straight line**?**

b What happens if she throws it harder**?**

c What happens if she fires a bullet horizontally**?**

Escaping from the Earth

Imagine firing a gun from the top of a very high mountain:

The bullet will fall back to Earth, just like a ball. It is pulled by gravity. This is shown at **A** in the diagram:

What if the bullet could be fired faster**?** It would go farther, but still fall to Earth. Look at **B** and **C**.

Suppose the bullet could be fired even faster, at 25 times the speed of sound. It would still fall towards Earth but, because the Earth is curved, it would stay the same height above the ground. Look at **D**.

It is now in orbit. It is a **satellite**.

d What can happen if it travels even faster than **D?**
Draw a diagram of this.

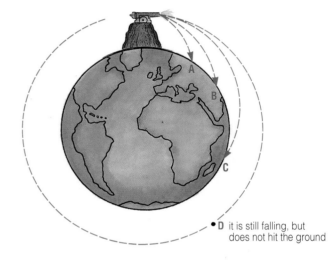

D it is still falling, but does not hit the ground

You can't do this with a gun, but you can with a **rocket**.
It needs a speed of about 29 000 km per hour (18 000 mph).

A satellite moves very fast, but it can seem to be standing still !
If the satellite is put at just the right height and speed, it takes **24 hours** to go round the Earth once.
This is the same time as the Earth takes to spin round once – so the satellite appears to stay over one place !
This is called a **geo-stationary** satellite.

Rockets

- Blow up a balloon and then let go.
  What happens**?** Why**?**

  As the air rushes backwards, the balloon moves forwards. A rocket works in the same way.

- Your teacher may show you a water rocket, using compressed air.
  What happens when the water is forced out**?** Why**?**

The space-shuttle taking off.

A communications satellite.

Using satellites

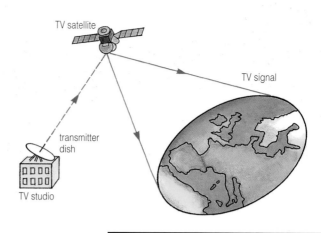

TV satellite

TV signal

transmitter dish

TV studio

Communications satellites can be used to send telephone messages or TV pictures:

We use a geo-stationary satellite. It moves with the Earth, and stays over the same place all the time.

You can use a 'dish' aerial on your house to get the signal.

e Why are the dishes used in the north of Scotland bigger than those used in the south of England?

Weather satellites are useful. They take photos of the weather, and send the pictures back to Earth by radio.

f Look at the weather picture shown below. Write down all the conclusions you can draw from it.

Land survey satellites are very useful. These are lower satellites that take photos in great detail. They can warn of forest fires and water pollution; show healthy and diseased crops; and help us to find oil.

Military satellites are used for spying.

Navigation (GPS) satellites are used by ships, planes, taxis, walkers. You can find where you are, anywhere on Earth, to within 10 metres !

Astronomy satellites carry telescopes. They can take very sharp pictures of planets, because they are outside the Earth's atmosphere.

The Earth seen from a satellite

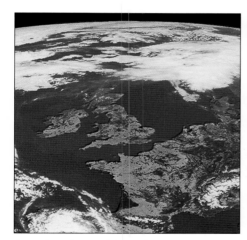

A weather picture of the UK/Europe. What conclusions can you draw?

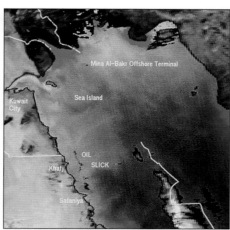

An oil slick polluting the sea. Which part of the world is this?

This is London. Can you see the bridges over the river Thames?

---

1 Copy and complete:
a) All objects are pulled to the Earth by . . . .
b) If it travels fast enough, a satellite can stay in . . . . even though it is falling towards Earth all the time.

2 Why do satellites not need to be streamlined?

3 The diagram shows a firework rocket: As it flies through the air, there are 3 forces on it. Copy the diagram.
a) Which 3 arrows show the 3 forces?
b) Label the 3 arrows, using these words: **weight   air resistance   thrust**
c) What can you say about these forces when the rocket is just taking off?
d) Why does the rocket come back down?

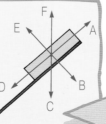

Things to do

The Solar System

The Sun is a star, like all the other stars in the sky.

a Why does the Sun look brighter than the other stars?

b How many hours does it take for the Earth to spin round once?

c Explain why we have day-time and night-time.

d The Sun 'rises' in the East. Which way are we travelling, now?

e At night, all the stars appear to move slowly to the West. Why?

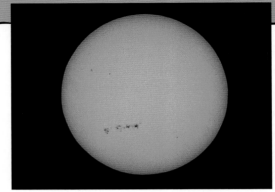

The Sun – our nearest star. On the same scale, the Earth is about the size of this full stop .

The diagram shows the Earth on its journey round the Sun:

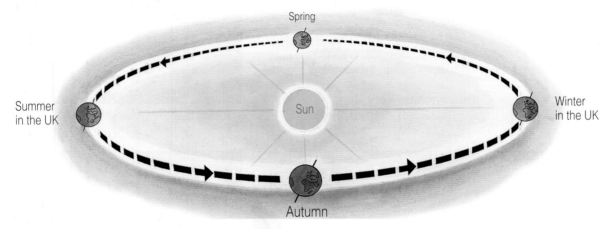

f How long does it take for the Earth to make one complete journey round the Sun?

g How many times does the Earth spin on its axis while it makes this journey?

h The Earth travels in an ellipse. Why does it not travel in a straight line?

The Earth's axis is always **tilted** at $23\frac{1}{2}°$, like this:

In summer, our part of the Earth is tilted towards the Sun.
You can see this in the diagram above.
This means that the Sun appears higher in the sky to us.

i Why is it warmer in summer?

j Why is winter colder?

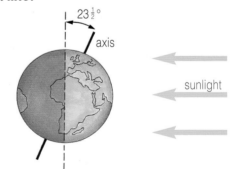

k The Moon is in orbit round the Earth. How long does it take for 1 orbit?

l Why does the Moon shine? What happens if it goes into the Earth's shadow?

Use a lamp and a ball to 'model' the Sun and the Earth.
Use your model to show: 1) day and night,
                          2) a year,
                          3) summer and winter.

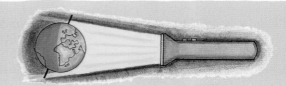

The planets

The diagram shows the planets orbiting our Sun (not to scale):

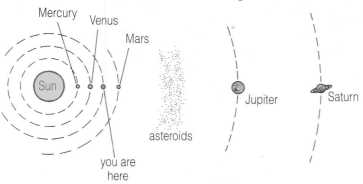

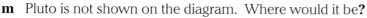

Mercury
Venus
Mars
Sun
you are here
asteroids
Jupiter
Saturn
Uranus
Neptune

m Pluto is not shown on the diagram. Where would it be?

n How many planets are there? Write down their names in order. Then find a way to memorise them.

o Which 2 planets are nearest to Earth? Which of these is hotter than Earth?

p Which 2 are the biggest planets? Which of these has rings round it?

q Which planet do you think is the coldest? Why is this?

r Which planet goes round the Sun in the shortest time?

s The planets travel in curved orbits. What is the name of the force that pulls them from a straight line?

t Planets and stars both look like bright dots in the sky. What difference is there in the way they send light to us?

u Planets are smaller than stars, but they often look as bright as stars. What conclusion can you draw from this?

Jupiter

The photo shows Voyager-2.
This is a space-probe or 'artificial satellite'.
It has been used to explore the Solar System.

v Why has it not been used to explore outside the Solar System?

w Why has it not carried people?

The Voyager-2 space-probe travelled at 20 000 mph. After 4 years it passed Saturn.

Things to do

1 Copy and complete:
a) The . . . . is the centre of the . . . . System.
b) The names of the 9 planets (in order) are:
c) The coldest planet is . . . . This is because it is the farthest from the . . . .
d) The planets do not travel in . . . . lines. Their orbits are . . . . This is because of the gravitational . . . . of the . . . ., pulling on each planet.
e) The . . . . shine only by reflected . . . ., like the Moon.

2 Here is a list of objects:
star   planet   universe   moon   galaxy
a) Put them in order of size (smallest first).
b) For each one, write a sentence to explain what it is.

3 Why do you think Pluto was the last planet to be discovered?

4 Explain why you think life developed on Earth and not on other planets.

Physics at Work

Athletics

Here is a distance–time graph for a sprinter:

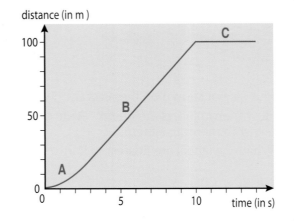

a What is happening in part C?

b How long is the race in
(i) distance? (ii) time?

c What was her average speed?

d Why is the graph curved at A?

e Can you sketch a speed–time graph for her?

Hydraulic brakes on a car

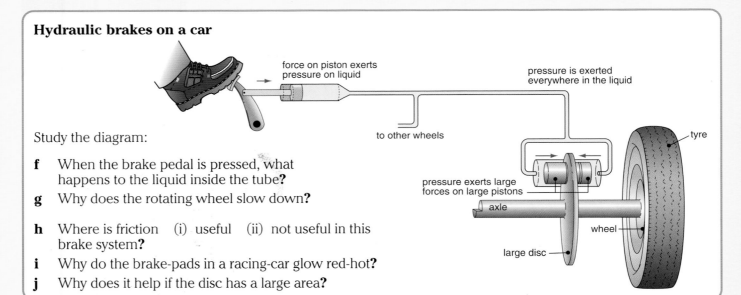

force on piston exerts pressure on liquid

pressure is exerted everywhere in the liquid

to other wheels

pressure exerts large forces on large pistons

axle

large disc

tyre

wheel

Study the diagram:

f When the brake pedal is pressed, what happens to the liquid inside the tube?

g Why does the rotating wheel slow down?

h Where is friction (i) useful (ii) not useful in this brake system?

i Why do the brake-pads in a racing-car glow red-hot?

j Why does it help if the disc has a large area?

Melanie pumps up her **bicycle tyre**. She notices that the pump becomes hot.

k Where did the energy come from to pump up the tyre?

l Explain how the air molecules exert a pressure on the walls of the tyre.

m The air in the tyre was warmed by the pumping. How does this affect the molecules of air?

Space shuttle

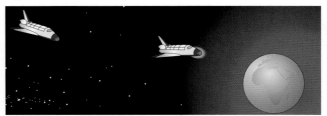

When the space shuttle (or a meteorite) enters the Earth's atmosphere, it glows red-hot.

n Explain why. Use the particle theory if you can.

Cycling

The photo shows a racing cyclist.

o Why is he wearing this odd hat?

p Why do some cyclists shave their legs?

q Where does a cyclist find friction
(i) helpful? (ii) not helpful?

r He is holding the handlebars near the centre.
Will this make it easier or harder to turn corners?

Sky-diving

There are 2 forces acting on the parachutist.

s What is the name of the force acting upwards?
t Name the force acting downwards.

u If the man weighs 600 N, and air resistance is
only 500 N, what is the resultant force?
v What happens in this case?

w What happens when his parachute opens?
x Can you explain this, using the particle theory?

Bungee-jumping

Look at this woman jumping off a bridge:

y What is the main force on her?
z Which way is it acting?

As she goes faster, the air starts to exert a force on her.
A What is this force called?
B Which way does it act?

C What stops her hitting the ground?
D Which way does this force act?

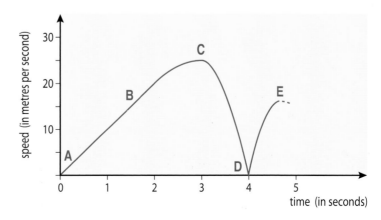

The speed–time graph below shows how she falls.

Point A was when she jumped off the bridge.

E At which point (B, C, D, E) is she
moving fastest?
F What is her highest speed?
G At which point has she got most
kinetic energy?

H At which point did she have most
gravitational potential energy?

I Is she moving at point D?
J At which point is the rope stretched
the most?

K Can you predict the shape of the
rest of the graph?

Forces and the Solar System

Ideas about Forces

One of the earliest scientists was a Greek called **Archimedes**. In about 260 BC he worked out the law of levers (the principle of moments).
He also discovered the idea of an upthrust in water, and why things float.
He discovered this in his bath, and was so excited that he ran naked into the street shouting "Eureka!" ("I have found it!").

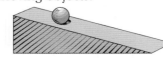

EUREKA! EUREKA! (The very first streaker)

Another famous Greek called **Aristotle** wrote about forces (see lesson 31f). He believed that objects will only keep moving as long as there is a force exerted on them. (This appears to be true in everyday life on Earth, because of friction.)

It wasn't until 2000 years later that **Galileo** actually did some experiments on moving objects.
In 1589 he rolled some balls down an inclined plane (a ramp).

He showed that a force causes a ***change*** in an object's motion (see lesson 31a).
If there is no force on an object (and so no friction), then the object just keeps on moving at the same speed. In practice there is usually a friction force, and this ***changes*** the speed of the object, and it slows down.

Isaac Newton was a great mathematician. He worked out 3 laws about forces, called the 3 laws of motion, which he published in 1686. He also worked out and published his law of gravitation (see lesson 31f). These laws let us calculate the effects of forces.

Ideas about the Solar System

Once upon a time, people believed the Earth was flat. But by 350 BC, **Aristotle** had good arguments for a round Earth. (For example, when a ship sails away, in any direction, you see the masts last of all.)

People believed that the Earth was at the centre of the universe. They believed that the Earth stayed still, and everything moved round it.

As time went by, astronomers observed the planets more and more carefully. They found it harder and harder to explain what they saw.

It wasn't until 1507 that a Polish monk called **Nicolaus Copernicus** took a fresh look at the problem. He saw a simpler way to explain the observations. He suggested that the ***Sun*** is at the centre and the planets move round it. This idea was very strongly opposed by the Church.

In 1609, **Galileo** used a telescope to observe Jupiter and its moons. What he saw convinced him that Copernicus was right. This led to Galileo's famous argument with the Church, when he was threatened with torture and forced to retract his ideas.

Since 1570, **Tycho Brahe** had been making accurate observations of stars and planets. **Johannes Kepler** looked at this data in detail. By 1609 he worked out that the planets must be moving in ***ellipses***, not the 'perfect circles' that everyone had believed.

Later **Isaac Newton** used the idea of gravity (see lesson 31f) to explain ***why*** the planets move in elliptical orbits, to form the Solar System.

Questions

1 Sketch a rubber duck floating in Archimedes' bath and mark on it:
   a) its weight b) the upthrust of the water.

2 Think about Galileo's experiments with a ramp.
   a) If you release a ball on a ramp, does it travel at constant speed? Describe its motion carefully.
   b) Does a ball roll faster down a steep ramp or a shallow ramp? Can you explain why?
   c) To reduce the effects of friction, would it be better to use a heavy ball or a light ball? Why?

3 Explain carefully how looking at a ship gives you evidence for a round Earth.

4 Give some reasons why you think people in the past "believed that the Earth was at the centre of the universe."

5 A space probe, far out in space, travels at a steady speed without using its engine. Why is this?

6 Choose one of the scientists and find out more details of his life.

Revision Summary

Forces and motion

- Forces are pushes and pulls. They are measured in newtons (N).
  Friction is a force which always tries to slow down movement.
  Air resistance can be reduced by streamlining.
  Weight is a force. It is the pull of gravity by the Earth, downwards.

- If 2 forces on an object are equal and opposite, we say they are **balanced** forces. In this case there is no resultant force.
  When the forces are balanced, then the movement of the object is not changed (it stays still, or stays moving at a steady speed).

- If the forces on an object are not balanced, there is a **resultant** force.
  This resultant force makes the object speed up, or slow down, or change direction.

- The speed of a car can be measured in metres per second or kilometres per hour.

$$\text{Average speed} = \frac{\text{distance travelled}}{\text{time taken}}$$

- The motion of a car can be shown on a distance–time graph:

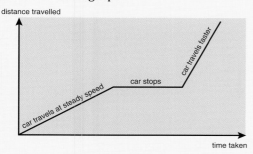

- Levers have many uses. A long spanner is easier to turn than a short spanner.
  The moment (or turning effect) of a force = force × distance of force from the pivot.

  The principle (or law) of moments says:

  In equilibrium, the anti-clockwise = the clockwise moments moments

- Pressure is measured in N/cm² or N/m² (also called a pascal, Pa).

$$\text{Pressure} = \frac{\text{force} \ (\text{in newtons})}{\text{area} \ (\text{in cm}^2 \text{ or m}^2)}$$

The Earth and beyond

- The Earth turns on its axis once in 24 hours. This is 1 day.
  This means that the Sun appears to rise in the East and set in the West. For the same reason, stars at night appear to move from East to West.

- The Earth travels round the Sun in an orbit, taking 1 year ($365\frac{1}{4}$ days).
  The Earth's axis is tilted (at $23\frac{1}{2}°$). This means that in summer the Sun is higher in the sky, and so day-time is longer and warmer than in winter.

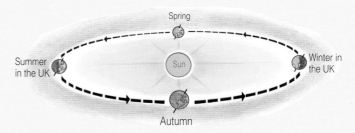

- The Moon moves round the Earth, taking 1 month for a complete orbit.
  The Moon shines because of sunlight on it.
  It shows different phases at different times of the month. If it goes into the shadow of the Earth, there is an eclipse of the Moon.

- The Sun is a star. It has 9 planets round it.

  The diagram above shows the order and the relative size of them (but they should be shown much further apart). This is the Solar System.

- A planet is held in orbit round the Sun by a gravitational force.
  The shape of each orbit is an ellipse.

- The Sun and other stars are very hot and make their own light.
  The planets and their moons shine only by reflecting the sunlight.

- Artificial satellites and space probes can be launched to observe the Earth and to explore the Solar System.

Questions

1 The graph shows how far a cyclist travels in 10 seconds:

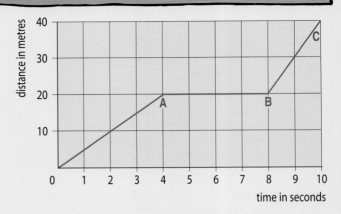

Use the graph to answer these questions.
a)   How far does she go in the first 4 seconds?
b)   What was her speed during the first 4 seconds?
c)   What was her speed between 4 and 8 seconds?
d)   What was her average speed for the whole journey?
e)   During which part of her journey was she travelling fastest?

2 The diagram shows an aeroplane. It has 4 forces on it:

The names of the 4 forces are
• the **lift** from the wings,
• the **weight** of the plane,
• the **drag** of the air resistance,
• the **thrust** of the engine.

a)   Sketch the plane and put the correct label against each force.
b)   If the lift is greater than the weight, what happens to the plane?
c)   If the thrust is greater than the drag, what happens?

3 The diagram shows a metre rule balanced on a pivot:

The weight of the rule is 1 N.
a)   Where does the weight of the rule act?
b)   Re-draw the diagram, showing the weight of the rule.
c)   How far is this force from the pivot?
d)   What is the value of F?
e)   What is the total force down on the pivot?
f)   What is the force exerted by the pivot on the rule?

4 Jackie has a pair of stilts:

She weighs 400 N and the stilts weigh 100 N.
Each of her shoes has an area of 150 cm^2.
The bottom of each stilt has an area of 25 cm^2.
Calculate the pressure on the ground in each of the diagrams:

(a)   (b)   (c)

5 A car with 4 wheels has the tyres at a pressure of 20 N/cm^2.
Each tyre has an area of 100 cm^2 in contact with the road.
a)   What is the weight of the car?
b)   If 1 kg weighs 10 N, what is the mass of the car (in kg)?

6 Paul says, "When you look at the stars, you are looking back in time." What does he mean?

Matter | 32

Everything around us is a solid, a liquid or a gas.
We ourselves are made of solid, liquid and gas.
These are the 3 states of matter.
But what do the states have in common?
How are they different?

In this topic you'll find out.

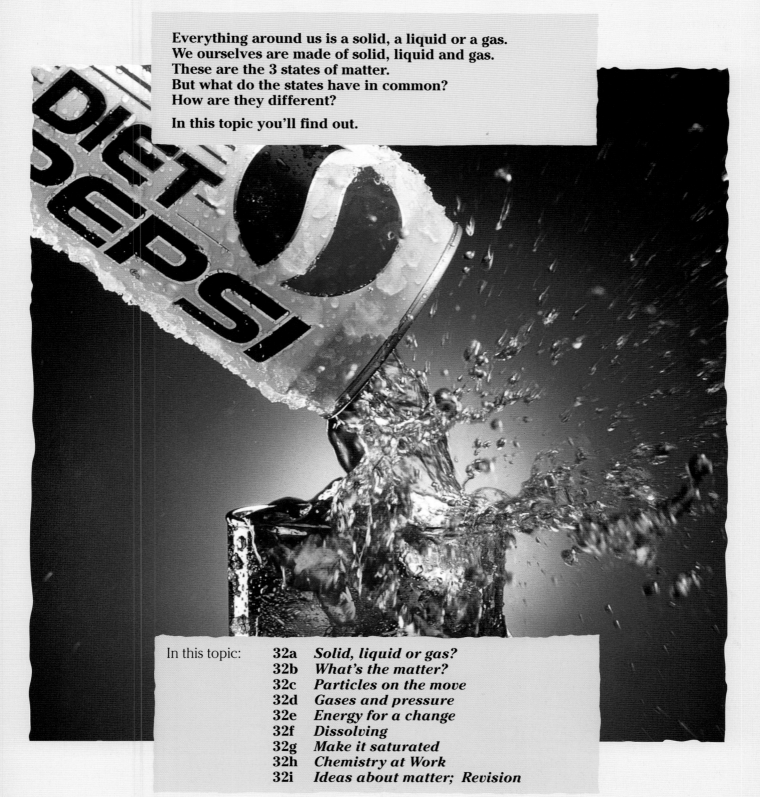

Solid, liquid or gas?

When did you last go to a fair?

▶ Look at the picture:

a Can you name:
   i)   2 solids,
   ii) 2 liquids,
   iii) 2 gases? (Clue: you might not be able to see the gases!)

Solid, **liquid** and **gas** are the **3 states of matter**.

Which state?

Think back to your work on solids, liquids and gases in Book 7.
Copy and complete the table. Use ✓ for yes and ✗ for no.
A few answers have been done for you.

Yes, It's a liquid!

Property	Solid	Liquid	Gas
Is it runny?		✓	
Is it hard?			
Is it heavy?			
Can it be poured? (Does it flow?)	✗		
Does it have a fixed shape?			
Does it have a fixed volume?			
Is it easily squashed?			✓
Is it easily stirred?	✗		✓
Is it dense? (Heavy for its volume)			

▶ Look at the table of melting points and boiling points:
At room temperature, 20°C, which element(s) are:
b solid?   **c** liquid?   **d** gas?

This bottle of cola contains gas:

e Where is the gas?

f What is the gas called?

g What happens when you open a can of fizzy drink . . .

Element	Melting point in °C	Boiling point in °C
chlorine	−101	−34
iodine	114	184
fluorine	−220	−188
bromine	−7	59

. . . straight from the fridge?   or   . . . just off the shelf?

Is there any difference?

Getting rid of the fizz

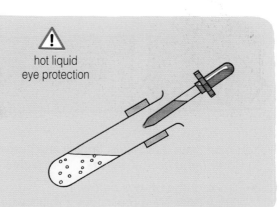

Quarter fill a test-tube with cold fizzy water.
Add a few drops of universal indicator.
What do you see?
The carbon dioxide dissolved in the water makes it a weak acid.

Warm the tube *gently* shaking a little all the time.
Let the fizzy water boil slowly.
Look at the colour of the universal indicator.
What do you see?
Try to explain what is happening.

Time the fizz

In this investigation you'll be working with a solid, a liquid and a gas.
Stomach powder is the solid. It is added to the liquid, water, and a gas is made.

Your task is to use this reaction to measure time.
Your device must measure 40 seconds exactly.
Plan how you can do this.
Your teacher will give you some stomach powder.
Show your teacher your plan. Ask for the other apparatus you need.
Each group can have a stop-clock for the tests.
The stop-clock will be taken away when your device is tested!

Which group is the most accurate?

Well, you said you wanted a watch for your birthday!

---

1 Copy and complete:
a) Solids have a . . . . shape.
b) Liquids and . . . . take the shape of the container.
c) Gases are . . . . dense than solids and liquids.
d) Solids and liquids are . . . . to squash.
e) . . . . and . . . . can be poured.
f) Solids and liquids have a . . . . volume.

2 Which properties of solids, liquids and gases are important for these sports?
a) rock climbing
b) water skiing
c) hot-air ballooning
d) hockey
e) ice-skating

3 Classify each of these as solid, liquid or gas at room temperature.

| paper | ice | mud | glass | smoke |
| air | wax | carbon dioxide | petrol | |

Are any hard to classify? Why?
Write about your ideas.

4 Sam filled a syringe with water. He held the end against a rubber stopper. He pushed the plunger.

He then did the test with air in the syringe.
Then he did the test with pieces of wood in the syringe. Describe what he would have noticed in each of the 3 tests.

Things to do

129

What's the matter?

You have seen that solids, liquids and gases behave in different ways.
In Book 7 you used ideas about **particles** to explain the differences.

▶ Look at the photos below.
How does each one suggest that matter is made of particles**?**

a Blue water**?** **b** Hot curry**?** **c** Sweet mug**?** **d** Lovely smell**?**

Particle tests

Now try these simple tests. For each one, write down what you notice.
What does each one tell you about particles**?** Write down your ideas.
Think about differences between solids, liquids and gases.

Purple shades

1. Take one large purple crystal. Put it in a test-tube.
Add 10 cm³ water. Cork the tube. Carefully shake it to
dissolve the crystal.

2. Take 1 cm³ of this solution in another test-tube.
Add 9 cm³ water. Cork the tube. Carefully shake it.

3. Repeat step 2 again and again. Do this until you can't see the
pink colour any more.

How many times did you repeat step 2**?**
What does this tell you about the particles in the crystal**?**

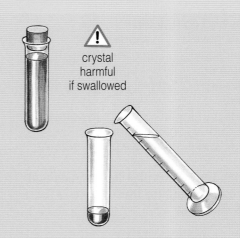

crystal
harmful
if swallowed

Lost in spaces?

Measure 25 cm³ sand in a measuring cylinder.
Measure 25 cm³ dried peas in another cylinder.
Predict the total volume when the 2 solids are added together
and mixed.

Now mix the 2 solids. Shake the substances well.
Let the mixture settle.
What is the ***total*** volume**?**

Warm air

Gently warm the tube of air for one minute.
What do you see?
As soon as you stop heating, lift the delivery tube
out of the water.

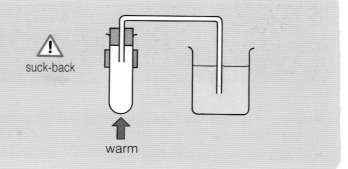

suck-back

warm

'Dry ice'

Have you seen 'dry ice' being used at pop concerts?
'Dry ice' is solid carbon dioxide.
The solid turns easily to gas. It is stored in pressurised containers.

A **small** volume of solid gives a **large** volume of gas.
e   What does this tell you about particles in solids and gases?

Rising balloons

A balloon rises if it is less dense than the air around it.

f   How does the air in a hot-air balloon become less dense than
the air outside?
Try to explain your idea by drawing particles.

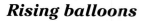

heat →   ?

cold air   hot air

1   Copy and complete.
Choose the correct word from the 2 in
brackets.
a)   All matter is made of . . . .
      (particles/solids)
b)   The particles are very . . . . (small/large)
c)   In a gas, the particles are . . . . (more/less)
      spread out than in a liquid.

2   Soluble aspirin tablets are used to treat
headaches.

What happens to the particles in the tablet
when it is dropped in water?
Draw pictures to help you to explain.
Use ○ for a water particle.
Use ● for an aspirin particle.

3   This coffee filter collects the coffee
grains. Why does the water pass
through the filter paper?

4   To make a balloon lighter than air
you could fill it with a light gas.
Hydrogen is a light gas.
a)   Why isn't hydrogen used to fill
      passenger balloons?
b)   Find out all you can about the
      Hindenburg.

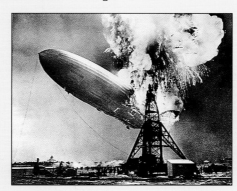

Things to do

Particles on the move

▶ Draw 3 diagrams to show how you think particles are arranged in a solid, a liquid and a gas.

How do your diagrams explain that:

a solids are hard to compress (squash)?
b gases are easy to compress?
c liquids can be poured?
d gases are the shape of their container?

In Book 7, you learnt that materials **expand** when they get hot.
They **contract** when they cool down.

e What does *expand* mean?
f What does *contract* mean?
g When a solid expands, what do you think happens to the particles?

▶ Look at your answers to **e**, **f** and **g**.
Use these to help you with the photo questions.

j Boiling water should not be poured into a cold glass. Why not?

h Why is mercury used in thermometers?

i Railway tracks contain small gaps. Why do they have these?

l Warming the jam jar lid may help to remove it. Why?

k Concrete roads have gaps between sections. Why are these filled with tar?

Watching for movement

Do particles move? Try some of these tests to find out.

A blue move?
Before you do this test, predict what will happen.

Put a few blue crystals in the bottom of a beaker.
Carefully pour water on the top.
Do not shake or stir.
Leave the beaker for a few days.
Draw pictures to show what happens.

Do you think particles move?
Write down or draw what you think happens to the particles.

Use some of these words to explain what happens.

dissolve   move
particles   spread
blue   mix
water   collide

Smoke signals?
Your teacher will show you this experiment.

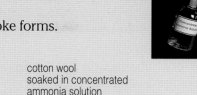

When fumes from the acid and ammonia meet, white smoke forms.

What do you think will happen in this experiment?
Predict **_exactly_** what you will see.

Your teacher will do this experiment.
Try to explain what you see.

cotton wool
soaked in concentrated
ammonia solution

cotton wool soaked
in concentrated
hydrochloric acid

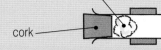

cork

A brown move?
Your teacher will show you the bromine experiment.

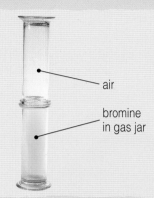

air

What happens when a gas jar of air is put on top of a gas jar of
bromine?
Do you think the particles move?
Write down or draw what you think happens to the particles.

bromine
in gas jar

Diffusion

Liquid and gas particles can move and mix. They do this without
being stirred or shaken. This is called **diffusion**.

Have you ever smelt freshly baked bread?
Particles of gas are released from the bread. They **diffuse** through
the air. You can smell the bread throughout the room.

The **_Watching for movement_** tests tell you about **_rates_** of
diffusion too.

m   Which diffuses faster, a gas or a liquid? Why?

1   Copy and complete:

a) 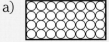   These are the particles
in a . . . .

b) 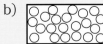   These are the particles
in a . . . .

c) 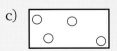   These are the particles
in a . . . .

2   Robert Brown was a Scottish scientist. He
studied pollen grains in water. Find out about
what he saw. This is called Brownian motion.

3   Helium is a lighter gas than air.
Gas particles can diffuse through balloon
rubber. This is why balloons go down.

Which balloon do you think will go down
first? Why?

Things to do

Gases and pressure

▶ Copy out each label. Say whether it is for a **solid**, a **liquid** or a **gas**. (Clue: there are 2 labels for each!)

The particles are far apart and arranged randomly.

The particles are close together but random.

The particles are very close together. They are in a regular pattern.

The particles move about quickly and in all directions.

The particles do not move about. They vibrate.

The particles move about.

▶ Look at the 2 labels you have chosen for gases. These tell you about **gas pressure**.

Gas pressure . . .

. . . keeps a balloon blown up.

. . . tells us about the weather.

. . . gives us a comfy bike ride!

Gas pressure

What causes the pressure? Particles help us to understand.
Think about gas inside a balloon.
The particles move around very quickly.
They move in all directions. Some particles hit each other.
Others hit the wall of the balloon. Those that hit the wall give a force on each unit of area of the balloon. This is called the **pressure** of the gas.
(Look at page 112 to remind yourself about pressure.)
The more often particles hit the wall, the greater the pressure.
The harder they hit the wall, the greater the pressure.

Think about gases

Make some predictions. Discuss these in your group.

1 Think of a gas in a closed box. What happens if you heat the gas? Do you think the pressure will increase or decrease? Try to explain using the idea of particles.

2 Think of a gas in a syringe. The plunger can move in and out. What happens to the plunger if you heat the gas? Try to explain using the idea of particles.

Check your predictions with your teacher.

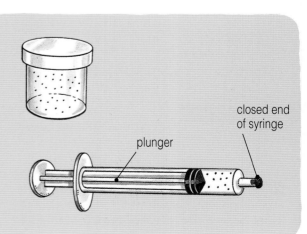

closed end of syringe

plunger

Moving gases

Your teacher will show you an experiment using a porous pot.
The porous pot lets gas particles (molecules) through its walls.
Your teacher will put some natural gas into the beaker.
The gas is lighter than air.
Think about the movement of gas molecules.

Try to explain what you see.
Use your ideas about gas pressure and diffusion.

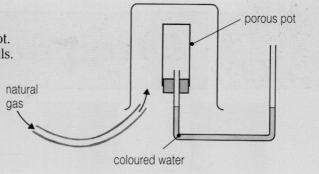

porous pot

natural gas

coloured water

Gases into liquids

Gases can be turned into liquids. One way to do this is to put the gas in a pressurised container. We say the gas is **compressed** or stored **under pressure**.

a   Why does *compressing* a gas turn it to a liquid?
Use particles to explain.

You have probably seen tankers like the one in the photograph:
This one is used to carry liquid nitrogen.

b   Why are gases stored and transported as liquids?

Liquid nitrogen is very useful. It is very cold.
Lots of foods are frozen by spraying them with liquid nitrogen.

c   Why do we freeze foods?

d   Are frozen foods good for you? Write about your ideas.

Propane and butane can also be stored as liquids.

e   What are these gases used for?

f   What are the dangers of these gases?

g   Why does the pressure in a butane cylinder fall when the temperature falls?

---

1   Copy and complete:
Particles in a gas . . . . quickly in . . . . directions. When they hit the . . . . of a container this is called the gas . . . . This is the . . . . on each unit of area. Gas particles move more . . . . when they are heated. As the gas is heated in the container, the pressure . . . .

2

PIZAZ SPORT - The all over deodorant body spray for men. Long lasting deodorant blended with the subtle intrigue of a Designer Fragrance.

Caution: Do not use near fire or naked flame. Do not pierce or burn even after use. Do not spray eyes or face. Keep out of reach of young children.

 CFC FREE

150ml e

Why shouldn't you put this near to heat?

3   Look at these boiling points of gases that are in the air.

xenon	$-108°C$	krypton	$-153°C$
argon	$-186°C$	nitrogen	$-196°C$
oxygen	$-183°C$	helium	$-269°C$
	neon	$-246°C$	

To collect the gases, air is cooled so it becomes liquid. The liquid air is slowly warmed so the gases boil off.

a)   Which 2 gases have the closest boiling points?

b)   When liquid air is warmed, which boils off first – oxygen, argon or nitrogen?

c)   What is this method of separating called?

d)   Which gas is the most common in the air?

e)   Which gas is needed for burning?

f)   Name 3 gases with similar properties. (Clue: use the periodic table.)

Things to do

Energy for a change

solid   liquid   gas

Water is usually found as a liquid. But water can be a solid (ice) or a gas (steam).
Ice, water and steam are the same chemical substance (H_2O).
When water turns into ice or steam we say it is **changing state**.

*distillation is
evaporation + condensation*

▶ Sketch the pictures of the 3 states of water. Write a label next
   to each arrow. Choose the correct label from this list:

> **boil (or evaporate)**   **melt**   **freeze**   **condense**

a At what temperature does water boil?
b At what temperatures does ice melt?

Is this true? Explain.

Liquids into solids

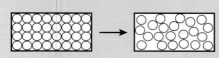   

How do you turn a solid into a liquid? How do you turn a liquid into a solid?
In this experiment you will make a solid melt by heating it. Then you
will let the liquid cool slowly. What do you think will happen?

- Put a few spatula measures of the solid in a test-tube.
- Clamp the tube in a warm water bath.
- Heat up the water bath until the solid melts.
- When the temperature of the liquid reaches 75°C,
  switch off your Bunsen.
- Leave the substance to cool.
- Record the temperature of the substance every minute
  as it cools.
- Stir carefully.
- Take readings every minute until the temperature
  reaches 50°C.
- Leave the apparatus to cool.

⚠ hot
eye protection

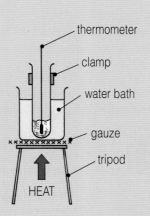

thermometer
clamp
water bath
gauze
tripod
HEAT

Plot a graph of your results.
Try to explain the shape of your graph.

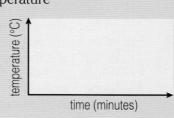

temperature (°C)

time (minutes)

Feeling cool?

Dip your finger into water.
Dip the same finger of the other hand into alcohol.
Hold your fingers out in front of you.

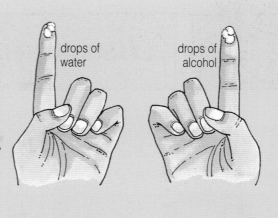

drops of water   drops of alcohol

c Which liquid cools your skin most?
d Which liquid evaporates faster?
e Try to explain these results using the idea of moving particles.
f What happens to the temperature of a liquid as it evaporates?
g You have thermometers, rubber bands, paper tissues, beakers and a stop-clock.
How can you use this apparatus to find out which liquid evaporates fastest – alcohol, water or propanone?

Hassan studied some ice melting.
He stirred crushed ice in a beaker.
He took the temperature of the ice every 2 minutes.
These are his results:

thermometer

beaker

ice

Time (minutes)	0	2	4	6	8	10	12	14	16	18	20
Temperature (°C)	-4	-2	0	0	0	0	0	0	0	2	5

h At what temperature did the ice melt?
i Ice melts when it is heated. Where did the heat come from in this experiment?
j Why didn't the temperature rise between 4 and 16 minutes? Explain what happens to the particles.

Salt lowers the freezing point of water.

k Why do we put salt on icy roads in winter?

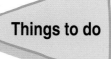
Things to do

1 Copy and complete using **heat** or **cool**:
a) To turn a solid to a liquid you need to . . . . it.
b) To turn a liquid to a gas you need to . . . . it.
c) To turn a gas to a liquid you need to . . . . it.
d) To turn a liquid to a solid you need to . . . . it.

2 Use the words from the box to describe
a) melting point   b) boiling point.

| solid | liquid | gas | temperature |

3 You looked at the water cycle in Book 8. Use the words below to help explain the cycle.

| evaporate | sea | Sun | cloud |
| rain | condense |

Draw a simple picture of the cycle.

4 Look at this heating curve for a solid substance X:

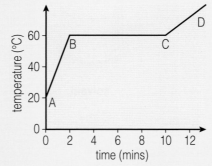

a) What is the state of X from:
i) A to B?   ii) B to C?   iii) C to D?
b) What is the melting point of X?
c) X is being heated. Why does the temperature stay steady between B and C?
d) What do you think happens if heating carries on after 12 minutes?

Dissolving

Do you like drinking tea?
There's a lot of science in action when you make tea.

▶ Look at what you do:

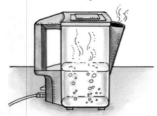

Boiling the water.

Brewing the tea.

Adding milk and sugar.

Write about the particles in each step shown above.
Where are they? What is happening to them?
Start with the water particles in the kettle. Finish with the particles
in your cup of milky sweet tea.
Try to use some or all of these words and phrases:

moving slowly	*moving more quickly*	*steam*	*diffuse*	*soluble*
insoluble	*close together*	*far apart*	*dissolve*	*mix*

Sugar dissolves in a hot cup of tea. It dissolves in the water.
It makes a **solution**. Sugar is **soluble**.
In a solution the substance which dissolves is the **solute**. Sugar is the **solute**.
The water dissolves the sugar.
The water is the **solvent**.

solute   +   **solvent**   ⟶   **solution**

Dissolving quickly

Think about all the things that affect dissolving.
How could you get a sugar cube to dissolve as
quickly as possible?

a   Make a list of your
    ideas.

b   Explain each idea
    in terms of particles.

Making a solution

Emma adds the salt to the water
in the beaker.

5.5 g of salt

water

c   When all the salt has
    dissolved, what is the
    reading on the balance?
    Explain this using the
    idea of particles.

d   How can Emma get
    the solid salt back?

In most solutions the solvent is water. But other substances can be solvents

Have you ever had any clothes dry-cleaned?
Dry cleaning uses solvents without water in them.
These are called non-aqueous solvents.

e What type of stains can dry-cleaning remove?

f Why don't we dry-clean **all** our clothes?

Nail varnish remover is another non-aqueous solvent.

g What is its chemical name?

MADE IN RUSSIA
57% VISCOSE/Вискоза
43% ACETATE/Ацетат
LINING/Подкладка
100% POLYESTER/
Полизфир

M20627

Ⓟ

PROFESSIONAL
DRY CLEAN
ONLY

Clean nails

Paint some nail varnish on a glass slide.
Leave it to dry for a few minutes.
Test the 3 solvents your teacher will give you.
Which is best at removing the varnish?

Some solutes are very soluble in a solvent but they may be **in**soluble in another solvent.
They have different **solubilities** in different solvents.

A stain remover

Plan an investigation on solvents.
Which solvent is best at removing stains?

⚠ Some solvents are very flammable.
Make sure there are no Bunsens alight in the lab.

Your teacher will give you some substances which stain.
Examples could be:

> ball-point pen   felt-tip pen   grease
>
> paint   grass   coffee   tea
>
> orange juice   tomato sauce

Ask your teacher to check your plan.
Then do the investigation.

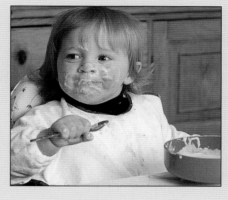

1 Copy and complete:
a) A substance which . . . . is soluble.
b) A substance which does not . . . . is insoluble.
c) solute + solvent → . . . .
d) Solvents without . . . . are non-aqueous.
e) Solutes have different . . . . in different solvents.

2 Which of these are soluble in water?
a) sand
b) salt
c) chalk
d) butter
e) wax
f) sugar
g) detergent

3 Sea-water is a solution. Name a solute and the solvent in sea-water.

4 What's the difference between these felt-tip pens?

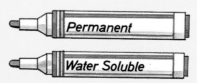

Permanent

Water Soluble

5 Tom is investigating the paints used in some oil paintings.
He uses chromatography to compare them.
How does he choose the best solvent to use?
List the properties of a good solvent for chromatography.

Things to do

Make it saturated

Nazia makes a solution from 4 g of salt and 100 g of water. Describe 2 ways she could make a solution which is *half* as concentrated.

Some solutions contain only *a little solute* in *a lot of solvent*. We say the solutions are **dilute**.
Some solutions contain *a lot of solute* in only *a little solvent*. We say the solutions are **concentrated**.

What happens if we heat a concentrated solution?

As more and more solvent evaporates, the solution becomes more and more concentrated.
Eventually it cannot become any more concentrated.
If more solvent evaporates, solute comes out of the solution.
We see solid forming. The solution is **saturated**.

A **saturated** solution is one in which no more solute will dissolve (at that temperature).

Plotting solubility curves

The amount of a substance that can dissolve in a certain amount of solvent (at that temperature) is called the **solubility** of the substance.

We can measure the solubility of a substance at different temperatures. If the information is plotted on a graph, it makes a **solubility curve**.

Use the information in the table to plot a solubility curve for potassium chloride:

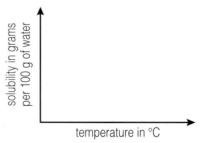

a What is the solubility of potassium chloride at 45°C?

b At what temperature does 36 g of potassium chloride dissolve in 100 g of water?

c At 80°C, how much potassium chloride dissolves in 1 kg (1000 g) of water?

d At 25°C, how much potassium chloride dissolves in 20 g of water?

e At 40°C, how much potassium chloride dissolves in 28 g of water?

f What happens to the solubility of potassium chloride as the temperature increases?

Temperature in °C	Solubility in grams per 100 g of water
0	28.0
10	31.0
20	34.5
30	37.5
40	40.0
50	43.0
60	45.5
70	48.5
80	51.0
90	54.0
100	56.5

This table shows how the solubility of potassium chloride changes with temperature.

Testing solubility

Plan a test to see which compound is the most soluble in water.

Think about:

- How will you make this a fair test?
- How will you make your solutions saturated?
- How will you measure how much solid dissolves?
- How will you make your results reliable?
- What apparatus will you use?
- How will you record your results?

Ask your teacher to check your plan.
You can then collect some compounds to test.

Which is the most soluble?

Solubility patterns

Scientists have measured the solubility of lots of compounds.
Some patterns can be seen. Look at the solubility table:
Use this table to work out answers to **g** to **l**.

Are these compounds soluble or insoluble in water:

g copper chloride?
h potassium carbonate?
i magnesium nitrate?
j lead sulphate?
k iron carbonate?
l ammonium sulphide?

Solubility Table	
• All sodium, potassium and ammonium compounds	are soluble
• All nitrates	are soluble
• All chlorides	are soluble (except $AgCl$, $PbCl_2$)
• All sulphates	are soluble (except Ag_2SO_4, $BaSO_4$, $CaSO_4$, $PbSO_4$)
• All carbonates	are insoluble (except Na_2CO_3, K_2CO_3, $(NH_4)_2CO_3$)
• All sulphides	are insoluble (except Na_2S, K_2S, $(NH_4)_2S$)

1 Explain the meanings of each of these words or phrases:
a) solution
b) saturated solution
c) solubility
d) solubility curve.

2 At 60°C, 40 g of copper sulphate dissolves in 100 g of water to make a saturated solution.
a) At 60°C, how much will dissolve in 250 g of water?
b) At 60°C, how much will dissolve in 46 g of water?
c) Why is the solubility of solids in water normally given only for temperatures between 0°C–100°C?

3 A hot, saturated solution of potassium nitrate in water is cooled to room temperature. Describe what you would see. (Use the graph for question 4 to help you.)

4 Look at these solubility curves:

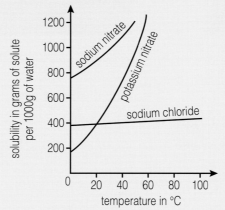

a) Which substance is the most soluble at room temperature?
b) Which substance is the least soluble at room temperature? (Explain your answer carefully!)
c) Which substance has a solubility which changes only a little with temperature?

Things to do

Chemistry at Work

32h

Useful mixtures of solids, liquids and gases

A **foam** is a mixture of a solid or a liquid with gas trapped inside it.
We see many foams in everyday life.
Look at the photos below:

A

B

C

D

E

F

G

a Which of the photos above show 'solid foams' and which show 'liquid foams'?

b Why is the mixture in photo A used inside furniture?

c How do you think that the gas gets inside furniture foam?

d All foam used to make furniture must be treated with a flame retardant. Why?

e Some types of foam are now banned for use in furniture. Explain why.

f In photo B, the gas trapped in the foam is carbon dioxide. Carbon dioxide extinguishes a flame. Why is the foam used?

g What is the liquid that you beat with a whisk when you make meringue?

h Why is the liquid in **g** beaten with a whisk to make meringue?

An **aerosol** is a gas with tiny droplets of liquid mixed in with it.
Do you use any aerosols?

Aerosols became very popular in the 1970s and 1980s.
People used them to put on their deodorant, their hair-spray
and to freshen the air with nice smells.
The gases used to propel the droplets of liquid were called
CFCs (an abbreviation for chlorofluorocarbons).

The CFCs were seen as 'wonder molecules'.
They were easy to make and completely harmless to use.
They were very unreactive.

However, scientists discovered that these CFCs were not as
harmless as was first thought.
Scientists found a hole appearing in the ozone layer – a layer
of gas in the atmosphere that protects us from harmful rays
from the Sun.
The CFCs were to blame! They were reacting with ozone gas
molecules. One CFC molecule could remove thousands of
ozone molecules.
Most countries have now banned their use.

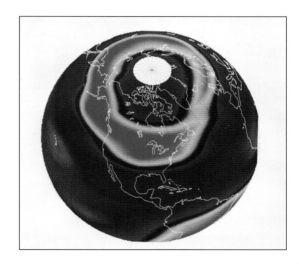

i   Why are aerosols an effective way to apply air freshener
to a room?

j   Which gases were used to carry the droplets of liquid out
of the aerosol cans?
Name the elements in these compounds.

k   Why is there a hole in the ozone layer?

l   Find out:
    i) the dangers of losing the ozone layer.
    ii) the importance of ozone in the history of life on Earth.
    iii) which gases we use now in aerosol cans.

Emulsions are mixtures of liquids that don't really mix well together!
For example, oil and water shaken up form an emulsion.
Emulsifying agents are added to foods to stop the oily liquids
separating from the watery solutions.

m   Carry out a survey of some food labels to identify which
foods contain emulsifying agents.

n   Where would you use an emulsion when decorating
your house?

o   Find out how the oil and water stay mixed in salad cream.

Matter

Early ideas about atoms

You already know a bit about **atoms**, but do you know where the word came from**?** The Greek word 'atomon' means something that cannot be divided up into smaller bits.
The first people to think that matter was made up of tiny particles were the ancient Greeks.
The idea was developed by **Democritus** who was born in 460 BC. He was a wealthy Greek philosopher.
He used the ideas of his teacher to think up a way of explaining the universe.

DEMOCRITUS

Democritus believed that there were two parts to the universe. These were the Void (just empty space) and Being (made up from atoms). He thought of atoms as particles that were:

- invisible (so small that we can't see them)
- eternal (they can't be destroyed)
- solid (they can't be squashed as there is no space in them).

But atoms can have different shapes and sizes.
He said that they could also move around in different ways and be positioned differently.

Armed with this theory, Democritus now had the tools to explain all about the world.

Explaining our observations using the ideas of Democritus

When something grows, this must be more atoms joining the ones already there. When something seems to disappear, atoms must separate and float off into the Void. This seemed logical to Democritus. What do you think**?**

You pour some water. Its atoms must be smooth and round so that they can slip past each other easily. On the other hand, the atoms in a piece of hard metal must be rough and jagged. Their sharp edges make it difficult for the atoms to slip past each other. They get locked together into a solid shape.

But the beauty of Democritus' theory of atoms was the fact that it could be extended to explain more and more things.
For example, 'atomists' could explain our senses. Imagine looking at a white object. They thought that the colour white was caused by atoms that were smooth and flat. They would ***not*** form a shadow, so the object appeared to be white.
They said that different tastes and smells were caused by different shapes and sizes of atom. For example, a bitter taste is caused by small atoms that are curved and smooth.
These atoms bump into tiny tubes in your tongue that contain atoms. These atoms bump into neighbouring atoms in the tube until the sensation arrives in your 'mind'.

You can see that Democritus had developed quite a powerful theory to make sense of the world . . . which he did until the ripe old age of 90!

Questions

1 Describe in your own words what all atoms have in common according to Democritus.

2 In what ways does Democritus say that one type of atom differs from another?

3 a) How did Democritus explain why an object looks white?
   b) How do you think he would explain an object that was black?

4 Using the ideas of Democritus:
   a) Draw the atoms in water.

   b) Draw the atoms in a piece of iron.
   c) Draw the atoms that cause a bitter taste.
   d) Have a go at drawing the atoms that might cause a sweet taste.

5 In what ways do your ideas about atoms differ from those of Democritus?

6 Find out about other ancient Greeks who contributed towards scientific thinking at that time.
   Write about their ideas and anything you can find out about their lives.

Revision Summary

Matter

solid	liquid	gas
Particles vibrate about a fixed position	Particles vibrate and change position	Particles move freely in all directions

heat / cool

Gas particles hit the walls of the balloon. This causes gas pressure.

Properties	Solid	Liquid	Gas
Fixed shape?	Yes	No – shape of container	No – shape of container
Fixed volume?	Yes	Yes	No – fills the container
Easily squashed (compressed)?	Very difficult	Can be compressed	Easy to compress
Flows easily?	No	Yes	Yes
Dense (heavy for its size)?	Yes	Less dense than solids	Less dense than liquids

$$density = \frac{mass}{volume}$$

- solid ⇌ liquid ⇌ gas
  (melts / freezes) (boils/evaporates / condenses)

Expanding and contracting

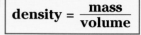

Particles stay the same size . . . they just get further apart or closer together.

- Different materials have different melting points, boiling points and densities.
- Most substances expand (get bigger) when they are heated.
  Most substances contract (get smaller) when they are cooled.
- Particles can move and mix themselves. This is diffusion.
- solute (soluble solid) + solvent (liquid) → solution
- The solubility of a solute is different ...
  - at different temperatures, and
  - in different solvents.

- A saturated solution is made when no more solid can dissolve in solution at that temperature.

Acids and alkalis

- Acids and alkalis are chemical opposites.
  Alkalis are bases (metal oxides, hydroxides or carbonates) which dissolve in water.
- We can use indicators to show which things are acids and which things are alkalis.
  Coloured berries, flower petals and vegetables make good indicators.
- Universal indicator is a mixture of indicators. Its colour gives you the pH number of the substance.

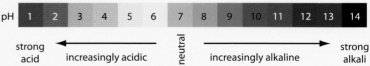

pH | 1 2 3 4 5 6 7 8 9 10 11 12 13 14

strong acid ← increasingly acidic — neutral — increasingly alkaline → strong alkali

- Acids can be changed into salts by chemical reactions.
  acid + metal → salt + hydrogen

  acid + base (alkali) → salt + water
  e.g. acid + metal oxide → salt + water
  e.g. acid + metal carbonate → salt + water + carbon dioxide
      (carbon dioxide gas turns limewater cloudy)
- The acid + base reaction is called neutralisation.
  e.g. sulphuric acid + potassium hydroxide → potassium sulphate + water
        (acid)   (base)   (salt)

  Neutralisations are useful reactions.
  e.g. Acids damage teeth. Toothpastes contain alkali to neutralise acids in the mouth.
  Some plants grow better in alkaline soil. Lime can be added to change the pH of the soil.
- Acids in the atmosphere can cause damage. Acid rain can corrode metal.
  It can dissolve rock (e.g. limestone).

Questions

1 Name some things in your body which are
a) solid   b) liquid   c) gas.

2 Dan's teacher drew some particle diagrams for his class.
But the labels got muddled.
Copy out the diagrams. Choose the right label to write under each diagram.

a)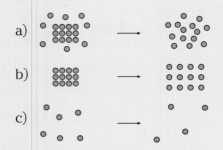

Labels

a solid expanding

a gas expanding

a sugar cube dissolving in water

b)

c)

3 **Fizzo** *is the fizziest orange drink you can buy. It leaves the others flat.*

Plan an investigation to see which drink contains the most fizz.

4 Look at the diagram opposite:

a) Explain how this apparatus could be used as a simple thermometer.
b) What happens to the water molecules as the temperature rises?
c) Could you use this to measure the temperature of boiling oil? Explain your answer.
d) Could you use this to measure the temperature inside a freezer? Explain your answer.

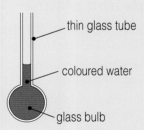

thin glass tube

coloured water

glass bulb

5 Some crushed ice is put in a beaker. It is left in a room at 25°C.

a) Sketch a graph to show how the temperature of the ice changes. Mark any important temperatures on your graph.
b) Explain what you would see in the beaker during the experiment.
c) Describe what happens to the water molecules during this experiment.
d) Why does ice float on water? What does this tell you about the molecules in ice and in water?

temperature

time

6 You have a solution of potassium nitrate in water.
The solution is saturated.
How can you find out the solubility of potassium nitrate at room temperature?
What apparatus will you need? Describe what you will do.
What measurements will you make?
Show how you will calculate the solubility.

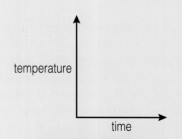

Variation 33

We inherit many of our features from our parents.
They are passed on from one generation to the next.

The same but different

Look at the kittens in the picture:
They are all from the same litter.

a In what ways do you think they look alike**?**

b In what ways do you think they look different**?**

▶ Look around at the people in your class.
   They have a lot in common: they are all human for a start!
   But they also have features that are different.
   Make a list of some of these differences.

Why do we look like we do?

We get some of our features from our parents. We **inherit** them.
Other features do not come from our parents.
These features are caused by the way we lead our life.
We call these features **environmental**.

Can you roll your tongue like the girl in the photograph**?**

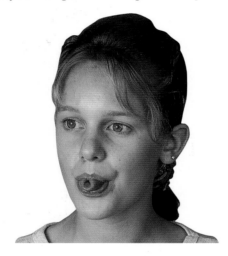

You can't learn how to do it. You have either inherited it from your parents or you haven't.

The soccer player in the photograph has a lot of natural ability.
Do you think that this is inherited or environmental**?**
But to be a top-class player, strength, agility and stamina are needed.
Do you think that these are inherited or environmental**?**

▶ Copy out the following list of features.
   Write (i) after those that you think are inherited,
   and   (e) after those that you think are environmental.

shape of nose	neat writing	freckles	hair colour
hair length	scars	skill at languages	an accent
eye colour	good at sport	blood group	size of feet

How do you measure up?

Nobody's the same, we are all unique!
Collect the following information about yourself and others in your class:

eye colour	height	left-handed *or* right-handed	shoe size
length of index finger	hair colour	tongue rolling	ear lobes

Record your findings.
Some things vary **gradually**.

c Draw a bar-chart to show the number of people in your class with different length index fingers. What do you find**?**

Other things are more **clear-cut**. For instance there are only a few different types of eye colour.

d Draw a bar-chart to show the number of people in your class with different colour eyes. What do you find**?**

▶ Look at the graph of the height of some pupils:

e How many children are less than 160 cm**?**

f What is the most common height**?**

g Do you think that the variation shown on the graph is gradual or clear-cut**?**

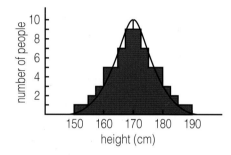

▶ Look at the graph of the hair colour of some pupils:

h What is the most common hair colour in the class**?**

i How is this graph different from the graph for height**?**

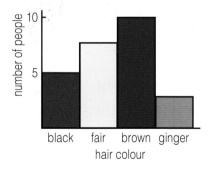

Things to do

1 Copy and complete:
We . . . . many features from our parents.
Other things, like being able to ride a bike, we . . . . during our lifetime. We say that they are due to the . . . .
Some variation, like height, is . . . . Other variation, such as eye colour, is . . . .

2 Libby has just come home from 2 weeks in Majorca.
Do you think her sun-tan is inherited?
Explain your answer.

3 Mike says "I think red hair and being good at sport are both inherited."
Do you agree or disagree? Give your reasons.

4 Look at the picture of a litter of puppies:
a) What features have the puppies inherited from their mother?
b) What features have the puppies inherited from their father?

A design for life

Have you ever heard someone say of a new baby, "Isn't she like her father?" or "Doesn't he have his mother's eyes?"

What things do you think you have inherited from your parents?

What's a chromosome?

How do we inherit things from our parents?

The **instructions** for designing a new baby are found in 2 places:

- the egg cell of the mother, and
- the sperm cell of the father.

a Which part of these cells do you think contains these instructions?

Most cells in your body contain a nucleus.
Each nucleus contains **chromosomes**.
It is the chromosomes that carry the instructions.

▶ Look at the photo:

b What do the chromosomes look like?

c Are they all the same size and shape?

d How many are there?

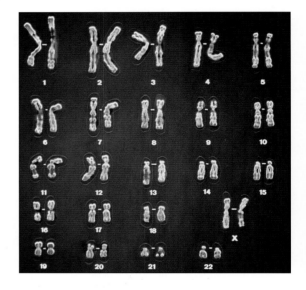

In most human cells there are 46 chromosomes.
We can put them into 23 pairs that are identical.

Halving and doubling

When a sperm cell or an egg cell is made, the chromosomes in each pair split up.

e So how many chromosomes will there be in the sperm or egg now?
Do you remember what happens when a sperm fertilises an egg?

▶ Look at the diagram:

f How many chromosomes does a fertilised egg contain?

g Where have these chromosomes come from?

h What do you think would happen at fertilisation if the sperm and the egg each contained 46 chromosomes?

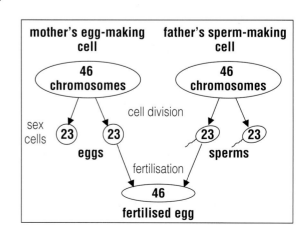

Looking at chromosomes

Scientists can make slides of human chromosomes.
Your teacher will give you a sheet showing what these
chromosomes look like.

- Count the number of chromosomes.
- Cut out your chromosomes and count them again to make sure
  you haven't lost any.
- Arrange them on a sheet of paper. Start with the largest and end
  with the smallest.
- Arrange your chromosomes in pairs according to size and
  pattern of banding.
- Stick down your chromosomes neatly in their pairs.

i   Are these chromosomes from a female or a male?

j   How do you know?

k   What do you think the bands on each chromosome might be?

Genes

Genes contain the instructions that we inherit.
Genes control certain features like eye colour.

▶   Look at the diagram:

l   How many genes do you think there are for each feature?

m   Where are they found?

n   What do you notice about the position of genes on a pair of
chromosomes?
Each band on a chromosome represents one gene.

Key to genes	
●	eye colour
✕	hair colour
▲	tongue rolling
■	height
●	nose length
✳	skin colour
■	making haemoglobin
⌄	build of body

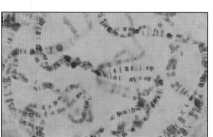

Things to do

1   Copy and complete:
Inside the nucleus of each cell there are
thread-like shapes, called . . . .
These are made up of . . . .
These . . . . contain instructions to control
how the . . . . works.
They also contain information which is . . . .
from one generation to the next.

2   How many chromosomes are there in a
human sperm or a human egg?
How many are there in other human cells?
Why do you think these numbers are
different?

3   Where are genes found?
What do genes do?
Genes are made of the chemical called DNA.
Try to find out what DNA stands for.

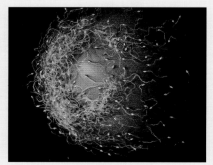

What's in a name?

What do the ox-eye daisy, the dog daisy and marguerite have in common?
The answer is that they are all the same plant.
But they have different names in different parts of Britain.

a Why do you think that using 'common names' can be confusing?

Well if you wanted to describe a particular plant or animal to someone in another country, you would be speaking in different languages.

Luckily we have a **binomial system** of naming living things.
This gives every living thing *2* names: the first name is the **genus** and the second name is the **species**.

For instance, Homo sapiens is the ***scientific name*** for a human.

b What do we mean by a species?

A species is a very similar group of individuals that can breed together and produce fertile offspring.
For example, all domestic dogs belong to the same species.
They may look different, but they can mate and give birth to cross-breeds that are perfectly healthy.

Grouping species

▶ Look at the diagram, which shows how we **classify** the grizzly bear.

c What is the largest group of individuals in the diagram?

d What is the smallest grouping in the diagram called?

Can you see that we can classify living things on the basis of their ***shared*** features?

e Use the diagram to list the groups in order of size. Start with the smallest and end up with the largest group.

The grizzly bear Ursus arctos | is part of the genus Ursus | of the family Ursidae | of the order of Carnivora | of the class of mammals | in the phylum vertebrates | in the animal kingdom

The name game

This game will help you revise invertebrate classification.

Choose a partner and sit opposite each other.

You will both be given 16 cards each with a picture and description of an invertebrate that lives in freshwater.

Lay out your 16 cards face-up on the table in front of you.

Your partner keeps his or her cards hidden and picks out **one** card, looks at it and places it in an envelope – so you don't know which it is.

You now have to ask questions based upon the pictures and descriptions to try and find out which invertebrate is in the envelope.

But your partner is only allowed to answer 'yes' or 'no'.

Write down the question that you ask each time.

Turn over the cards that you eliminate with each question.

Eventually you will identify the invertebrate chosen by your partner.

Now swap roles and see how many questions your partner needs to ask to identify the invertebrate that you choose.

The person with the **fewest** questions wins **'The name game!'**

Things to do

1 Copy and complete:
A group of organisms that can mate and produce . . . .
offspring is called a . . . .
The study of how we put living things into groups is called . . . .
It uses the . . . . system by giving every living thing 2 names.
The first is called the . . . . name and the second the . . . . name.
We classify living things on the basis of their . . . . features.

2 The Arthropods are a phylum of jointed-legged animals.
a) Can you name the 4 main classes?
b) Give an example of an animal from each of these classes.

3 The Plants are classified into 4 main groups.
a) Can you name each of these groups?
b) Give an example of a plant from each group.

4 The vertebrates make up one phylum.
a) What feature do all vertebrates have?
b) Name the 5 main classes of vertebrates.
c) Give an example of an animal from each of these classes.
d) To which class of vertebrates do each of the following belong:
   i) a turtle?   ii) a bat?   iii) a whale?
   iv) a salamander?   v) a snake?

To which class of Arthropods do these belong?

Pick and mix

Vicki's dad keeps racing pigeons.
She helps to look after them.
They are related to wild pigeons, but have been specially bred.
They have to fly long distances but always return home.

a What features do you think have been bred into racing pigeons?

Selective breeding means that we breed in the features that we want and breed out the features that we don't want.

▶ Write down a list of animals and plants that humans have selectively bred.
Why do you think humans have selectively bred these animals and plants?

Calypso fruit

A new type of fruit has been discovered on a tropical island.
It has an amazing taste, but only when it is just ripe.
The skin is covered with hairs and it is difficult to remove.
It has a bright orange colour that often attracts birds.
The number of its seeds varies and they are very bitter.
It is said to be very good for the digestion since it contains a lot of fibre.
The calypso fruits are hard to pick because the stem has lots of thorns.

b Draw a diagram of what you think the calypso fruit looks like.
c What features would you try to breed out?
d What features would you keep?
e What would your calypso fruit look like after selective breeding?

This little piggy . . .

Our modern pig is descended from the wild pig.

▶ Look at the photos:

Bacon pig

Wild pig

f Which features do you think have been bred into the modern pig?
g Which features do you think have been bred out of it?
h Do you think the modern pig could survive in the wild?
Give your reasons.

Supercow!

Farmers can now breed better cattle.
New breeds of cattle produce more milk and more beef.

Artificial insemination means that sperm can be taken from the best bulls and put directly into the best cows.
This means that the farmer no longer has to keep bulls of his own.

i Why do you think this is an advantage to the farmer?

Eggs from the best cows can be removed and fertilised with bull sperm in a test-tube.
The fertilised egg is then put back into the mother cow.
These are called **embryo transplants**.

j What do you think are the advantages to breeders of:
   i)   artificial insemination?
   ii) embryo transplants?
k Why do you think it is important to keep alive some of the old-fashioned breeds of cattle?

In your groups, discuss whether you think that artificial insemination and embryo transplants should be used on farm animals.

---

1 Make a list of 5 animals or plants that you think have been 'improved' by selective breeding. For each one, say how you think this is useful to humans.

2 A lot of cereals originally came from the Middle East.
What features do you think have been bred into varieties that are grown in Britain?

3 What features do you think have been bred into these dogs:
a) pekingese?   b) sheep dog?
c) bloodhound?

4 Humans have selectively bred modern varieties of wheat from wild wheat.
These have greater yield, improved disease resistance and ripen over a shorter time.
How do you think these 3 features have helped the farmer?

Things to do

Biology at Work

The Human Genome Project

The Human Genome Project is a six-billion dollar venture involving over 1000 scientists from 50 countries around the world. Its aim is to trace every single human gene and find its particular position on a chromosome.

a   What is a gene and what does it do?
Genes are found on chromosomes.

b   What are chromosomes? (Hint: see page 150)?

c   Where are chromosomes found?

Dr. John Sulston, director of the Sanger Centre where the British genome work was based

In June 2000, the human genome was completed:
3 billion 'chemical letters' that spell out all the human genes.
Scientists will be able to use the information to understand how people are affected by certain diseases and target early treatment. Cancer scientists have begun to catalogue the DNA changes in cancer cells in the hope of developing totally new treatments.

d   How do cancers form in the body?

e   How do cancer cells spread through the body?

f   Give 2 ways in which cancers are currently treated?

The Human Genome Project will help create new drugs to treat heart disease, immune disorders, muscular dystrophy, birth defects and degenerative nervous diseases.

g   Find out more about some of these diseases.

h   Use the internet to find out more about the Human Genome Project.

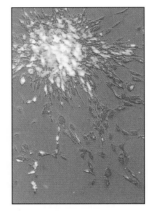

Cancer cells breaking away from a tumour.

In vitro fertilisation (IVF)

Explain how each of the following could stop a couple having children:

i   The man cannot make enough sperms.

j   The woman's egg tubes can become blocked.

In vitro fertilisation can often help these couples. ('In vitro' means 'in glass'.)

k   What is meant by fertilisation?

l   Why do you think this technique is called IVF?

First the woman is injected with hormones to make her produce eggs.

m   How do you think the eggs are removed from her body?

The eggs are then kept in a solution containing food and oxygen at the correct temperature.

n   Why do you think this is?

Look at the diagram:

o   Write a paragraph to explain exactly how IVF is carried out.
Sometimes more embryos form than can be used.
Many people think that it is wrong to destroy these extra embryos.

p   What do you think? Write about your thoughts.
Sometimes these extra embryos are frozen. They can then be used later if the first embryos do not grow.

q   Do you think that it is right to do this? Write about your thoughts.

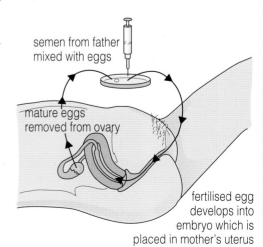

semen from father mixed with eggs

mature eggs removed from ovary

fertilised egg develops into embryo which is placed in mother's uterus

The GM food debate

Genetically modified (GM) food in the form of soya products, tomato purée or vegetarian cheese has probably been eaten by most people already.

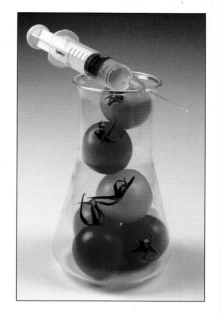

What are GM foods?

Genetic engineering has allowed sections of DNA to be removed from some plants and transferred into other plant cells.

r   What chemicals are used to remove and transfer this DNA?

GM foods – the benefits

- **Solving global hunger** – crops can be developed with the genes that give them tolerance of drought, frost and salty soil.

s   How does this help solve food shortage?

- **Environmentally friendly** – genetic modification can give crops resistance to insect pests, weeds and diseases.

t   How can this help the environment?

Crops can be developed that are able to take up nitrogen better.

u   How can this help the environment?

- **Consumer benefits** – GM food can be produced with better flavour, better keeping qualities and which need fewer additives.

v   How do these qualities help suppliers and consumers?

GM foods – the concerns

Opposition to the increased use of GM foods has come from the following areas:

- **Environmental safety** – there are worries that GM crops may become successful weeds and transfer their genes to related plants.

w   How might a plant that develops insect-resistant genes become a weed?

- **Food safety** – there are concerns that the proteins that GM food genes can produce could be transferred to microbes in the human intestine.

x   How might this prove to be a threat to human health?

- **Changes in farming structure** – there has been a trend, over the past decades, towards larger more intensive farms.

y   Why might the production of GM foods favour wealthy farmers?

- **Biodiversity** – the control of plant breeding could result in fewer varieties of plant species being available to farmers.

z   Why could the reduced use of old varieties and their wild relatives put more plants in danger of attack by pests and diseases?

- **Animal health** – there is increasing resistance to any developments in the use of farm animals that could affect their welfare.

A   **Either** research further aspects of the benefits and concerns of GM foods on the internet **or** set up a debate with groups arguing these benefits and concerns about this new biotechnology.

Greenpeace activists destroying a GM trial crop

33f Variation

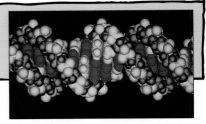

Ideas about DNA

Chromosomes are always found inside the nucleus. When the cell divides, they split lengthways and provide an identical copy of each chromosome for the 2 new cells.

Each chromosome is now known to be made up of an extremely long coiled thread of the chemical **DNA**. Sections of the DNA making up a chromosome are called **genes**.

Genes are the code for the production of certain characteristics, e.g. eye colour.

In the 1950s a great deal of work was being carried out by scientists to discover the nature of DNA.

Erwin Chargaff analysed samples of DNA and made firm conclusions about its chemical make-up.

In 1952, **Frank Hershey** and **Martha Chase** proved that it was the DNA in viruses that controlled characteristics.

X-ray diffraction techniques

In 1953, **Rosalind Franklin** and **Maurice Wilkins** used X-ray diffraction to work out more about how the atoms inside the DNA molecule were arranged.

This technique involved firing a beam of X-rays into crystals of DNA.

The X-rays hit the atoms and were scattered, making a pattern on a photographic plate.

They were able to use the X-ray diffraction photos to help build up a picture of the structure of DNA.

The double helix

The molecular structure of DNA was finally worked out by **James Watson** and **Francis Crick**, working in Cambridge in 1953.

They used all the latest information including Chargaff's results and the X-ray diffraction pictures of Franklin and Wilkins.

This meant piecing together cut-out models of the molecules involved and fitting them together.

After months of discussion and painstaking manipulation of the model, they were able to build a 3-D model of the structure of DNA.

It turned out to be a beautiful 'double helix' shape.

Each helix could separate from the other and make an exact copy of itself. This meant that chromosomes and genes could also make exact copies of themselves when cells divided.

Watson and Crick with their DNA model

Questions

1 Explain what is meant by each of the following words:
a) chromosome b) DNA c) gene

2 a) What controls inherited features?
b) Give 3 examples of features that are controlled by genes.

3 a) What features are controlled by the way we lead our lives?
b) Give 3 examples of features that are affected by our environment.

4 Why do you think so many scientists were working to discover the nature of DNA in the early 1950s?

5 Explain the X-ray diffraction techniques used by Franklin and Wilkins.

6 What is meant by the phrase 'double helix'? Why is it sometimes compared with a spiral staircase?

7 Why was it important that any model of DNA should be able to make an *exact* copy of itself? (Hint: think about what happens to chromosomes when a cell divides.)

8 Try to find out more about the work of:
a) Hershey and Chase, or b) Franklin and Wilkins, or c) Watson and Crick. You could use books, ROMs or the internet.

Revision Summary

Variation

- A species is a group of plants or animals that are able to reproduce fertile offspring (offspring that are able to breed).

- There is variation between *different* species, e.g. differences between dogs and cats.

- There is also variation between individuals of the *same* species, e.g. differences between domestic dogs.

- We inherit some features from our parents, e.g. eye colour.

- Other features are caused by our environment, e.g. a sun-tan.

- Some variation is *gradual*, e.g. height, whilst other variation is *clear-cut*, e.g. hair colour.

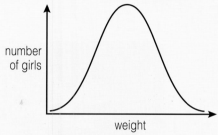

- Living things can be put into groups that have similar features.

- Animals with backbones are called vertebrates. They include fish, amphibians, reptiles, birds and mammals.

- Animals without backbones are called invertebrates. They include the jellyfish group, flatworms, roundworms, segmented worms, molluscs, arthropods (jointed-legged animals) and the starfish group.

- The main plant groups include the mosses, ferns, conifers and flowering plants.

- Some plants reproduce by making seeds, others by making spores.

- Useful features can often be bred *into* some animals and plants; less useful features can often be bred *out*. Selective breeding can produce new varieties of plants and animals.

- Scientists have been able to selectively breed high yield crops that are resistant to frost and resistant to disease.

- For years farmers have selectively bred cattle for their meat and milk, sheep for their wool, and pigs for their meat.

Growing up

- At adolescence our bodies and our emotions change.
  A boy starts to make sperms, grow body hair and his voice deepens.
  A girl starts to make eggs, her breasts develop and she starts having periods.

- These changes are controlled by chemicals produced in our bodies called hormones.

- The sperm tube carries sperm to the penis; glands add fluid to make semen.

- The egg tube carries an egg to the uterus every month.

- The male sperm nucleus contains characteristics of the father and the female egg nucleus contains characteristics of the mother.

- During love-making, sperms are placed into the vagina.

- At fertilisation the sperm penetrates the egg and its nucleus joins with the egg nucleus.

- If the egg is fertilised it passes down the egg tube and settles into the uterus.

- The fertilised egg grows first into an embryo and then into a fetus.

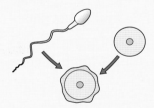

- The placenta acts as a barrier to infections and harmful substances.

- The placenta gives the fetus food and oxygen and removes carbon dioxide and waste chemicals.

- The fluid sac acts as a shock absorber to protect the fetus.

- The muscles in the wall of the uterus contract during birth, pushing out the fetus and placenta through the vagina.

- The baby is fed on milk from the mammary glands, which provide nutrients and protect the baby from infection.

- If an egg is not fertilised, the uterus lining breaks down and leaves through the vagina. This is called a period, which occurs about once a month.

Questions

1 What features do you think that you have inherited from
a) your mother? b) your father?
If you have a sister or brother, have they inherited the same features?

2 Bob and Baz are identical twins:
What features have they inherited from their parents?
What features are the result of their environment?

3 Some pupils did a survey on the size of foxglove fruits.
Here are their results:

Length of fruit (mm)	20	21	22	23	24	25	26	27	28	29
Number collected	4	6	14	22	30	26	18	12	12	3

a) Draw a bar-chart of their results.
b) What sort of variation do you think this shows?

4 Cloning involves taking some pieces of tissue from a parent plant and growing them in sterile conditions in nutrient agar.
a) Why will the cloned plants be 'genetically identical' to the parent?
b) Why are the clones grown in sterile conditions?
c) Explain how plants grown in this way can:
(i) be produced quickly ii) be free from disease (iii) have the 'good' qualities of the parent plant, e.g. disease-resistance.
d) Find out and write about any examples of animal cloning.

5 Breeding racehorses is a million-pound industry.
What sort of features do you think would be bred into a champion racehorse?

6 If animals of 2 different species mate they produce a **hybrid**.
The tigon resulted when a tiger and a lion mated in captivity:
a) What do you think were the parents of a leopon and a zeedonk?
b) Invent your own animal from 2 different species and draw it.
c) Hybrids are usually sterile (they cannot produce offspring).
Why do you think that the survival of some species would be threatened if they bred with other species in the wild?

tigon

7 Look at the table of 2 breeds of sheep:

Feature	Welsh Mountain breed	Border Leicester breed
adult mass (kg)	30–32	73–77
number of lambs born per female (ewe)	1	2
temperament	wild	docile
fleece per ewe (kg)	1	3
growth rate	slow	fast

a) What features do you think have been bred into the Border Leicester?
b) How do these make it a successful sheep?
c) Hill farmers often cross Welsh Mountain ewes with Border Leicester rams. Why do you think this is?

Chemical reactions 34

Chemical reactions keep you alive.
Today you'll probably be eating food made by chemical reactions.
Reactions may also be keeping you warm.

Some reactions are so powerful they can put a rocket into space . . . .

What a change!

What can you remember about **chemical changes?**
a Write down 3 things that might happen in a chemical change.

Scientists talk about 2 kinds of changes –
chemical changes and **physical changes**.
In a **chemical change** a new substance is made.
It's not easy to get the substance you started with back again.
We say the change is **irreversible**.
In a **physical change** no new substance is made.
We say the change is **reversible**.

▶ Look at the photos of some changes.
   For each one, say if you think it is a chemical change, or a
   physical change. Explain why.

b   **c**   **d**

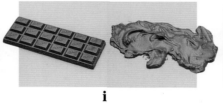

e   **f**   **g**

h   **i**   **j**

When a new substance is made, a chemical reaction must happen.
This is a **chemical change**.
The new substance is called a **product**.
You have seen lots of chemical reactions already.
Do you remember burning magnesium?

| magnesium + oxygen ⟶ magnesium oxide |
| $2\,Mg$ + O_2 ⟶ $2\,MgO$ |

▶ Copy and complete these word equations for reactions:

   copper + ... ⟶ copper oxide

   iron   + ... ⟶ iron chloride

Try balancing these symbol equations:

.... Cu + O_2 ⟶ .... CuO

.... Fe + ... Cl_2 ⟶ .... $FeCl_3$

When a substance changes state it changes into a different form.
It may look different but it is still the same substance.
This is a **physical change**.

Does the mass change?

Do you think **mass** changes . . . during a physical change?
. . . during a chemical change?
Predict what your conclusions will be before you do each test.

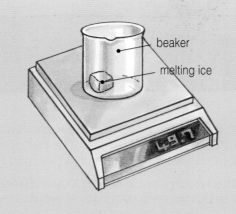
beaker
melting ice

Test 1 – A physical change
- Put a cube of ice in a beaker.
- Quickly put the beaker on the top-pan balance. Measure its mass.
- Leave the beaker until the cube has half melted. Measure its mass again.
- When the ice has all melted, measure its mass again.

What do you notice about the mass?

Test 2 – A chemical change
- Half fill a small tube with dilute sulphuric acid. Carefully put it inside a small conical flask.
- Measure out 25 cm³ of barium chloride solution in a measuring cylinder.
- Carefully use a teat pipette to transfer the solution into the flask.
  Do not drop any solution into the test-tube.
- Put a stopper on the flask. ***Do not let any acid spill into the solution.*** Measure the mass of the apparatus.
- Now tip the flask very gently so the 2 liquids mix. How do you know there is a reaction? Measure the mass of the apparatus again.

What do you notice about the mass?

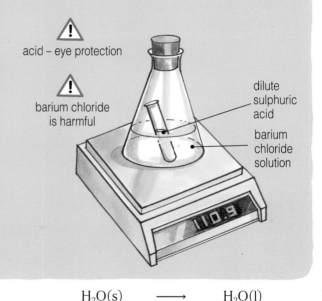
acid – eye protection
barium chloride is harmful
dilute sulphuric acid
barium chloride solution

In a **physical change**, the mass stays the same. This is because no new substance is made. The substance just changes its form.

$$H_2O(s) \longrightarrow H_2O(l)$$
solid ice → liquid water

In a **chemical change**, the *total* mass stays the same. This is because the new substances must be made from the substances already there. The chemical elements are just combining together in different ways.

$$BaCl_2 + H_2SO_4 \longrightarrow BaSO_4 + 2HCl$$

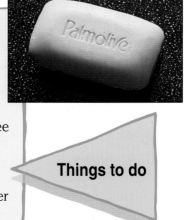

---

1 Copy and complete:
a) In a . . . . change, a new substance is made.
b) In a . . . . change, no new substance is made.
c) In a chemical change, the total mass . . . .
. . . .
d) In a physical change, the mass . . . .
. . . .

2 Melting is a physical change.
a) Describe what happens to the particles as a solid melts.
b) Describe what happens to the particles as a liquid boils.
c) Use your answers to a) and b) to explain why the mass stays the same in a physical change.

3 Which of these are chemical changes?
a) Making soap from vegetable oil.
b) Boiling some water.
c) Burning natural gas.
d) Making aluminium cans from aluminium metal.
e) Making coffee by adding water to coffee powder.
f) Making glass from sand.
g) Baking clay.

4 When hydrogen burns in oxygen, water is made.
$$2H_2 + O_2 \longrightarrow 2H_2O$$
The mass stays the same.
Use the equation to explain why.

Things to do

Making salts

The word *salt* probably makes you think of something you put on your chips!
But in science a **salt** is much more than this.

In this lesson you can make lots of *different* salts.
To do this you will start with an **acid** and a **metal**.

a   Write down everything you know about acids.
Include these words if you can.

| pH | alkali | strong | red | weak | neutral |

b   Write down everything you know about metals.
Include these words if you can.

| shiny | conductor | strong | electricity | heat | hard |

Reacting acids with metals

Try these tests with hydrochloric acid and metals.
Make a table to record your results.

Put 5 test-tubes in a rack.
Put about 2 cm³ of dilute hydrochloric acid in each test-tube.
Clean the metal samples with sand paper.
Add the metal samples to the acid as shown.

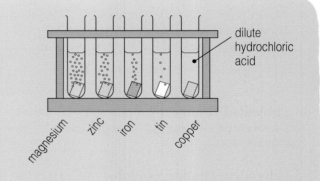

dilute hydrochloric acid

magnesium   zinc   iron   tin   copper

c   How do you know if there is a reaction?
d   What is the name of the gas given off?
e   How can you test for this gas?

If the metal does not react, put the tube in a beaker of hot water.
See if the metal reacts with *warm* acid.

f   You could use dilute sulphuric acid now instead of
dilute hydrochloric acid.
What do you think would happen?
Ask your teacher if you can check your idea.

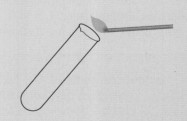

g   What do you think would happen with dilute nitric acid and metals?

When a metal reacts with an acid a **salt** is made.

magnesium + hydrochloric acid ⟶ ***magnesium chloride*** + hydrogen
Mg + $2HCl$ ⟶ $MgCl_2$ + H_2

magnesium + sulphuric acid ⟶ ***magnesium sulphate*** + hydrogen
Mg + H_2SO_4 ⟶ $MgSO_4$ + H_2

magnesium + nitric acid ⟶ ***magnesium nitrate*** + hydrogen
Mg + $2HNO_3$ ⟶ $Mg(NO_3)_2$ + H_2

sulphuric acid is H_2SO_4
hydrochloric acid is HCl
nitric acid is HNO_3

164

Salts made from **sulphuric acid** are **sulphates**.
Salts made from **hydrochloric acid** are **chlorides**.
Salts made from **nitric acid** are **nitrates**.

Making zinc sulphate

An acid can be changed to make a salt. The change is a ***chemical reaction.***

acid – eye protection

Carry out this experiment to make crystals of a salt. You can use the Help Sheet.

Add zinc powder to dilute sulphuric acid and stir.

When no more zinc dissolves, filter the mixture.

Carefully evaporate the filtrate to half its original volume.
Then leave it to cool.

eye protection

sulphuric acid	+	zinc	⟶	zinc sulphate	+	hydrogen
(**acid**)		(**metal**)		(**salt**)		

h Look at the photos. Which one shows the hydrogen being made**?**

i Why should you keep adding zinc until ***no more dissolves?***

j What do you see when you evaporate and then cool the solution**?**

k What is the name of the solid made? This is the product.

l Try to write a symbol equation for the reaction.

Acids are corrosive

---

1 Copy and complete:
a) Acids have pH number . . . . than 7.
b) Acids react with metals to make . . . . and hydrogen.
c) acid + ... ⟶ salt + ...
d) Hydrogen gas . . . . with a . . . . spill.
e) Sulphates are made from . . . . acid.
f) Chlorides are made from . . . . acid.
g) Nitrates are made from . . . . acid.
h) To make zinc chloride we use . . . . and . . . . acid.

2 Acid and metal reactions are used to make lots of salts.
a) Why can't we make copper sulphate this way?
b) Why can't we make sodium sulphate this way?

3 Some solutions were tested with pH paper:

solution	A	B	C	D	E
pH value	9	1	5	13	7

a) Say whether each solution is acidic, alkaline or neutral.
b) What colour does the pH paper turn with i) D? ii) E? iii) B?
c) Which solution is the most acidic?
d) Which solution could be pure water?

| 1 | 2 | 3 | 4 | 5 | 6 | 7 | 8 | 9 | 10 | 11 | 12 | 13 | 14 |

4 Acid rain causes problems. Think about the reactions of acids.
a) What happens when acid rain falls on metal?
b) Limestone is calcium carbonate. What happens when acid rain falls on limestone rock?

Things to do

Acids and bases

We can make a **salt** by reacting acid with metal.

▶ Copy and complete these word equations:

a zinc + nitric acid ⟶

b iron + hydrochloric acid ⟶

c magnesium + sulphuric acid ⟶

Take care with the next one!

d copper + hydrochloric acid ⟶

There are other ways to make salts.
We can react acids with **bases**.
Bases are the oxides, hydroxides and carbonates of metals.

▶ Name the bases with these formulae:

e MgO   **f** $CuCO_3$ **g** $Ca(OH)_2$

The base **neutralises** the acid.

Try matching your products to these formulae $FeCl_2$ $MgSO_4$ $Zn(NO_3)_2$

Calcium Carbonate   Copper Oxide   Sodium Hydroxide

acid	**+**	**base**	⟶	**salt**	**+ water**
sulphuric acid	+	magnesium oxide	⟶	magnesium sulphate	+ water
H_2SO_4	+	MgO	⟶	$MgSO_4$	+ H_2O

If the base is the metal **carbonate**, we get another product.

Look at the reaction of magnesium carbonate with acid:

h What causes the fizzing in the reaction?

i How can you test for this gas?

sulphuric acid	+	magnesium carbonate	⟶	magnesium sulphate	+	carbon dioxide	+	water
H_2SO_4	+	$MgCO_3$	⟶	$MgSO_4$	+	CO_2	+	H_2O

j Which elements are found in all carbonates?

Your teacher may let you try some other 'carbonate + acid' reactions.
We can use this reaction to prepare carbon dioxide in the laboratory.

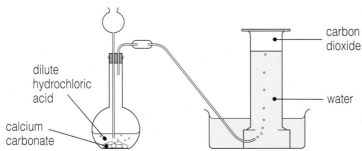

dilute hydrochloric acid

calcium carbonate

carbon dioxide

water

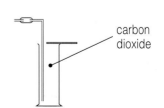

carbon dioxide

The carbon dioxide can be collected **over water**. It is only slightly soluble in water.
We can collect it by **downward delivery**. The gas is heavier than air.
It is colourless, so it is difficult to tell when the gas jar is full.

These are the general word equations for acid + base reactions:

acid + metal oxide ⟶ salt + water

acid + metal hydroxide ⟶ salt + water

acid + metal carbonate ⟶ salt + carbon dioxide + water

Try using an acid + base reaction to make a salt. You can use the Help Sheet.

Making copper sulphate

 ! acid – eye protection

Add copper oxide to warm dilute sulphuric acid and stir.

When no more copper oxide dissolves, filter the mixture.

Carefully evaporate the filtrate to half its original volume. Then leave it to cool. ⚠

eye protection

sulphuric acid + copper oxide ⟶ copper sulphate + water
   (**acid**)   (**base**)   (**salt**)

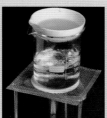

k How can you tell there is a chemical reaction here?

l Why should you keep adding copper oxide until *no more dissolves*?

m Which substance is left in the filter paper?

n What is the name of the solid made? This is the product.

If the base is copper carbonate you can still make copper sulphate the same way. (You don't have to warm the acid though.)

sulphuric acid + copper carbonate ⟶ copper sulphate + carbon dioxide + water

o What causes the fizzing in this reaction?

---

1 Copy and complete:
a) Bases are the oxides, ... or . . . . of metals.
b) Bases neutralise . . . .
c) acid + carbonate makes . . . . gas
d) . . . . + metal oxide makes a salt.

2 You have 5 test-tubes containing different gases. The gases are:

nitrogen oxygen carbon dioxide
hydrogen   air

How can you identify each gas?
Describe the tests and the results.

3 There are 3 bottles and 3 labels!
The labels have come off the bottles!
You have samples of lime water, copper carbonate and red litmus paper.
How can you use these to identify the liquid in the bottles?
Describe what you would do.

Things to do

Salt of the Earth

Some salts can be used as fertilisers.
The 3 main chemical elements in fertilisers are:
nitrogen (N), phosphorus (P) and potassium (K).
The elements are in **compounds** in the fertiliser.
On fertiliser bags you often see numbers. These are **NPK** ratios.
They tell you how much nitrogen, phosphorus and potassium
the fertiliser contains.
16.8.24 means 16%N, 8%P, 24%K.

▶ Look at these bags of fertilisers:
a Which of these fertilisers:
   i)   contain nitrogen**?**
   ii) contain phosphorus**?**
   iii) contain all 3 elements**?**

b What do fertilisers do**?** Why do we use them**?**

Using fertilisers

Rupa and Tim are talking about fertilisers.

I think it's best to put the fertiliser in the soil before you plant the seeds.

No. You should plant the seeds first and then add the fertiliser.

Who do you think is right**?**
Plan an investigation to find out.
In the next activity you can make a fertiliser.
You can use it to carry out your investigation.

Making a fertiliser

You can make a simple fertiliser called ammonium sulphate
in the lab.

Ammonium sulphate has the formula $(NH_4)_2SO_4$
c Which chemical elements does it contain**?**

Ammonium sulphate is a salt. It is made by neutralising an acid.
In Book 7 you learnt that **alkalis** neutralise acids.
An **alkali** is a special kind of base – it dissolves in water.

The reaction to make a fertiliser is a **neutralisation**.

acid + alkali ⟶ salt + water **(base)**

Sodium hydroxide is a base. It is also an alkali.

Copper oxide is a base. It is **not** an alkali.

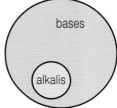

Making ammonium sulphate

 acid – eye protection

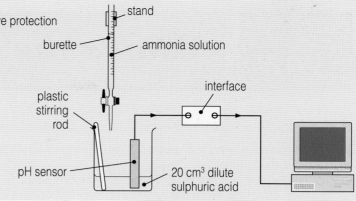

1. Put 20 cm³ of dilute sulphuric acid into a beaker.
   Put a pH sensor into the acid. Note the pH reading.
   Start recording.

2. Fill a burette with ammonia solution.
   Add 2 cm³ of ammonia solution to the acid.
   Stir very carefully with a plastic stirrer.
   Be careful not to touch the sensor with the stirrer.

3. Keep adding ammonia solution 2 cm³ at a time.
   The sensor will measure the pH as it changes.

4. Keep adding ammonia solution until the pH reaches 7 (neutral) or just over.
   Stop recording. Remove the sensor. The acid has been neutralised.
   You have a solution of ammonium sulphate.

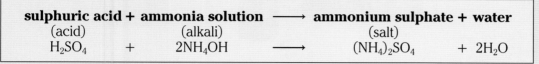

sulphuric acid	**+**	**ammonia solution**	⟶	**ammonium sulphate**	**+ water**
(acid)		(alkali)		(salt)	
H_2SO_4	+	$2NH_4OH$	⟶	$(NH_4)_2SO_4$	+ $2H_2O$

5. **!** hot   Pour the solution into an evaporating basin.
   Carefully evaporate the water from the solution by heating it on a water bath.
   Evaporate until only half of the original solution is left.

6.  Leave the basin to cool.
   Crystals of ammonium sulphate will form slowly.
   Filter the crystals from any solution left.
   Dry them between filter papers.

What does your fertiliser look like?
You can use this fertiliser to carry out your investigation (page 168).

---

1 Copy and complete:
a) 3 common elements in fertilisers are ...., ... and ....
b) NP fertilisers contain .... and ....
c) An .... is a base that dissolves in water.
d) Ammonium sulphate is made from dilute .... acid.

2 Look at these NPK values for 4 fertilisers:

0.24.24	15.15.21	25.0.16	27.5.5
1	2	3	4

a) Which fertiliser contains most nitrogen?
b) Which fertiliser contains least nitrogen?
c) Which one is NK fertiliser?
d) Which fertiliser contains the same % of nitrogen as phosphorus?
e) Fertilisers can cause water pollution. Explain why.
f) Plants also need small amounts of:
   Ca Mg Na Cu Zn S Fe
   Name these elements.

3 Visit a garden centre. Look at packets of fertilisers recommended for growing
i) fruit (e.g. tomatoes)
ii) grass
iii) flowers
a) Make a list of NPK values for these fertilisers.
b) Can you draw any conclusions about the elements needed to grow certain crops?

4 What are **organic vegetables**?
Why do some people want to buy these even if they are more expensive?

Things to do

What's the use?

Some reactions are useful. Others, like rusting, are not useful.

▶ What makes a reaction useful? Write down your ideas.
Look at the photos opposite:
They all show the results of a chemical reaction.
Say whether you think the reaction is *useful* or *not useful*.
Explain why.

Neutralisation

acid + base ⟶ salt + water

This is a **neutralisation**.
You know that neutralisation can be a useful reaction.
Fertiliser can be made this way.
Other acid + base reactions are useful too.

a

b

c

d

e

f What does 'milk of magnesia' do?
g How is toothpaste used in a neutralisation?
h Why can you treat a wasp sting with vinegar?

Making quicklime

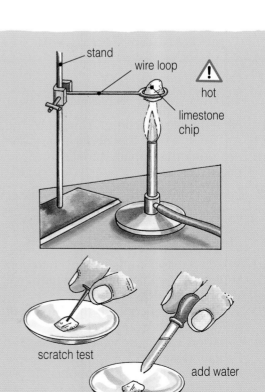

stand

wire loop

hot

limestone chip

scratch test

add water

Here's a chance for *you* to carry out a useful reaction.

Take 2 limestone chips which look similar.
Heat one chip strongly in a hot Bunsen flame.
Heat it for 10 minutes. Then let the chip cool.
Compare the heated and unheated chips:
• Appearance – what do they look like?
• Do they scratch easily? Use an iron nail to test.
  (Don't touch the solids.)
• Add 2 drops of water to each chip and test with pH paper.
• Add one drop of dilute acid to each.

Record all your results in a table.
Do you notice any difference between the chips?

⚠ acid

When you heated the limestone chip it decomposed (broke down).
Two products were made in the reaction:

calcium carbonate	⟶	calcium oxide	+	carbon dioxide
limestone		quicklime		
$CaCO_3$	⟶	CaO	+	CO_2

i What happened to the carbon dioxide?
j Quicklime is an alkali. Sometimes farmers use it on soil. Why?

Burning fuels

k Why does Emma think that burning is a useful reaction?

l Does this reaction spoil our planet?
What does Jop mean?

Your teacher may show you this experiment:

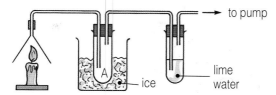

You can burn fuels containing carbon and hydrogen.

m What do you see in tube A?

n How can you test if this is water?

o What happens to the lime water?

If there is enough oxygen, the fuel makes carbon dioxide (CO_2).
This is a **combustion** reaction.

If there is not enough oxygen the combustion is *incomplete*.
This means carbon monoxide (CO) is also made.
Some carbon (C) itself may be given off too.
This is soot. It makes the flame look smoky.

Car exhaust fumes contain carbon monoxide.

Global warming

Global warming is caused by the **greenhouse effect**.

Carbon dioxide is a 'greenhouse gas'. It is important because
it traps heat that would otherwise escape into space.
It keeps the Earth warm for us.
But we are disturbing the natural balance of carbon dioxide
in the atmosphere. We are making so much of it that the
Earth is warming up very quickly.

p How are we making so much carbon dioxide?

q What will be the effects if global warming continues?

r What could we do to reduce global warming?

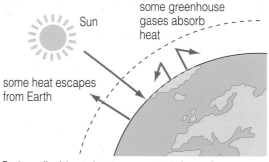

Carbon dioxide and water vapour are 'greenhouse gases'.

Things to do

1 Copy out each description of a reaction.
Which reaction best fits the description?
Match the reaction to its description.

Description	Reaction
● A useful reaction which can make some nasty products.	● Fermenting sugar
● A slow reaction which is not useful.	● Burning a fuel
● A slow reaction which makes alcohol.	● Rusting of iron

2 Carbon dioxide and water vapour are
'greenhouse gases'.
Find out the names and formulae of some
other greenhouse gases.

3 Find out about these fuels:

wood   ethanol   hydrogen

Make a list of the advantages and
disadvantages of each one.

4 Ethene has the formula C_2H_4.
It can be made from crude oil.
a) Find out about useful products from
reactions of ethene.
b) Ethene burns in air. What will the
products be?

Finding the energy

Do you enjoy November 5th?
Bonfire night is about chemical reactions!
▶ The chemical reactions in fireworks transfer energy.
Write about all the energy transfers in the photo.

Most chemical reactions **give out** energy.
They are called **exothermic** reactions.
But some reactions **take in** energy from the surroundings.
These are called **endothermic** reactions.

Your mouth feels cold when you eat sherbet.
The reaction of sherbet with water is **endothermic**.
The reaction takes in heat energy from your mouth so it cools it down.

Energy in or out?

Try some of these reactions. See what happens to the temperature.

1. Dissolve some citric acid in 50 cm³ water.
Note the temperature of the solution.

Add crushed limestone to the solution, one spatula measure at a time. Stir and note the temperature after each addition. Add 5 spatula measures in total.

What do you notice?
Is this an exothermic or endothermic reaction?

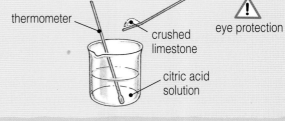

2. Repeat experiment 1 but add sodium bicarbonate (sodium hydrogencarbonate) instead of crushed limestone.
What do you notice?
Is this an exothermic or endothermic reaction?

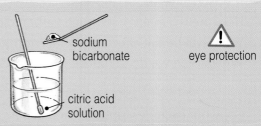

3. Measure 25 cm³ of dilute sulphuric acid into a beaker.
Note the temperature of the solution.

Add 5 cm³ of sodium hydroxide solution to the acid. Stir and note the temperature of the solution. Repeat this until 30 cm³ of sodium hydroxide have been added.
What do you notice?
Is this an exothermic or endothermic reaction?

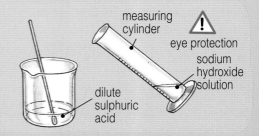

4. Light a Bunsen burner.
Natural gas burns.
What do you notice?
Is this an exothermic or endothermic reaction?

Do **not** measure the temperature of the flame. Just observe.

Lab in chaos

⚠️ eye protection

Five glass bottles are in the lab.
They all contain colourless liquids.
Four have lost their labels. One is labelled ***dilute sulphuric acid***.

You have only 2 beakers and one thermometer.
How can you find out which of the 4 solutions are alkalis?
Write a plan for your teacher.
Have your plan checked. Then do it!

Energy is always transferred when a chemical change takes place.
Sometimes we can observe this
 – the temperature may change
 – we may see light or hear sound.

Think about these energy changes from chemical reactions.

You may have seen these in camping shops.
They keep your hands warm for several hours.

a How do you think they work?

Have you ever bought one of these?
They are popular at outdoor concerts.

b How do you think they work?

c Why is this so useful?

But sometimes the energy transfer can be a problem.
Look at the newspaper extract.

d What should you do if you smell a gas leak?

Explosion wrecks home!

Workmen who picked their way through the rubble of a house demolished by a gas explosion yesterday found 94-year-old Mrs Ivy Shepherd still standing in the kitchen where she had been eating a cheese sandwich.
The roof and timbers had collapsed around Mrs Shepherd, a widow, but she was unharmed and her only complaint was of the dust in her white hair and a torn apron.
She was taken to hospital in Worthing, West Sussex, for a check-up but was later released.

---

1 Copy and complete:
a) Chemical reactions which give out energy are called . . . .
b) Chemical reactions which take in energy are called . . . .
c) In an . . . . reaction the temperature of the reaction mixture rises.
d) In an . . . . reaction the temperature of the reaction mixture falls.
e) Burning a fuel in air is an . . . . reaction.
f) Neutralisation is an . . . . reaction.
g) Dissolving sherbet in water is an . . . . reaction.

2 Spirit burners can be used to burn liquid fuels safely in the lab.
Plan an investigation to compare the amount of energy transferred when different fuels are burnt.

— burning fuel

— wick

— fuel

3 Is respiration an exothermic or endothermic reaction?
How do you know?

Things to do

What's your reaction?

In Books 7, 8 and 9 you have met lots of chemical reactions.

▶ Remind yourself of some reactions. Copy and complete these word equations:

a   iron + oxygen ⟶ . . . . (rust)

b   acid + metal ⟶ . . . . + ...

c   acid + carbonate ⟶ salt + ... + ...

d   acid + base ⟶ . . . . + water

e   fuel + oxygen ⟶ . . . . + ... + energy

Do you remember about **displacement** reactions?

▶ Rosie tested 4 metals to see which would react with solutions of metal sulphates.
Use the reactivity series to predict her results.
Use a copy of the table. Put a tick (✔) if the metal reacts.
Put a cross (✗) if the metal does not react.

zinc	iron	magnesium	copper	
			✗	copper sulphate
		✗		magnesium sulphate
	✗			iron sulphate
✗				zinc sulphate

Reactivity series

potassium
magnesium
zinc
iron
tin
copper

Displacement reactions and energy

Compare the energy changes when different metals are added to copper sulphate solution.
Plan your investigation.
• How will you make your tests fair?
• How will you measure the energy changes?
Have your plan checked by your teacher. Then carry it out.

Look closely at your results. Look at the reactivity series.
Do you notice a pattern?

Don't throw that away. I need it to fill up the car.

The future

What about the future? New chemical reactions will make new materials.

. . . making petrol from paper?

It is possible to make oil from waste paper. At the moment the oil is just suitable for boiler fuel. But in the future it may be possible to change this to petrol and plastic.

. . . hydrogen to fuel a car?

The hydrogen reacts with oxygen to drive the engine.

. . . a cure for flu?

Scientists are using computers to help them design a molecule which may cure flu.

A best seller

- Make a class-book about **chemical reactions**.

- Your teacher will ask your group to write one section of the book.

- Design your pages carefully. They will need diagrams, cartoons and photos to make them interesting.

- Remember that someone will need to make the cover.

- What will your book be called?

Sections

reactivity series   energy changes

physical change   combustion

safety

respiration

rusting   fermentation

symbol equations

photosynthesis

neutralisation

word equations

chemical change

salts

---

1 Copy and complete using a word from the box:

| hydrogen | oxygen | combustion |
| neutralisation | fermentation | |

a) . . . . is a reaction in which a fuel burns in air.
b) Reacting acid and metal makes . . . .
c) . . . . is the making of alcohol from sugar.
d) Respiration uses . . . . gas.
e) The reaction between an acid and a base is . . . .

2 Chemical reactions don't always happen. Think about the reactivity series. Predict whether a reaction will take place in each case.
a) magnesium + iron oxide
b) zinc oxide + copper
c) copper sulphate + zinc
d) magnesium sulphate + copper

3 Link the raw material in the list with the made material on the right, e.g. sand is used to make glass.

Raw material	Made material
sand	steel
oil	glass
iron ore	copper
malachite	paper
wood	plastic

4 Use books and ROMs to find out how some of these things are made.
a) soap
b) bread
c) polythene
d) glass
e) yoghurt.

Things to do

Chemistry at Work

Combustion

Rockets escaping the gravitational pull of the Earth need fuels that burn very fiercely.
Liquid hydrogen and liquid oxygen are used.
It was a leak in the fuel tanks that caused the space shuttle disaster in 1986.

a Write a word equation for hydrogen reacting with oxygen.

Hydrogen is sometimes called the fuel of the future.

b Why are we searching for fuels to take the place of petrol and diesel?

c Which common compound could be a useful source of hydrogen in the future?

d Find out how we can get hydrogen from the compound in question **c**.

e Explain why burning hydrogen will be better for our environment than burning petrol.

f Write about some of the problems that we will have to overcome if we do ever use hydrogen as a major fuel in the future.

Neutralisation

You know that an acid and an alkali react together.
You might have used one of these neutralisation reactions to make ammonium sulphate.

g Name the acid and alkali used to make ammonium sulphate.

h Is ammonium sulphate:
  i) a metal?
  ii) a non-metal?
  iii) a salt?
  iv) an alkali?

The chemical formula of ammonium sulphate is $(NH_4)_2SO_4$.
It is used as a fertiliser (see page 168).

i Which important element does ammonium sulphate provide for plants?

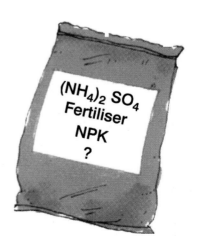

What are the NPK values for ammonium sulphate?

Another important fertiliser is ammonium nitrate.
Its formula is NH_4NO_3.

j   How many different elements are there in ammonium nitrate?

k   How many atoms are there in a molecule of nitric acid, HNO_3?

l   Write a brief method you could use to make ammonium nitrate in the lab. You must bear in mind that ammonium nitrate can explode if you heat the solid too strongly.

In industry the reaction is carried out as shown below:

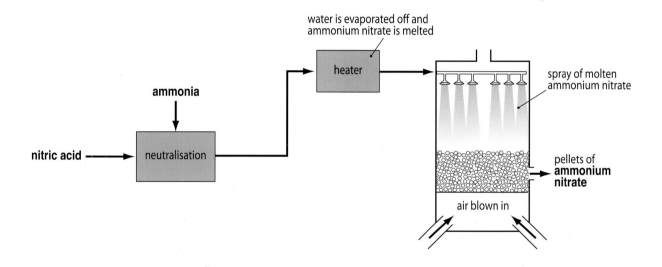

m   Find out the chemical formula of ammonia.

n   Find out the chemical formula of nitric acid.

o   Write a word equation for making ammonium nitrate.

p   Find out all the raw materials you would need to make ammonia and nitric acid in industry.

q   Describe the ideal site to put a fertiliser factory that manufactures ammonium nitrate.
Think about the raw materials you will need and anything else you feel is important.
Explain all your reasoning.

r   Why is the plant in the photograph situated well away from any houses?

s   Write a letter to your local council which has just given planning permission for a fertiliser factory next to your school.

t   Find out about the pollution that fertilisers like ammonium nitrate can cause.

Chemical reactions

The plastics revolution

Have you ever wondered what life would be like without plastics?

We can trace the start of the 'plastic age' to a chemist named **Leo Baekeland**. He was born in Belgium in 1863, but worked in America where he made his fortune.

Leo was a chemist with a sharp eye for a business opportunity. His first invention, in the 1890s, was a new type of paper for making photographs. This set Leo up for life when he sold the rights to make the paper for a million dollars.

However, Leo did not settle for a quiet life in his mansion in New York State. In a converted barn on his estate, he set about his next project. At that time, ten-pin bowling was becoming very popular in the USA. The wooden floors of the bowling alleys were varnished with a substance called shellac. This was imported from Asia, where beetles left a sticky liquid on trees. The liquid was collected, heated and filtered to make the varnish. Leo tried to make a new varnish that could be manufactured from chemicals.

He investigated chemicals you could get from coal-tar and wood alcohol. Thirty years earlier a German chemist had discovered a thick, gooey substance as he tried out reactions to make new dyes. To Adolf von Baeyer this was just a nuisance. But Leo could see its potential for use as his new varnish. Not only would it help the budding sport of ten-pin bowling, but it would signal the start of the plastics industry.

When Leo heated up the gooey liquid it turned even thicker. If he did the reaction under pressure it made a hard, translucent solid. He could mould this into any shape he liked.

In 1907, he had made the first synthetic plastic! It had taken him 3 years and thousands of failed experiments, but his perseverance paid off in the end.

Leo the chemist quickly became Leo the business-person. He patented his new plastic and gave it the trade name 'Bakelite'. He formed a company to make and sell the plastic.

A new customer would help Leo make another fortune. The electricity industry was just starting to grow. Plans to get electricity into homes were being drawn up, but there was a problem. The early insulation material used was shellac. Leo could make moulded electrical insulators from his new plastic. By doing this he played a big part in changing life in the last century.

People were quickly using the new plastic for everything from buttons to telephones. You might have seen old-fashioned radio or TV sets made from a hard brown plastic. This was Bakelite. But Leo could make his plastic in a variety of colours. It even became trendy to wear Bakelite jewellery. Plastics had arrived in our lives!

Questions

1 How was Leo Baekeland's chemical research influenced by business opportunities?

2 What do you think were the characteristics of Leo Baekeland that made him a wealthy man?

3 Make a list of all the plastic things you have used so far today.
   How would your life today be different without plastics?

4 Most plastics nowadays are made from products we get from crude oil.
   How do you think the plastics industry will develop in the next 50 years?

5 Do some research to find out about either:
   a) The problems of plastics waste and how we might solve them, or
   b) The life and work of Wallace Carothers.

Revision Summary

Chemical reactions

- Scientists talk about 2 kinds of changes – chemical changes and physical changes.

- In a chemical change, one or more new substances are made. But there is no change in the total mass before and after the reaction. The same atoms are still there but they are combined in different ways. Chemical changes are usually difficult to reverse.

- In a physical change, no new substances are made. There is no change in mass. Physical changes are usually easy to reverse.

- Word equations show us the reactants and products in a reaction.
  e.g. magnesium + oxygen (reactants) → magnesium oxide (products)
       $2 Mg$ + O_2 → $2MgO$

  iron + chlorine → iron chloride
  $2 Fe$ + $3 Cl_2$ → $2 FeCl_3$

  iron + sulphur → iron sulphide
  Fe + S → FeS

- There are different **types** of reaction,
  e.g. when something gains oxygen, this is an **oxidation**.

- Some reactions are very useful to us,
  e.g. – setting superglue.
       – burning a fuel to keep us warm.

- Some chemical reactions are not useful to us,
  e.g. – iron rusting when it reacts with air and water.
       – fossil fuels making acid rain when they burn.

- Reactions which take in energy from the surroundings are **endothermic**.
  Reactions which give out energy are **exothermic**.

Acid rain has damaged these trees.

Reactivity Series

- Metals can react with:
  – oxygen to make oxides,
    e.g. copper + oxygen → copper oxide
  – water to make hydrogen gas,
    e.g. sodium + water → sodium hydroxide + hydrogen
  – acid to make hydrogen gas,
    e.g. magnesium + hydrochloric acid → magnesium chloride + hydrogen
  (Hydrogen gas 'pops' with a burning splint.)

Caesium reacts violently with water.

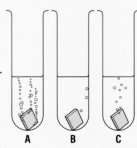

potassium
sodium
calcium
magnesium
zinc
iron
tin
copper

- We can use these reactions to put metals in a league table of reactivity.
  This is called the Reactivity Series.
  e.g. magnesium is reactive – it is high up in the series.
       gold is unreactive – it is low in the series.

- A metal high in the Reactivity Series can displace one lower, from a solution of its salt.
  e.g. zinc displaces copper from copper sulphate solution
  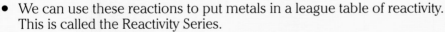
           zinc   + copper sulphate → zinc sulphate   + copper
      (silver-grey)   (blue solution)   (colourless solution) (pink/brown)

- The Reactivity Series can be used to make predictions about reactions.
  Q. magnesium + copper oxide → ?
  A. magnesium is more reactive than copper – so it displaces copper.

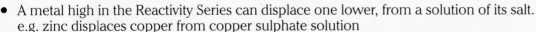
      magnesium + copper oxide → magnesium oxide + copper
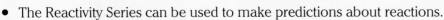
      (silver-grey)   (black)   (grey-white)   (brown)

Metal A reacts fastest with acid. It is the most reactive. Metal B is the least reactive.

Questions

1 Which of these are physical changes?
   a) Adding water to orange squash.
   b) Burning petrol in a car engine.
   c) Getting salt from sea water.
   d) Making detergent from crude oil.

2 Gavin heated some magnesium ribbon in air.
   He measured the mass of solid before and after heating.
   Here are his results:
   Mass of solid before heating = 0.24 g
   Mass of solid after heating   = 0.40 g
   a) Copy and complete the word equation for the reaction:
      magnesium + ... $\longrightarrow$ magnesium oxide
   b) Name the solid product of the reaction.
   c) Try to explain Gavin's results.

3 Explain how you could make a sample of solid magnesium sulphate
   starting with magnesium ribbon and dilute sulphuric acid.
   Write a method. Draw diagrams.

4 You have used lots of chemicals to carry out reactions.
   Some chemicals are dangerous. They must be used very carefully.
   They have hazard labels on their containers.
   Look at the hazard labels opposite. Draw sketches of them.
   Explain what each hazard label tells us.

5 Name the products of these reactions:
   a) iron + sulphuric acid
   b) zinc carbonate + sulphuric acid
   c) magnesium oxide + nitric acid
   d) sodium hydroxide + hydrochloric acid

6 Stomach powders help to neutralise acids in your stomach.
   Plan an investigation to find out which stomach powder is the
   best value for money.

7 Handwarmers are okay, but . . . .
   Invent some self-warming soup for winter walks.
   a) Design a can of soup which can warm itself when opened.
   b) Make an advertisement for your invention.

8 Can scientists help to solve some of the world's problems?
   Imagine *you* could make some new materials to solve these
   problems.
   What would you want your new materials to do?
   Make a list of your ideas.

Electricity and Magnetism

35

Electricity is important to all of us.
Our lives would be very different without it.

We use electricity to transfer energy from one place to another.
We use it for lighting and for heating.

And we can use electricity to make magnets – which we use
every day in radios, TVs, and many other things.

In this topic:

In series

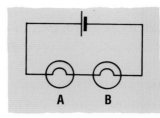

▶ The diagram shows a circuit with 2 bulbs in **series**:

a What does each symbol stand for**?**

b What can you say about the current through **A** and the current through **B?**

c What happens if bulb **B** breaks**?** Why**?**

d Draw a circuit diagram of 3 bulbs in series.

Bulbs in series

Energy from a battery

A battery pushes electrons (−) round the circuit:

The flow of electrons is called a **current**. The size of the current is measured in amperes (amps, A).

e What meter would you use to measure the current**?**

The electrons transfer energy from the cell to the bulbs. The higher the **voltage** of the battery, the more energy the electrons can transfer:

f What meter would you use to measure the voltage**?**

The energy transferred by the electrons is used to heat up the filament. Some of this heat energy is transformed to light energy, which is then transferred by radiation.

g Draw an Energy Transfer Diagram for this circuit.

A conductor lets electrons pass through it easily. It has a low **resistance**.
An insulator has a high resistance. The electrons cannot move through the insulator, so there is no current.

h Write down the names of 3 conductors and 3 insulators.

i 'Mains' voltage is 230 V. Why is this dangerous**?**

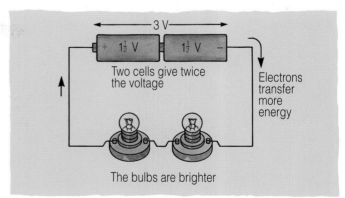

▶ Here are some of the symbols used in circuit diagrams.

j Copy the symbols and label each one.

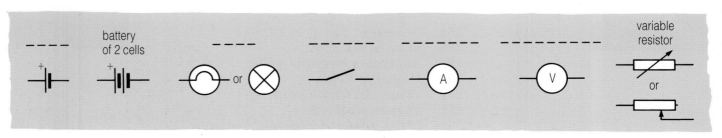

Reading ammeters

The diagrams show two ammeters:

What are the readings **k**, **l**, **m**, **n**, **o**, and **p**?

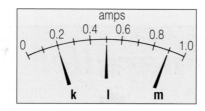

Measuring currents

Here is a series circuit:

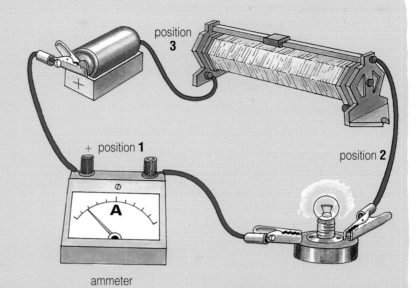

- Draw a circuit diagram for it.

- Then connect up the circuit. Make sure the + terminal of the ammeter is connected to the + terminal of the battery.

- Adjust the variable resistor to make the bulb as bright as possible.
  What is the reading on the ammeter?

- Disconnect the ammeter and then re-connect it in position 2.
  What is the reading now?
  What is the reading on the ammeter if it is in position 3?
  Write a sentence to describe what you found.

- Now connect a second bulb in **series**.
  What happens to the brightness of the first bulb?
  What happens to the current through the ammeter?
  Explain why you think this happens, using the words:
  current   electrons   resistance

- Predict what would happen if you added a third bulb in series. Try it if you can.

- With just one bulb, use the variable resistor to reduce the current until the bulb is not quite glowing.
  What is the reading on your ammeter now?

ammeter

Position of ammeter	Current (amps)
1	
2	
3	

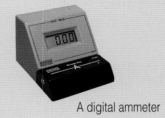

A digital ammeter

1 Copy and complete:
In a **series** circuit,
a) The current is the . . . . through each part of the circuit. It is not used up.
b) If you add extra bulbs, the current is . . . . and the bulbs are . . . . bright.
c) If you add extra cells, the electrons have . . . . energy and bulbs shine . . . . brightly.
d) An ammeter measures the . . . . in a circuit, in . . . . or A.
e) A battery pushes . . . . round a circuit. The size of the push is measured in . . . ., by using a . . . .
f) A good conductor has a . . . . resistance.

2 An ammeter is connected in series with a battery, a switch and a bulb.
a) Draw the circuit diagram.
b) If the ammeter reads 0.8 A, how much current passes through the bulb?
c) A second bulb is connected in series. Draw the circuit diagram.
d) The ammeter reading is now 0.4 A. How much current passes through each bulb now?
e) Explain why this current is less than before.

3 The ampere and the volt are named after André Ampère and Alessandro Volta. Find out more about these people and what they did.

Things to do

In parallel

▶ The diagram shows a circuit with 2 bulbs connected in **parallel**:

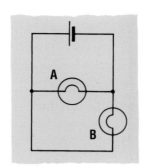

When the electrons travel from the battery, *some* of them go through bulb **A**, and the rest of them go through bulb **B**.

a What happens if one of the bulbs breaks**?**

b Draw a circuit diagram of 3 bulbs in parallel.

c Now re-draw your circuit with 3 switches, one to control each bulb.

d Then add a fourth switch to switch off all the bulbs together.

Bulbs in parallel

Measuring currents

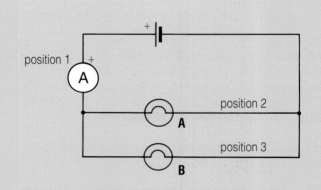

- Connect up this circuit, with the **ammeter** in position 1:
  Take care to connect the ammeter correctly.

- What is the reading on your ammeter**?**

- Then connect the ammeter in position 2.
  What is the current through bulb **A?**

- Then find the current in position 3.

- What do you notice about your results**?**
  Explain this, using these words:
  current   electrons   resistance

Notice the ammeter is always in series in the circuit.

Calculating currents

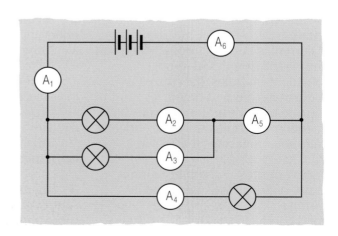

Look carefully at this circuit:

Suppose you are told the readings on 3 of the ammeters are:
$A_2 = 1\ A$ $A_3 = 1\ A$ $A_4 = 1.5\ A$

e What is the reading on ammeter A_5**?**

f What is the reading on ammeter A_6**?**

g What is the reading on ammeter A_1**?**

h If more cells are put in the circuit to increase the voltage, what would you expect to happen to each of the ammeter readings**?**

Measuring voltages – 1

Connect up this circuit with a cell and
2 bulbs in parallel:

A **voltmeter** is connected *in parallel*
with the bulbs.

Use your voltmeter to measure:
- the voltage across bulb **1** (V_1),
- the voltage across bulb **2** (V_2),
- the voltage across the cell (V_3).

What do you find?

Can you explain this?

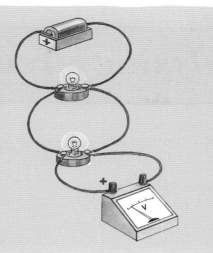
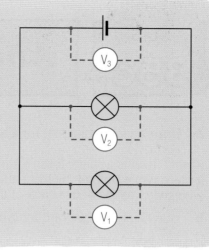

Measuring voltages – 2

Now connect 2 bulbs in series with a cell as shown:

Use your voltmeter to measure:
- the voltage across bulb **1** (V_1),
- the voltage across bulb **2** (V_2),
- the voltage across the cell (V_3).

What do you notice about your results?

Try a third bulb in series. What do you find now?

Notice that the bulbs are in series but the voltmeter
is *always in parallel* with a component.

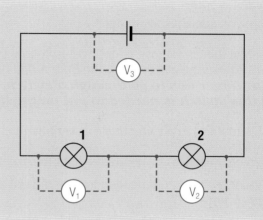

Calculating voltages

In this circuit, a voltmeter connected across the cell
reads 3 V. A voltmeter placed across bulb **A** reads 2 V.

i   What is the voltage across bulb **B**?

j   Which bulb do you think gets more energy? Why?

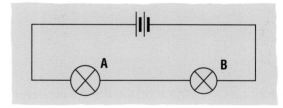

---

1   Copy and complete:
a) An ammeter measures the . . . . passing
through a component, so it is always
put in . . . . with the component.
b) A voltmeter measures the . . . . across a
component, so it is always put in . . . . ,
across the component.

2   Here is a circuit with 3 ammeters:

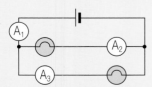

If ammeter A_1 shows 0.5 A and A_2 shows
0.3 A, what is the reading on A_3?

3   Draw a circuit diagram to show how
two 6 volt bulbs can be lit brightly from
two 3 volt cells.

4   Here is a circuit with 4 voltmeters:

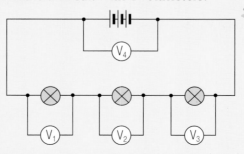

If voltmeters V_1, V_2, V_3 all show 2 V,
what is the reading on V_4?

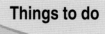

Things to do

a Draw a circuit diagram for a torch.

Rashid invents a safety torch for people walking at night. It has a white bulb at the front and a red bulb at the rear, with switches to control each of them separately.

b Draw a circuit diagram for him.

Luke suggests this circuit for Rashid's torch:

c Will it work?

d Can you see a disadvantage?

To analyse the circuit, use your finger to follow the path of the electrons from the cell through the bulb A and back to the cell. *If your finger has to go through a switch, then this switch is needed to put on the light.*

Use this method to answer these questions:

e Which switches are needed to light the green lamp?

f Which switches are needed to light the red and blue lamps together?

g What happens if both switches 3 and 7 are closed?

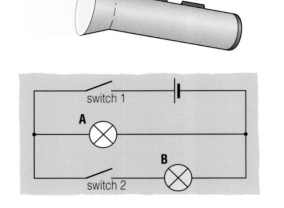

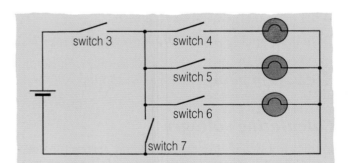

h How can you switch on the buzzer and the lamp?

i What happens if only switches **P** and **R** are closed?

j Re-draw the circuit so that the fan, lamp and buzzer each have their own switch.

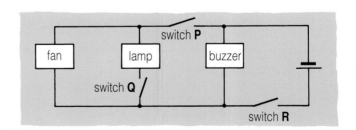

k Draw a circuit with a battery of 2 cells, a switch, an ammeter, 2 bulbs, and a variable resistor, all in series. Add a voltmeter in parallel with one of the bulbs.

In this circuit, 2 of the lamps have been **short-circuited** by a thick wire:

l What happens when the switch is closed?

m Re-draw the circuit so only lamp **Z** is short-circuited.

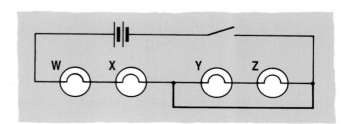

Two-way switches

The diagram shows a switch that can be in position A **or** in position B.

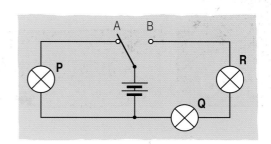

n What happens if the switch is in position A?

o What happens if the switch is in position B?

The diagram shows a mains circuit in a house, with two 2-way switches:
Wire C can be connected to either A or B.
This circuit is often used for the lighting on a staircase.

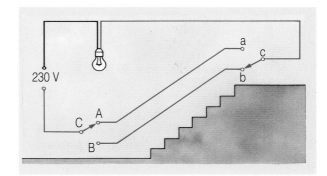

p In the diagram, is the lamp on or off?

q Describe how the circuit works, using the letters on the diagram in your answer.

r What are the advantages of this circuit?

Here is the diagram for a motor in a toy crane:

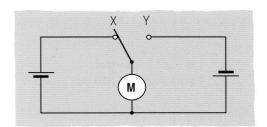

s What do you notice about the cells?

t What happens if the switch is moved from X to Y?

Here is a more complicated circuit:

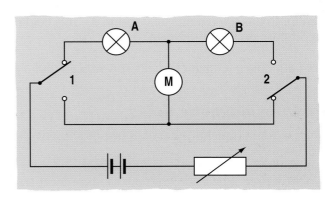

u Copy and complete this table.

Switch 1	Switch 2	Bulb lit?	Motor turns?
up	down	A	forwards
up	up		
down	up		
down	down		

v What would be the effects of varying the resistor?

---

1 Draw a circuit containing a cell, a switch and 3 bulbs labelled A, B and C. Bulbs A and B are in series, and C is in parallel with A. The switch controls only bulb C.
When all the bulbs are lit, which one is the brightest?

2 Draw a circuit with a 2-way switch, a cell, a bulb, and a motor so that in one position the bulb is on and in the other position the motor is on.

3 In these circuits, all the bulbs are the same:

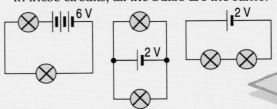

a) Which circuit has the dimmest bulbs?
b) Explain why this is, using the words:
   current   voltage   resistance

Things to do

Magnetic fields

You can use a magnet to pick up paper-clips, but not paper. Paper is not magnetic.

a Which of these are magnetic: wood, iron, plastic, steel, cloth, a coin, copper wire, nickel, iron oxide**?**

The diagram shows a magnet on a cork, floating on water:

b Which direction will the magnet point to**?**

c What is the name of this instrument**?**

a magnet on a floating cork

The ends of the bar magnet are called **poles**.

d Which end of a magnet is the N-pole**?**

e If another magnet is brought near, so that its N-pole is near the N-pole of this magnet, what happens**?**

f What happens if a S-pole is brought near a N-pole**?**

We say that: **Like poles repel,
Unlike poles attract**.

The magnets exert a force on each other without touching. This is because a magnet has a **magnetic field** round it. Iron and steel are affected by a magnetic field.

The Earth has a magnetic field round it. This field makes a compass point to the North.

We cannot see a magnetic field, but we can plot a map of it.

Plotting magnetic fields

Put a magnet under a sheet of paper, as shown:

Sprinkle a few iron filings over the paper, and then tap the paper. The iron filings act like tiny compasses.

Look carefully at the pattern that appears:

- Sketch the shape of this field.
  The curved lines are called **field lines** or lines of force.

- Use a small 'plotting compass' to follow a field line from the N-pole to the S-pole.

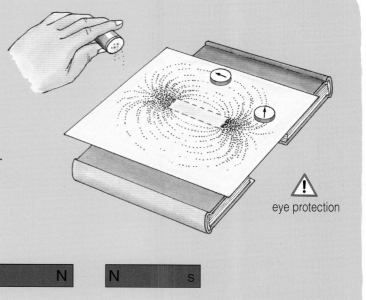

eye protection

Now find the shape of the magnetic field when 2 magnets are placed in line, with

a) The two N-poles near each other like this:
b) A N-pole near a S-pole.

Your teacher can give you a Help Sheet.

Electro-magnetism

In 1820, a Danish scientist called Hans Oersted discovered that:
an electric current produces a magnetic field.

In this experiment, a large current is passed up the thick copper wire.
Iron filings are sprinkled on the card to show the shape of the magnetic field:

Plotting compasses show the direction of the field lines.

g What happens if the current is reversed?

h What happens to the compasses when the current is switched off?

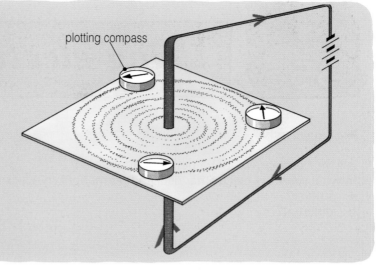

plotting compass

The magnetic field from a single wire is very weak. To make it stronger, the wire is made into a **coil**, or **solenoid**.

The field round a coil

Iron filings are sprinkled on a card round a coil:

i What happens when the current is switched on?

j What do you notice about the shape of the magnetic field? (Hint: see the opposite page.)

The compasses show the direction of the magnetic field.

k What happens if the current is reversed?

l What happens to the compasses when the current is switched off?

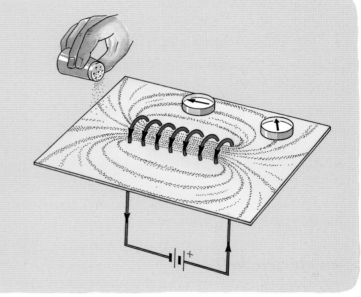

A coil like this is an **electro-magnet**.
An electromagnet usually has an iron **core**, which becomes magnetised and makes a stronger electromagnet.

You will use an electromagnet in the next lesson.

---

1 Copy and complete:
a) Like poles . . . . Unlike poles . . . .
b) The Earth has a magnetic . . . . round it.
c) A magnetic . . . . can be produced by an electric . . . .
d) The . . . . field round a straight . . . . is in the shape of circles.
e) The field round a coil (or . . . .) has the same shape as the . . . . round a bar . . . .
f) An electromagnet only works if a . . . . is flowing through the . . . .

2 Drink cans are usually made from either steel or aluminium. In a metal re-cycling plant they need to be separated. Design a machine to do this.

3 In the diagrams below, **A, B, C, D** are compasses. In diagram (a), a current is flowing **down**, into the paper.
In diagram (b), there is no current flowing.
Copy the diagrams and draw in the direction of each compass needle.

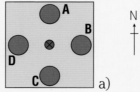
a)

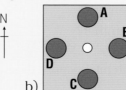
b)

4 Plan an investigation to see if iron can be made into a magnet more easily than steel. How would you make it a fair test?

Things to do

Using electromagnets

▶ Explain what is happening in this photo:

Is it an electromagnet or a permanent magnet?
In what ways are electromagnets and permanent magnets
a similar?
b different?

Investigating electromagnets

Plan an investigation to find out **what affects the strength of an electromagnet**.

- What things can you vary?
  Choose **one** of these, and plan your investigation.

- How will you make it a fair test?

- How will you measure the strength of your electromagnet?

Show your plan to your teacher, and then do it.
!Do not use electricity at more than 12 volts!

- If you have time, investigate the other variables.

Electromagnets have many uses.

An electric bell

This is used in doorbells, burglar alarms, and fire-bells.

Study the diagram:

c When the switch is closed, there is a complete circuit. What happens to the electromagnet?

The iron bar is on a springy metal strip which can bend.

d What happens to the iron bar?
e What happens to the hammer?

There is now a gap in the circuit, because the iron bar is not touching the contact.

f What happens now?

g Why does the bell ring for as long as the switch is closed?

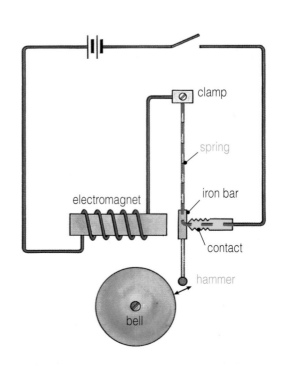

clamp

spring

iron bar

electromagnet

contact

hammer

bell

A relay

This is a switch operated by an electromagnet.
It is used when you want to use a small current
to switch on a larger current.

Study the diagram:

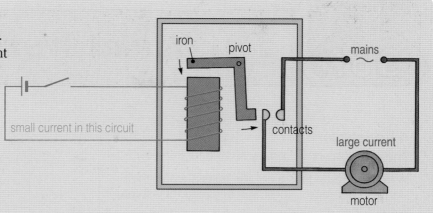

There are 2 circuits here.

h When a current flows in the blue circuit,
what happens to the core of the coil?

i What happens to the iron bar?

j What happens to the contacts in the
red circuit?

k What happens to the motor?

The motor might be the starter-motor in a car, or
the motor in a washing-machine, or in an electric train.

A circuit-breaker

This is an automatic safety switch.
It cuts off the current if it gets too big.

Study the diagram:

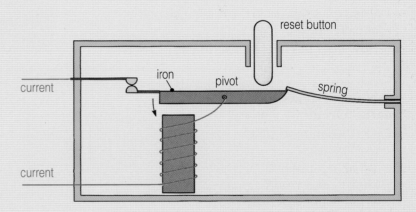

l What happens to the electromagnet when
the current is flowing?

m If the current is big, what happens to
the iron bar?

n What does this do to the current?

o How would you re-set this circuit-breaker?

p To make it switch off at a lower current,
how would you change the electromagnet?

Electromagnets are also used in loudspeakers, in motors, in cassette-recorders,
and in computers to store data on the computer discs.

---

1 Copy and complete:
The strength of an electromagnet can be
increased by:
a) increasing the number of turns on the . . . . ,
b) increasing the . . . . , or
c) using an . . . . core.

2 Design a relay that would use a small
current to turn *off* a big current. Draw a
labelled diagram of your design.

3 Door-chimes use an electromagnet to
make a 'bing-bong' sound. When the switch
is pushed, an iron rod hits one chime (a metal
tube). When the switch is released, the rod
springs back to hit the other chime tube.
Draw a labelled diagram to show how this
could work.

4 Design a machine that could separate full
and empty milk-bottles on a conveyor belt.

Things to do

Physics at Work

A lie detector

The diagram shows a very simple lie detector:

When a person tells a lie, the resistance of their skin can decrease – perhaps because they sweat with embarrassment.

a Use the words below to explain how it works.

voltage   current   resistance   milli-ammeter

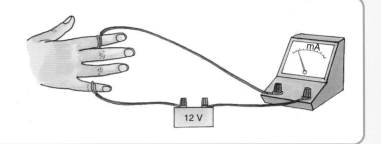

Car fuel gauge

Look carefully at the diagram:

b What happens to the float as the petrol is used up?

c What does this do to the resistance of the circuit?

d How does this affect the ammeter?

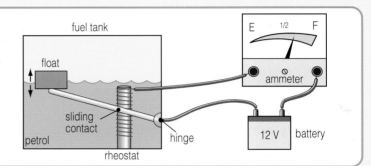

The diagram shows part of a **'mains' circuit** for a house:

e Are the lamps in series or in parallel?

f What is a fuse for?

g How does it work?

h What happens if fuse A 'blows'?

i How does the staircase circuit work?

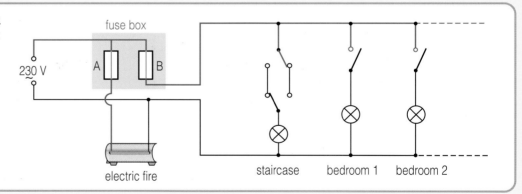

Electric car

j Draw an Energy Transfer Diagram for this electric car.

k It has re-chargeable batteries in it. Explain how its energy probably comes from the Sun.

The Earth has a magnetic field:

l What do you notice about the shape of the field?

m Which way does a compass point?

n Near the North Pole of the Earth, is there a magnetic N-pole or S-pole?

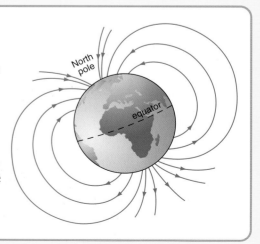

Electromagnetic relay

Analyse the diagram carefully:

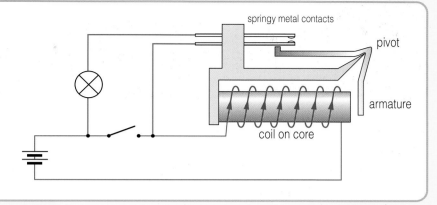

o Name suitable materials for the wire of the coil, and for the core.

p Give 2 reasons why iron would be a good choice for the armature.

q Explain, step by step, what happens when the switch is closed.

r When the switch is opened, the bulb stays on. Explain why.

s Draw a diagram to show how a relay could be used to set off a large fireworks display safely.

t Explain how it works.

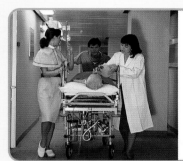

In a hospital, the corridor doors need to be open most of the time, so trolleys can move easily. But in a fire, the doors should be closed to stop the fire spreading.

u Draw a diagram to show how electromagnets can help.

Loudspeaker

The diagram shows a simple loudspeaker:

If a current is passed through the coil from A to B, the coil becomes an electromagnet and is attracted to the bar magnet.

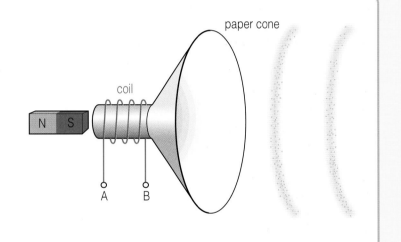

v What happens if a current is reversed so it passes from B to A?

w What happens if the current is reversed, to and fro, 50 times in each second?
(This is called *alternating current*.)

x What difference would you hear if the current was alternating 1000 times per second?

y What difference would you hear if the current was bigger?

Microwave oven

Microwaves are dangerous, and the oven must not work while the door is open.

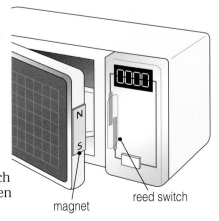

z Why are the 2 contact strips inside the **reed switch** made of iron?

A Why does the oven not work when the door is open?

B Why does the reed switch complete the circuit when the door is shut?

Two-tone door chime

Look at this circuit:

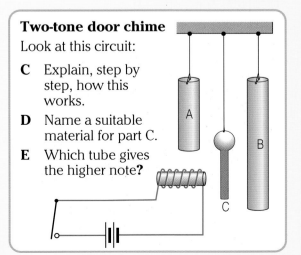

C Explain, step by step, how this works.

D Name a suitable material for part C.

E Which tube gives the higher note?

Electricity and Magnetism

35g

Ideas about Electricity

2500 years ago, a Greek called **Thales** experimented with a piece of amber resin. He found that if he rubbed it, it would attract tiny pieces of paper, just as your comb can. (Amber was called *elektron* in Greek.)

Much later, in 1660, **Otto von Guericke** invented a rubbing machine that would make sparks.

In 1752, **Ben Franklin** had an idea while looking at lightning. He suggested that the clouds were charged with electricity . . . but he had no evidence. In a very dangerous experiment he flew a kite in a storm and found electricity was conducted down the wet string.

In 1791, **Luigi Galvani** noticed that a dead frog's leg twitched if touched by 2 different metals at the same time.

Alessandro Volta followed up this idea, and in 1800 he invented the first battery: He used 2 metals (silver and zinc) with blotting paper (soaked in salt water) between the metals.

Volta and his battery

Now that a steady current could be used, electricity was studied by many scientists, including **André Ampère** and **Georg Ohm**.

Ideas about Magnetism

The first magnets were pieces of rock (iron oxide) called *lodestone*. About 1000 years ago, sailors began to use a lodestone as a compass.

In 1600, **William Gilbert** (Queen Elizabeth I's doctor) published the results of his experiments with magnets. He built a model of the Earth in lodestone and used it to show the Earth acts as if it has a bar magnet inside it.

Ideas about Electromagnetism

Scientists suspected a link between electricity and magnetism. But it wasn't until 1820 that **Hans Ørsted** showed how a current can affect a compass needle. This was the first ammeter.

In 1821, **Ampère** used a coil to make the first electromagnet.

Michael Faraday came from a poor home, but got a job as a lab assistant. He soon became the greatest experimenter in Physics.

Michael Faraday

In 1821 he invented the electric motor.

He also invented the idea of using 'lines of force' (or 'lines of flux' or 'field lines') to give a picture of a magnetic field. This is a very important idea. It is used by modern scientists to picture other fields, such as gravitational fields.

By 1831, after many experiments, Faraday discovered the transformer and the generator. This is a machine for making electricity (it is sometimes called a dynamo or an alternator). You may have one on your bicycle. It converts kinetic energy to electrical energy. It is vital to modern society.

In 1879, **Thomas Edison** invented the electric light bulb.

In 1897, **J. J. Thompson** did an important experiment with a cathode ray tube (a kind of TV tube). By using a magnetic field to bend the beam of current inside the tube, he showed that a current is really a flow of negative electrons.

Questions

1. Where do you think the word electricity came from?

2. Draw an Energy Transfer Diagram for
   a) a motor and   b) a generator.
   In what ways are they opposites?

3. a) Draw a labelled diagram of one of Volta's cells.
   b) One of his cells gives a voltage of 1.8 V.
      How did he get a voltage of 9 V?

4. The nerves in your body use electricity. How does Galvani's experiment support this idea?

5. Use the dates shown above to draw a time-line.

6. How did Edison's light bulb change people's lives?

7. The article says the generator 'is vital to modern society'. Explain what this means, with examples.

8. Choose one of the scientists and find out more details of his life.

9. Scientists work in many different ways. Use the article above to list as many ways as you can.

Revision Summary

Electricity

- For an electric current to flow, there must be a complete circuit.

- A conductor lets a current flow easily.
  A good conductor has a low resistance.
  An insulator does not let a current flow easily.
  It has a high resistance.

- Circuit diagrams are drawn using symbols:

- An electric current is a flow of tiny electrons.
  It is measured in amperes (amps or A), using an ammeter.
  An ammeter must be connected in series in a circuit. It should have a low resistance.

- Voltage is measured by a voltmeter, placed across a component (in parallel).
  It should have a high resistance.

- In a series circuit, the same current goes through all the components:

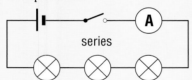

series

- To pass more current you can
  – add more cells pushing the same way,
  – reduce the number of bulbs in series.

- In a parallel circuit, there is more than one path.
  Some electrons go along one path and the rest go along the other path.

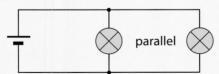

parallel

  To find the current in the main circuit, add up the currents in the branches.

- The electric current (flow of electrons) transfers energy from the cell to the bulbs.
  A bigger voltage means a bigger transfer of nergy.
  In the bulb the energy is transformed to heat and light energy.

- A fuse is used to protect a circuit. It melts if too much current flows, and breaks the circuit.

Magnetism

- The end of a compass that points North is called the North pole (N-pole) of the magnet.

- Two N-poles (or two S-poles) repel each other.
  An N-pole attracts an S-pole.

- Iron and steel can be magnetised. Other magnetic substances are nickel, cobalt and iron oxide.

- You can find the shape of the magnetic field round a bar magnet by using iron filings (or small plotting compasses).
  The shape is shown by 'lines of force' or 'field lines'.

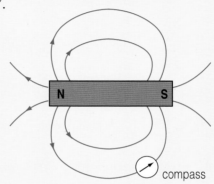

compass

- The Earth has a magnetic field round it.
  A compass points along the field.

- A current in a coil produces a magnetic field like a bar magnet. It is an electromagnet.

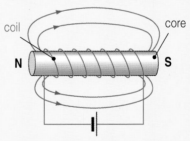

coil   core

N   S

- The strength of an electromagnet can be increased by:
  (1) increasing the current in the coil,
  (2) increasing the number of turns on the coil, and
  (3) using an iron core.
  Reversing the current, reverses the North and South poles.

- In a relay, a small current in the coil of an electromagnet is used to switch on a bigger current.

- In an electric bell, an electromagnet is used to attract an iron bar so that it breaks the circuit repeatedly. The vibrating iron bar makes the bell ring.

Questions

Ben Franklin

1 Benjamin Franklin (1706–1790) was a scientist who helped to write the American Declaration of Independence ("... *we hold these truths to be self-evident: that all men are created equal* ..."). He risked his life flying a kite in a storm and invented the lightning conductor.
   a) Find out all you can about him, and what he discovered.
   b) How have our ideas about electricity changed since he was alive?

2 This circuit is used to dim a light:

While the light is being dimmed, what happens to
   a) The current in the lamp?
   b) The resistance of the variable resistor?
   c) The voltage across the lamp?

3 The diagram shows an electrical circuit:

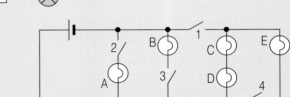

   a) What happens if only switch 1 is closed?
   b) What happens if only switches 3 and 4 are closed?
   c) How would you light bulbs A, C and D?
   d) If all the switches are closed, which bulb(s) are dimmest? Why?

4 In the circuits shown, all the cells are identical, and all the bulbs are identical:

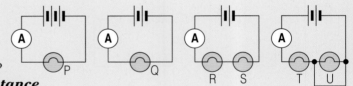

   a) Which bulb would be brightest? Why?
   b) Which bulb would not be lit? Why?
   c) Which ammeter would show the lowest reading? Explain why, using the words **voltage** and **resistance**.

5 Danny connected a battery in series with a switch, an ammeter, a variable resistor and a coil of wire. Then he connected a voltmeter to measure the voltage across the coil.

   a) Draw a circuit diagram of his circuit.

The table shows his results as he altered the variable resistor:

   b) Plot a large graph of the current against the voltage, drawing the line of 'best fit'.
   c) Which result(s) do you think could be wrong and should be checked?
   d) What would be the current if the voltage was 8.4 V?
   e) What conclusion(s) can you draw from the graph?

Current (A)	0.4	0.7	1.2	1.5	1.9	2.4	2.8
Voltage (V)	1.9	2.9	4.9	6.3	8.0	10.1	11.8

6 Rachel tested 2 electromagnets, one with 20 turns and one with 60 turns on the coil. She counted how many nails each electromagnet could hold up at different currents. Here are her results:

Current (A)		0	0.5	1.0	1.5	2.0	2.5	3.0	3.5	4.0
Number of nails	20-turns	0	1	4	9	15	21	27	33	38
	60-turns	0	4	12	27	42	55	61	64	64

   a) Plot a graph for each electromagnet (on the same axes).
   b) Describe what happens when the current is increased in
      i) the 20-turn coil,
      ii) the 60-turn coil.
   c) Can you explain this?

Rocks and Minerals

36

The ground we walk on is made of rock.
The Earth's crust is made up of 3 types of rock.
The study of these rocks tells us a lot about the history of the Earth.

In this topic, you will find out about how rocks are formed and re-formed in a constant cycle of change.

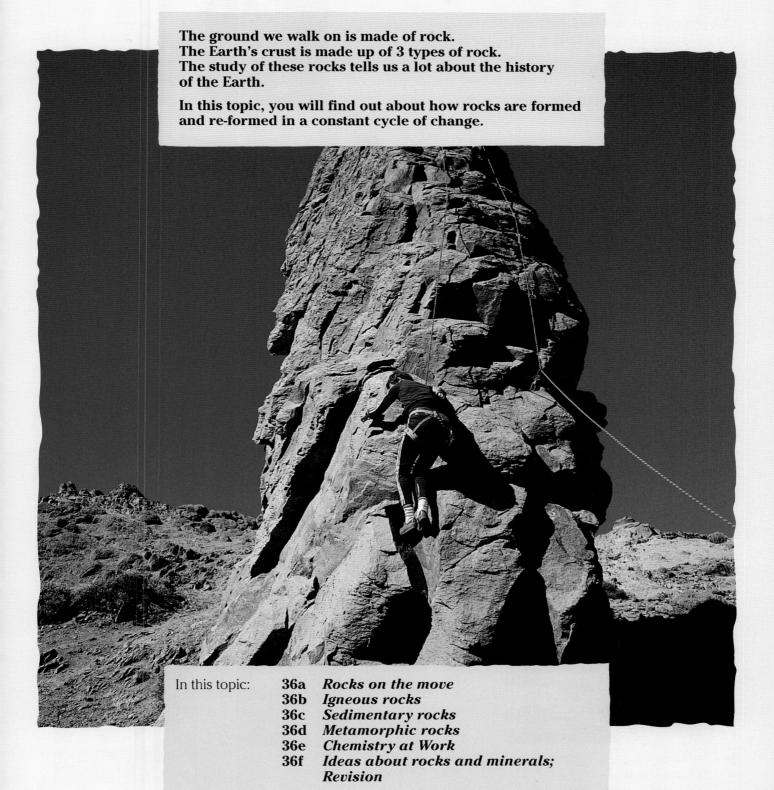

Rocks on the move

The photos show minerals and rocks.
Do you know the difference?

A **mineral** is a single substance. It has a formula.
It has a name.
But most **rocks** are **mixtures**. They contain
different minerals.

▶ Look at the photos:

a Which do you think are minerals?

b Which do you think are rocks?

malachite

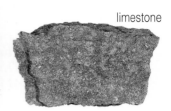
limestone

rock salt

basalt

iron pyrites

calcite

granite

But you told me to pick some rock!

Weathering

All rocks slowly crumble away.
The process is called **weathering**.
All the rocks in the pictures are being **weathered**. They are breaking up.

c

d

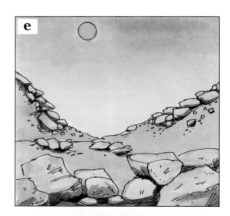
e

f

g

h

▶ Say what you think is causing the weathering in each of the
pictures **c** to **h**.

There are 3 types of weathering:
- physical
- chemical
- biological.

▶ Look at the descriptions of how rocks are broken. For each one, say whether it is physical, chemical or biological weathering.

i. Animals dig around rocks. The rocks break.

j. Cracks in rocks fill with water. The water freezes and expands. A piece of rock breaks off.

k. Oxygen in the air reacts with iron in rocks. Iron compounds form. The rock is weakened.

l. Soil gets trapped in cracks in rocks. Plants start to grow. The roots of the plants break the rocks.

m. Acid rain reacts with minerals in the rocks.

n. Rocks can get very hot in daytime. They cool at night. The minerals in the rock expand and contract at different rates. The rock cracks.

Weathering with acid

Test some rock samples with acid.
- Which of the rocks react with acid?
- What do you see?
- Which of your samples might contain a carbonate? How do you know?

Erosion

Small pieces of weathered rock can get moved from place to place.
Mostly wind, rivers and the sea do this.
We say the rocks are **transported** to another place.
As the rocks move, they wear away other rocks.
This is called **erosion**.
The rocks then settle somewhere else. They are **deposited**.

This way for rocks

Which rock erodes the fastest?

Use a nail to see which rock is the softest.
Make sure you do a fair and safe test.
Put the rocks in order of how fast they erode.

Things to do

1 Copy and complete. Use the words in the box:

> deposit   erosion   minerals
> transported   weathering

Most rocks are mixtures of . . . .
Rocks crumble due to . . . .
They are worn away by . . . .
Rock pieces are . . . . to another place.
They . . . . in another area.

2
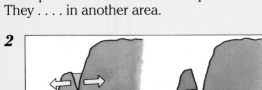

What do you think these diagrams show?
Copy them out. Try to explain this process.

3 Write down the causes of:
a) weathering b) erosion.

4 Make a list of rocks used for building.

5 Coves form when the sea erodes rocks.

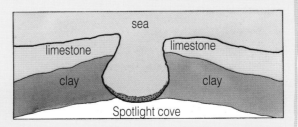
sea
limestone   limestone
clay   clay
Spotlight cove

Which is the harder rock around the cove?
Limestone or clay?

Explain how you know this.

Igneous rocks

Igneous rocks are made from **magma**. This is a molten (melted) material from deep underground.
Magma rises to the surface of the Earth. It can erupt at the surface to form a **volcano**.
The molten rock that erupts is called **lava**. It cools *quickly* at the surface to form solid rock. Some magma never reaches the surface. It cools *slowly* surrounded by rocks underground. It forms solid rock.

▶ Volcanoes can be dangerous.
But some people choose to live on the slopes of volcanoes.
Why do they do this?
Make a list of your ideas.

Igneous rocks are made up of crystals.
The crystals may be tiny or quite large.
Why does the size of crystal vary?
Does it depend on how fast the magma cools?
Try the next experiment to find out.

Crystal clues

We can't easily melt rocks in the lab!
Use salol to be your melted rock for this test.

⚠ Care – the water will still be hot.

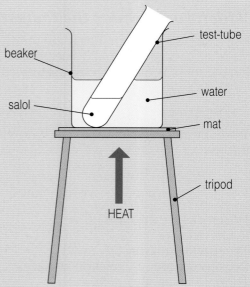

* Half fill a beaker with water.

* Put a solid called *salol* into a test-tube.
  It should be about 3 cm deep.

* Put your test-tube into the beaker of water.

* Heat the water to melt the salol.

* When the salol has melted, switch off your Bunsen burner.

* Ask your teacher for a *cold* glass slide.
  This has been kept in the fridge.

* Use a pipette to put 3 drops of melted salol on to the cold slide.
  Use a magnifying glass to watch carefully.
  You will see salol crystals form.

Crystals can form when a liquid cools.

* Now get a *warm* slide. Repeat your experiment.

a On which slide did the salol cool faster?

b On which slide did the bigger crystals form?

c Write a summary of your findings.

Comparing rocks

Your teacher will give you some rock samples.
Look carefully at the rocks.

Make a table to show your answers to the following:

- Describe the appearance of each rock.
- Decide which of the rocks are igneous rocks.

For the igneous rocks:

- How quickly did the magma cool to form each rock?
  How do you know?
- Did the rock form by cooling **above** or **below** ground?

▶ Look at these statements about igneous rocks.
They describe how the rock forms.
Put them in the right order. Copy out your answer.

Inside the Earth is magma. This is very hot molten rock.
Lava cools quickly. It makes igneous rocks with small crystals.

The volcano erupts
It makes igneous rocks with large crystals.
Some magma does not get to the surface.

It cools slowly underground.
Then magma comes to the surface of the Earth. It is called lava.

Igneous rocks are hard. They are used to surface roads. They are usually coated with tar.

d Igneous rocks do not contain fossils. Why not?

Density of rocks

Measure the density of the samples of granite and gabbro.
Granite is 'silica-rich'. Gabbro is 'iron-rich'.

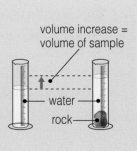

volume increase = volume of sample

water
rock

e Which of these rocks is the denser?

Now measure the density of the other igneous rocks.
Decide whether the rocks you test are relatively
'silica-rich' or 'iron-rich'.

---

1 Copy and complete:
a) Molten rock is called . . . .
b) Molten rock erupting from a volcano is called . . . .
c) Fast cooling of a liquid makes . . . . crystals.
d) Slow cooling of a liquid makes . . . . crystals.

2 Use books and ICT to help you with this.
a) What is a volcano?
b) Imagine that you are a newspaper reporter. You have been sent to report on an erupting volcano. You are the first at the scene. Write the report for your newspaper.

3 Find out about:
a) volcanoes in the world which are 'active'.
b) a famous volcanic eruption. (How did this affect local people? What happened to the environment?)

Things to do

Sedimentary rocks

Are you all OK?

Yes, we're just weathered.

Rocks are slowly weathered. They break into pieces.

▶ What causes weathering? Draw a spider diagram of your ideas.

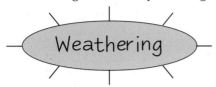

Weathering

The weathered rocks are moved by wind, rivers and the sea. They are **transported** to another place. When these settle (**deposit**), they are called **sediments**.
The sediments can be fine grains, like sand. They can be larger fragments, like pebbles.
Over time, layers of sediment build up. The sediment is squeezed by the weight of new layers above. Any water is squeezed out. The minerals dissolved in the water are left behind. These minerals **cement** the grains together. The solid sedimentary rock forms.

When seas or lakes run dry, sediments form. The water evaporates.

Look at the diagram:

a Which is the newest sediment deposited?

b Which is the oldest rock?

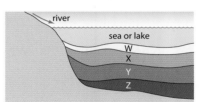

river

sea or lake

W
X
Y
Z

Layers of sedimentary rock forming.

Sand and sandstone

Look closely at the samples of damp sand and sandstone.
Use a hand lens or microscope.
How are the grains held together?

Squash the wet sand. Look for the water being squeezed out.
You can see how the sediments stick together.

Looking at sedimentary rocks

Look carefully at the rock samples your teacher gives you.
These are all sedimentary rocks.
Use books or ROMs to identify them.

Make a list of *features* of sedimentary rocks (appearance, texture, etc.).

c Name the rock made from pebbles.

d Name the rock made from mud.

e Fossils are often found in sedimentary rock. Why?

Testing limestones

Your teacher will show you some samples of limestones.
Are the limestones the same or different?

Plan the tests you will do to answer the questions below.
Be sure you know which measurements to make.

- What do the limestones look like?
- Do they soak up water?
- What are their densities?
- How much carbonate do they contain?

Ask your teacher to check your plans.
Then carry out the tests.
Record your results in a table.

f Are all limestones the same?

g Why do you think this is?

h Are your results reliable? How can you improve these tests?

▶ Look at the statements below.
  They describe how sedimentary rocks form.
  Put them in the right order. Copy out your answer.

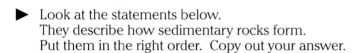

> Rocks can crumble.
> They make small particles.

> The pressure and the
> mineral cement stick
> the particles together.

> The particles settle
> in another place.
> They form a layer.

> Water is squeezed
> out. The minerals
> left in the sediment
> act like cement.

> The lower layers get pressed together.

> The particles are carried away
> by rivers or wind.

> Other layers get put on top of them.

> The solid rock forms slowly.

Things to do

1 Draw a cartoon strip to show the process of forming a sedimentary rock. Start with a piece of weathered rock. Finish with the solid lump!

2 A river carries rock fragments from a mountain to the sea. Describe 2 ways in which the fragments change as they are moved.

3 Why can the presence of fossils be useful in the investigation of rocks?

4 Imagine that a limestone quarry is opening near you. You are a local newspaper reporter. Write a balanced report about the quarry. Explain why the quarry is important. Write about problems that might arise.

Metamorphic rocks

Metamorphic rocks can be formed from igneous, sedimentary or other metamorphic rocks.

Some rocks are buried deep underground. They are hot. They feel pressure from rocks above them.
Sometimes the heat and pressure are so great that the mineral structures of the rocks change. The particles in the buried rock form new crystals.
Metamorphic rock is formed.
These changes happen when the rock is still solid. It does not melt.

Sometimes rocks are 'baked' by magma.

a What is magma?

The rocks close to the magma get very hot. The high temperature can change the mineral structure of the rock. It becomes **metamorphic** rock.

The minerals in metamorphic rocks line up in bands.

What's changed?

Sedimentary rocks can become new metamorphic ones.
Your teacher will give you some rock samples.
Look at the rocks with a hand lens.
Match the **sedimentary** rock with the **metamorphic** rock it makes.

Choose one matching pair of rocks.
Describe the differences between the rocks.

▶ Look at this rock face diagram:
It shows 3 types of rock.

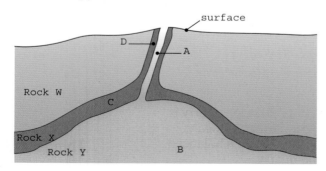

b Which rock is sedimentary?

c Which rock is igneous?

d Which rock is metamorphic?

e The rock at A cooled more quickly than the rock at B. How does that affect its appearance?

f Why is the band of rock thicker at C than at D?

3 rock types!

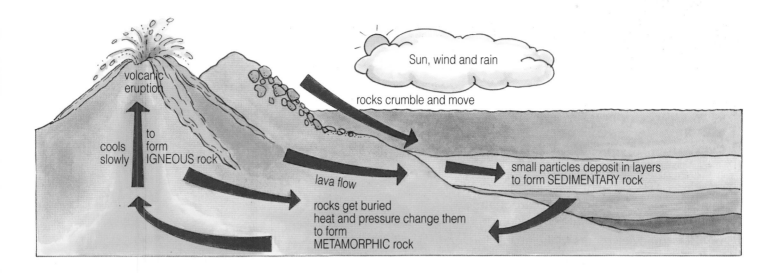

volcanic eruption

cools slowly / to form IGNEOUS rock

lava flow

rocks get buried
heat and pressure change them
to form
METAMORPHIC rock

Sun, wind and rain

rocks crumble and move

small particles deposit in layers
to form SEDIMENTARY rock

g This is called the **rock cycle**. Why do you think this is**?**

Identifying rocks

These could be features to look for:

Igneous	Sedimentary	Metamorphic
Hard	Can be soft and crumbly (but not always!)	Hard
Made of crystals No layers	Made of lots of grains	Made of bands or sheets Splits into layers
No fossils	May contain fossils	May contain distorted fossils

- Use these ideas to sort some rock samples into groups.
- Name as many of the rocks as you can.
- Use books or ROMs to list some uses of these rocks.

1 Copy out the 2 lists of rocks.
Use a line to join each sedimentary rock
with the metamorphic rock it makes.

Sedimentary	Metamorphic
limestone	quartzite
sandstone	marble
shale	slate

2 Fossils found in metamorphic rock are
often distorted. Why?

3 You must get permission for this first!
Visit a local garden centre or builder's yard.
Make a list of the rocks you see.
How are the rocks used?

4 Find out some information about
earthquakes.
a) What causes earthquakes?
b) What is the ***epicentre*** of an
earthquake?
c) What is the ***Richter scale***?
d) What is a ***seismometer***?
e) Why is San Francisco at risk from
earthquakes?

Things to do

Chemistry at Work

Limestone

Limestone is a sedimentary rock made from the shells of sea creatures.

a Describe how limestone was formed.

Limestone cottages

Limestone is made of calcium carbonate.
Calcium carbonate has the chemical formula $CaCO_3$.

b How many elements make up calcium carbonate?

Limestone is a very important rock.
Blocks of it are used to construct buildings.

c Why are many old limestone buildings in cities showing bad signs of weathering?

Limestone is used to make cement, mortar and concrete for these buildings

We also use limestone to make other building materials, such as **cement**. Cement is then mixed with more rock products to make **mortar** and **concrete**.

When we make **cement** the limestone is ground up into a powder and heated with clay. A little calcium sulphate is then added to it.

d Find out how clay is formed in nature.

The mixture is heated in large rotating kilns.
Look at the diagram opposite:

When limestone is heated it breaks down into calcium oxide and carbon dioxide gas is given off.

e Write a word equation to show what happens when limestone is heated.

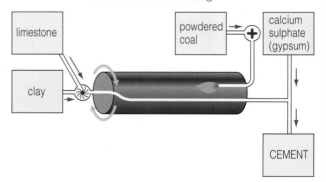

Mortar is made by mixing cement powder with sand, then adding water to make a thick paste.
It is the material that binds the bricks together when a house is built.

Concrete is made from a mixture of cement, sand and gravel or small stones. As with mortar, we then add water and mix it all together.
Reinforced concrete is made when we need large blocks, such as for building motorway bridges. The concrete is set in moulds with iron rods running through them.

f What might happen if the iron rods inside the concrete blocks started to rust?

Using mortar

Using concrete

Minerals

A mineral is a substance found in the Earth's crust.
Rocks are usually mixtures of minerals.

Mohs' scale is used to compare the hardness of different minerals.
It was first compiled by Friedrich Mohs, a German scientist,
in 1822.

Look at the table below:

Number on Mohs' scale	Mineral	Approximate relative hardness
1	Talc	1
2	Gypsum	3
3	Calcite	9
4	Fluorite	21
5	Apatite	45
6	Orthoclase, feldspar	72
7	Quartz	100
8	Topaz	200
9	Corundum (ruby and sapphire)	400
10	Diamond	1600

g How many times harder than ruby is diamond**?**

Look at the photos below:

Engraving glass

Diamond tipped mining cutters.

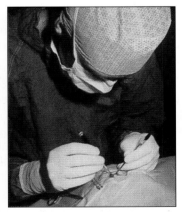

A surgeon using diamond coated instruments

h Why is diamond chosen for these uses**?**

Gemstones are minerals that are hard and attractive.
They can be cut along certain planes to make flat surfaces on the stone.
Diamond is a very expensive gemstone.

i Quartz is a mineral found in sand.
Why are most gemstones over 7 on Mohs' scale**?**

j Do some research to find out about one particular gemstone.
You might choose your birth-stone.
Try to find what it is made from, how hard it is and where
it is found.

Mary Anning – fossil hunter (1799–1847)

Can you imagine the excitement of discovering the fossil of a complete ichthyosaurus? Mary Anning had that thrill when she was only 11 years old.

She carefully uncovered a fossil her brother had spotted earlier. To her surprise the remains of the reptile were 30 metres long! The fossil is now in the Natural History Museum in London.

Mary has been described as the greatest fossil collector ever. She was one of the first *palaeontologists* (people who study fossils and evidence from prehistoric times).

Mary's father made furniture for a living but the family struggled to make ends meet. It is thought that her mother had as many as 10 children, but only Mary and her brother survived. Her father collected fossils to sell to tourists in their home town of Lyme Regis in Dorset. This helped to bring in a little more money but the family were in debt when he died in 1810.

However, the family were skilled fossil hunters and Mary eventually took over the business.
Even the dog was involved! Mary trained her dog to stay at the spot where she found a fossil while she went off to get her digging tools. Unfortunately the dog was killed in the line of duty when it was buried in a landslide.
She did manage to scrape a meagre living for the family with the support of a small grant from the government.

It is thought that the tongue-twister: 'She sells sea shells on the sea shore' refers to Mary Anning.

But Mary has not really gained the recognition that her discoveries and great knowledge about fossils deserve. Can you think why?

At this time, men dominated British society. They had all the best jobs and women were treated as second-class citizens.
Poor people were also looked down upon by those with wealth and power. The world of science reflected these attitudes. So you can see why Mary might have struggled to get credit for her work. She was not rich, had received little formal education and was a woman!

However, she did win the respect of scientists of her time. It helped when she discovered the first ever fossil of a plesiosaur. A famous French scientist doubted her discovery. But once he had checked it out himself he agreed that Mary's new fossil was an important find. This helped to get her and her family accepted by fellow scientists as part of their 'club'.
She could argue on equal terms with eminent geologists.
She was made an honorary member of the Geological Society of London before she died.

Questions

1 Not much was written about Mary Anning's contribution to science for many years after her death.
Why do you think she has only recently gained recognition for her work?

2 How are fossils formed?

3 Explain the chances of finding fossils in:
a) sedimentary rocks,
b) metamorphic rocks, and
c) igneous rocks.

4 Find out why Lyme Regis is a good place to find fossils.

5 What evidence can we find about the history of the Earth from fossils?
In your answer include information about the theory of plate tectonics.

Revision Summary

Rocks and minerals

- Most rocks are mixtures. They contain different minerals.

- All rocks slowly crumble away. They are weakened by the weather. This process is called weathering.
  Weathering can be caused by water, wind and changes in temperature.
  Rocks expand as they get hotter and contract when they get cooler.

- The small pieces of rock rub against each other as they are moved, e.g. by wind and rivers.
  They wear away. This process is called erosion.
  The rock pieces can be transported and deposited in another place.

- There are 3 main types of rock – igneous, sedimentary and metamorphic.
  The 3 types form in different ways.

Conglomerate is a sedimentary rock.

Slate is a metamorphic rock.

Gabbro is an igneous rock.

- Igneous rocks form when melted (molten) substances cool. They are hard and are made of crystals.
  Larger crystals form when the cooling is slow. Granite is an igneous rock.

- Sedimentary rocks form in layers. They are made when substances settle out in water.
  In hot weather, water from seas and lakes can run dry. A sediment can form in this way.
  Sometimes these rocks contain fossils. The rocks are usually soft. Sandstone is a sedimentary rock.

- Metamorphic rocks are made when rocks are heated and/or squashed together.
  They form very slowly. They are usually very hard. Marble is a metamorphic rock.

- Over millions of years, one rock type can change into another. The rocks are recycled.
  We call this the rock cycle.

Basalt has small crystals.
It is formed from lava.

Granite has larger crystals.
It is formed from magma.

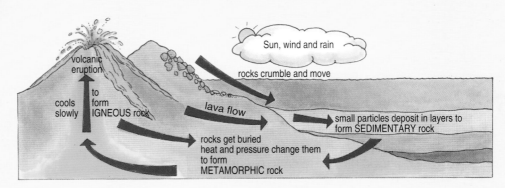

Questions

1 Write a worksheet for Year 9 pupils.
Show how to test rocks for:

- hardness
- porosity (how easily they soak up water)
- density.

You should include diagrams and instructions.
You could use cartoons. You could include questions too.

2 A gem is a precious mineral. It can be cut and polished.
Then it can be used in jewellery.
a) What makes a mineral precious?
b) Name as many gems as you can.

3 Explain how each of these rocks is formed:
a) granite
b) conglomerate
c) slate.

4 Sea defences can be used to limit coastal erosion.
Concrete can be used to build them.
Concrete is made from sand, cement and gravel mixed with water.
Plan an investigation to test different concrete mixes.
Which will make the best sea defence?
(You must be able to do your tests in the lab.)

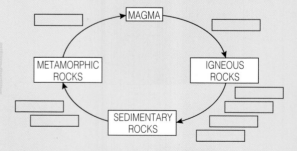

5 Look at the simple rock cycle:
Choose words from the list below to put labels in the boxes.

| heat | melting | erosion | deposition | pressure |
| weathering | transportation | crystallising |

6 Find out about geological time periods.
During your research, try to answer the questions below.
a) In which period were there lots of sea animals, but no life on land?
b) In which period did the Ice Age occur?
c) Which period lasted from about 135 million to 65 million years ago?
d) In which period did reptiles start to appear on Earth?
e) Which geological time period are we in today?

In the cretaceous period, great reptiles roamed the Earth.

Test tips

The national Tests usually take place in May in Year 9. As the date approaches, make sure that you are fully prepared.

Before the Tests:

- Plan your revision timetable.
  Your teacher can advise you on how much time you spend on each subject and when to start.

- Revise your work carefully.
  You can use the Revision Summary pages at the end of each topic. These cover the main points from all your work in Years 7, 8 and 9.

- You can revise your Year 9 work by working through Question 1 in 'Things to do' at the end of each double page.
  Make sure you can fill in all the missing words.
  If you get stuck, ask your teacher for some help.

- Ask your teacher for copies of the Tests from earlier years.
  Try to do as many as you can, and time yourself.

- Make sure that you have the correct equipment needed for the Tests.
  This is usually:
  pen, pencil, rubber, ruler, protractor and calculator.
  A watch is also useful, so that you can pace yourself in each Test.

During each Test:

- Read each question carefully.
  Make sure that you understand what each question is about and what you are expected to do.
  For example, if it asks for **one** answer, give only **one**.

- Sometimes you are given a list of alternatives to choose from.
  Make sure you choose the right number – if you include more answers than you are asked for, any wrong answers will cancel out your right ones!

- How much detail do you need to give?
  The question gives you clues:
  - Give short answers to questions which start:
    '*State ...*' or '*List ...*' or '*Name ...*'.
  - Give longer answers if you are asked to '*Explain ...*' or '*Describe ...*' or if you are asked '*Why does ... ?*'.

- The number of marks shown on the page usually tells you how many points the marker is looking for in your answer.

- The number of lines of space is also a guide to how much is needed in your answer.

- Don't explain something just because you know how to! If you are not asked to explain it, you won't gain any extra marks and you will just waste time.

- If you find a question too hard, go on to the next question. But try to write something for each part of every question.

- If you have spare time at the end, use it wisely to check over your answers.

Sc	Science test
KEY STAGE **3**	**Paper 1**
TIER **5–7**	

Please read this page, but do not open the booklet until your teacher tells you to start. Write your name and the name of your school in the spaces below. If you have been given a pupil number, write that also.

First name _____

Last name _____

School _____

Glossary

Abrasion
When a surface is worn away by rubbing.

Absorb
When light, sound or another form of energy is taken in by something, e.g. black paper absorbs light energy, or when digested food is absorbed into the blood from the small intestine.

Acceleration
The rate at which an object speeds up.

Acid
A sour substance which can attack metal, clothing or skin. The chemical opposite of an alkali.
When an acid is dissolved in water its solution has a pH number less than 7.

Adaptation
A feature that helps a plant or an animal to survive in changing conditions.

Adolescence
The time of change from a child to an adult, when both our bodies and our emotions change.

Aerobic respiration
The process that happens in cells whereby oxygen is used to release the energy from glucose.

Air resistance
A force, due to friction with the air, which pushes against a moving object, e.g. air resistance slows down a parachute.

Alkali
The chemical opposite of an acid. A base which dissolves in water. Its solution has a pH number more than 7.

Amphibian
An animal that lives on land and in water. It has moist skin and breeds in water.

Amplitude
The size of a vibration or wave, measured from its mid-point. A loud sound has a large amplitude.

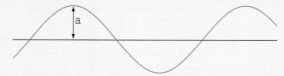

Anomalous result
A result that does not follow the general pattern in a set of data.

Antagonistic muscles
Muscles that work in pairs.
When one muscle contracts the other relaxes, e.g. your biceps and triceps.

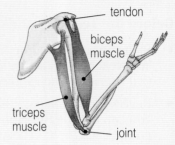

Antibiotic
A useful drug that helps your body fight a disease.

Artery
A blood vessel that carries blood away from the heart.

Asteroids
Small planets and pieces of rock hurtling through space. There is a belt of asteroids between Mars and Jupiter in the Solar System.

Atom
The smallest part of an element. All atoms contain protons and electrons.

Atomic number
The number of protons in each atom of an element. Elements are arranged in the periodic table in order of this atomic number.

Axis
The Earth spins on its axis. It is an imaginary line passing through the Earth from the North Pole to the South Pole.

Bacteria
Microbes made up of one cell, visible with a microscope. Bacteria can grow quickly and some of them cause disease, e.g. pneumonia.

Balanced forces
Forces are balanced when they cancel out each other (see page 106). The object stays still, or continues to move at a steady speed in a straight line.

Base
The oxide, hydroxide or carbonate of a metal. (If a base dissolves in water it is called an alkali.)

Biased
Results that unfairly tend to favour one set of variables over another. For example, a survey that includes many more boys than girls when you are looking for a general pattern.

Biomass fuel
Fuel (e.g. wood) made from growing plants.

Boiling point
The temperature at which a liquid boils and changes into a gas.

Braking distance
The distance a car travels *after* the brake is pressed.

Bronchus
One of the tubes at the bottom of the wind-pipe (trachea) that lead to the lungs.

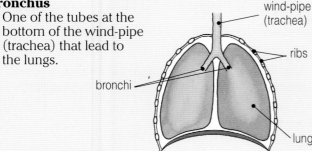

Capillaries
Tiny blood vessels that let substances like oxygen, food and carbon dioxide pass into and out of the blood.

Carbohydrate
Your body's fuel. Food like glucose that gives you your energy.

Carnivores
Animals that eat only other animals – meat-eaters.

Catalytic converter
Device fitted to a car's exhaust system to reduce the pollutant gases given out.

Caustic
A caustic substance is corrosive.

Cell membrane
The structure that surrounds a cell and controls what goes in and out.

Cell wall
The strong layer on the outside of a plant cell that supports the cell.

Cells
The 'building blocks' of life, made up of a *cell membrane*, *cytoplasm* and *nucleus*.

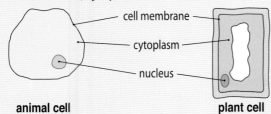

Charges
See *Electric charges*.

Chemical change
A change which makes a new substance, e.g. coal burning.

Chemical energy
The energy stored in substances, e.g. foods and fuels are useful stores of chemical energy.

Chlorophyll
A green chemical in plants used to trap light energy for photosynthesis.

Chloroplasts
Tiny, round structures found inside plant cells. They capture light energy and use it to make food in photosynthesis.

Chromatography
A method used to separate mixtures of substances, usually coloured ones.

Cilia
Very small threads or hairs on the surface of some cells.

Classify
To sort things out into different groups or sets.

Clone
Genetically-identical living things.

Combustion
The reaction which occurs when a substance burns in oxygen, giving out heat energy.

Community
The group of animals and plants that we find in a particular habitat.

Competition
A struggle for survival. Living things compete for scarce resources, e.g. space.

Component
One of the parts that make up an electric circuit, e.g. battery, switch, bulb.

Composition
The type and amount of each element in a compound.

Compound
A substance made when 2 or more elements are chemically joined together, e.g. water is a compound made from hydrogen and oxygen.

Conductor
An electrical conductor allows a current to flow through it. A thermal conductor allows heat energy to pass through it. All metals are good conductors.

Control variables
The factors we must keep the same during an investigation to make sure we carry out a fair test.

Convection
The transfer of heat by currents in a liquid or a gas.

Correlation
The strength of the link or connection between two variables being investigated.

Corrosive
A corrosive substance can eat away another substance by attacking it chemically.

Cytoplasm
The jelly-like part of the cell where many chemical reactions take place.

Dependent variable (or outcome variable)
When you do a fair test, this is the factor that you measure or observe in each test, in order to see the effect of varying another factor.
For example, if you investigate 'How does temperature affect the time taken for sugar to dissolve?', then the dependent variable is the time taken.

Diffusion
The process of particles moving and mixing of their own accord, without being stirred or shaken.

Digestion
Breaking down food so that it is small enough to pass through the gut into the blood.

Dispersion
The splitting of a beam of white light into the 7 colours of the spectrum, by passing it through a prism.

Displacement
When one element takes the place of another in a compound. For example,

magnesium + copper sulphate → magnesium sulphate + copper

This is called a displacement reaction.

Dissipation of energy
When energy is spread out by being transferred to lots of different places.

Distillation
A way to separate a liquid from a mixture of liquids, by boiling off the substances at different temperatures.

Dormant
Inactive, e.g. a dormant volcano is one which has not erupted for a long time.

Drag
Friction caused by an object travelling through a liquid or gas. For example, friction caused by air resistance.

Drug
A chemical that alters the way in which your body works, e.g. alcohol, cannabis, nicotine, solvents.

Dynamo
A machine that transfers kinetic energy to electrical energy.

Eclipse
A *lunar eclipse* is when the shadow of the Earth falls on the Moon.

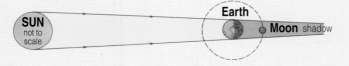

A *solar eclipse* is when the Sun is blotted out (totally or partially) by the Moon.

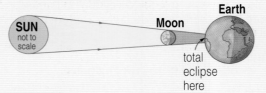

Ecosystem
A group of animals and plants plus the habitat in which they are found.

Egestion
Getting rid of indigestible food from the gut.

Egg
Female sex cell.

Electric charges
A positive or a negative charge can be given to an insulated object by rubbing it. A + charge repels another + charge, but attracts a – charge.

Electric current
A flow of electric charges (electrons).
It is measured in amps (A) by an ammeter.

Electro-magnet
A coil of wire becomes a magnet when a current flows through it. (See page 189.)

Electron
A tiny particle with a negative charge.

Element
A substance that is made of only one type of atom.

Embryo
A fertilised egg grows into an embryo and eventually into a baby.

Endothermic
A reaction that *takes in* heat energy from the surroundings.

Energy transfer
See *Transfer of energy*.

Enzymes
Chemicals that act like catalysts to speed up digestion of our food.

Epidemic
The spread of a disease through a community.

Equation
A shorthand way of showing the changes that take place in a chemical reaction

e.g. iron + sulphur → iron sulphide
$$Fe + S \rightarrow FeS$$

Equilibrium
A balanced situation, when all the forces cancel out each other.

Erosion
The wearing away of rocks.

Evaluate
   a) Your method,
      to judge how effective the method you used was in collecting reliable data.
   b) Your conclusion,
      to judge how strong the evidence is that you have used to draw a conclusion.

Exhale
To breathe out.

Exothermic
A reaction that *gives out* heat energy to the surroundings.

Fat
Food used as a store of energy and to insulate our bodies so we lose less heat.

Fermentation
The reaction when sugar is turned into alcohol.

Fertilisation
When sex cells join together to make a new individual, e.g. a sperm and an egg, or a pollen grain nucleus and an ovule nucleus.

Fertilisers
The nutrients that can be added to the soil if they are in short supply.

Fetus
An embryo that has developed its main features, e.g. in humans after about 3 months.

Fibre
Food that we get from plants that cannot be digested. It gives the gut muscles something to push against.

Filtration
A process used to separate undissolved solids from liquids.

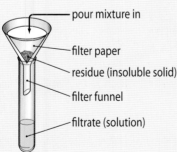

pour mixture in

filter paper

residue (insoluble solid)

filter funnel

filtrate (solution)

Flowers
The organs that many plants use to reproduce by making seeds.

Food chain
A diagram that shows how food energy is passed between plants and animals.

Food web
A diagram that shows a number of food chains linked together.

Formula
A combination of symbols to show the elements which a compound contains, e.g. MgO is the formula for magnesium oxide.

Fossil
The remains of an animal or plant which have been preserved in rocks.

Fossil fuels
A fuel made from the remains of plants and animals that died millions of years ago, e.g. coal, oil, natural gas.

Frequency
The number of complete vibrations in each second. A sound with a high frequency has a high pitch.

Friction
A force when 2 surfaces rub together. It always pushes against the movement.

Fuel
A substance that is burned in air (oxygen) to give out energy.

Fungi
Moulds, such as yeast or mushrooms, that produce spores.

Fungicide
A chemical which kills fungi that attack crops.

Fuse
A safety device in an electrical circuit. It is a piece of wire that heats up and melts, breaking the circuit, if too much current passes through it.

Gamete
The male or female reproductive cells.

Gas
A substance which is light, has the shape of its container and is easily squashed. The particles in a gas are far apart. They move quickly and in all directions.

Genes
Found in chromosomes, they control the inherited features of living things.

Gestation
The time from fertilisation to birth, e.g. in humans the gestation period is about 40 weeks.

Global warming
The build up of 'greenhouse' gases that is causing the temperature of the Earth to increase.

Gravity, gravitational force
A force of attraction between 2 objects. The pull of gravity on you is your weight.

Group
All the elements in one column down the periodic table.

Habitat
The place where a plant or animal lives.

Haemoglobin
The substance in red blood cells that transports oxygen around the body.

Herbicide
A chemical used to kill weeds that are in competition with a crop.

Herbivores
Animals that eat only plants.

Hibernate
To remain inactive throughout the winter months.

Igneous rock
A rock formed by molten (melted) material cooling down.

Image
When you look in a mirror, you see an image of yourself.

Immune
Not being able to catch a particular disease because you have the antibodies in your blood to fight it.

Inhale
To breathe in.

Inherited
The features that are passed on from parents to their offspring.

Independent variable (or input variable)
The factor that you choose to change in an investigation.
For example, if you investigate 'How does temperature affect the time taken for sugar to dissolve**?**', then the independent variable is the temperature.

Indicator
A substance that changes colour depending on the pH of the solution you add it to.

Insecticide
A chemical that kills insects that feed on crops.

Inspire
To breathe in.

Insulator
An electrical insulator does not allow a current to flow easily. A thermal insulator does not let heat energy flow easily.

Intestine
Tube below the stomach where food is digested and absorbed.

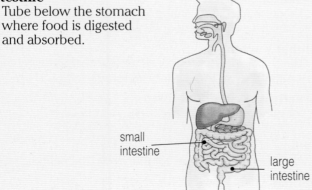

small intestine

large intestine

Invertebrate
An animal without a backbone.

Joint
The point where 2 bones meet. Joints usually allow movement.

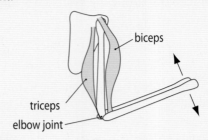

biceps

triceps

elbow joint

Kinetic energy
The energy of something which is moving.

Law of reflection
When light rays bounce off a mirror:

angle of incidence = angle of reflection.

Lava
Molten rock ejected from a volcano.

Lever
A simple machine that produces a bigger force or movement than we apply.

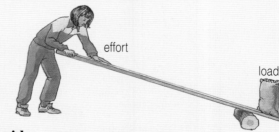

effort

load

Liquid
A substance which has the shape of its container, can be poured and is not easily squashed. The particles in a liquid are quite close together but free to move.

Lungs
The organs in our body that collect oxygen and get rid of carbon dioxide.

Magma
Hot molten rock below the Earth's surface.

Magnetic field
The area round a magnet where it attracts or repels another magnet.

Magnetic material
A substance which is attracted by a magnet, e.g. iron and steel.

Magnify
To make bigger.

Mammal
Warm-blooded animals with fur or hair that suckle their young.

Mammary glands
Where mammals produce the milk for their young.

Melting point
The temperature at which a solid melts and changes into a liquid.

Menstruation
The discharge of blood and lining of the uterus from the vagina.
This happens at the end of each menstrual cycle in which an egg has not been fertilised.

Metal
An element which is a good conductor and is usually shiny, e.g. copper.

Metamorphic rock
A rock formed by heating and compressing (squeezing) an existing rock.

Migration
Moving from one place to another in different seasons to avoid adverse or harsh conditions.

Millennium (plural: millennia)
A period of one thousand years.

Mixture
A substance made when some elements or compounds are mixed together. It is *not* a pure substance.

Molecule
A group of atoms joined together.

a molecule
of water, H_2O

oxygen atom

hydrogen atom

Moment
The turning effect of a force.

Moment = force × distance from the pivot.

Muscle
Structures that contract and relax to move bones at joints.

Neutral
Something which is neither an acid nor an alkali.

Neutralisation
The chemical reaction of an acid with a base, in which they cancel each other out.

Non-metal
An element which does not conduct electricity.
(The exception to this is graphite – a form of carbon which is a non-metal, but it does conduct).

Non-renewable resources
Energy sources that are used up and not replaced, e.g. fossil fuels.

Nucleus of a cell
A round structure that controls the cell and contains the instructions to make more cells.

Nutrients
The chemicals needed by plants for healthy growth, e.g. nitrates, phosphates.

Omnivores
Animals that eat both plants and animals.

Opaque
An opaque object will not let light pass through it.

Orbit
The path of a planet or a satellite.
Its shape is usually an ellipse (oval).

ellipse

Organ
A structure made up of different tissues that work together to do a particular job.

Organism
A living thing, such as a plant, an animal or a microbe.

Ovary
Where the eggs are made in a female.

Oviduct
A tube that carries an egg from the ovary to the uterus.

Oxidation
The reaction when oxygen is added to a substance.

Ozone depletion
The destruction of the ozone layer in our atmosphere.
Ozone protects us from the Sun's harmful ultra-violet radiation.

Palisade cells
Cells in which most photosynthesis takes place.
They are found in the upper part of a leaf.

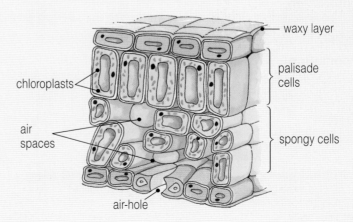

waxy layer

palisade cells

chloroplasts

air spaces

spongy cells

air-hole

Parallel circuit
A way of connecting things in an electric circuit, so that the current divides and passes through different branches. (See page 184.)

Pathogen
An organism that causes disease in another species, e.g. viruses or bacteria.

Period (1)
When the lining of the uterus breaks down and blood and cells leave the body through the vagina.

Period (2)
All the elements in one row across the periodic table.

Periodic table
An arrangement of elements in the order of their atomic numbers, forming groups and periods.

Pesticide
A chemical that kills insects, weeds or fungi that damage crops.

pH number
A number which shows how strong an acid or alkali is. Acids have pH 1–6 (pH 1 is very strong acid). Alkalis have pH 8–14 (pH 14 is very strong alkali).

Photosynthesis
The process by which green plants use light energy to turn carbon dioxide and water into sugars:

$$\text{carbon dioxide} + \text{water} \xrightarrow{\text{light and chlorophyll}} \text{sugar} + \text{oxygen}$$

Physical change
A change in which no new substance is made. The substance just changes to a different state, e.g. water boiling.

Pitch
A whistle has a high pitch, a bass guitar has a low pitch.

Placenta
A structure that forms in the uterus allowing the blood of the baby and the blood of the mother to come close together.

Pollination
The transfer of pollen from the anthers to the stigma of a flower.

Population
A group of animals or plants of the same species living in the same habitat.

Porosity
The ability to absorb a liquid such as water, e.g. sandstone is a porous rock.

Potential energy
Stored energy, e.g. a bike at the top of a hill has gravitational potential energy.

Predator
An animal that hunts and eats other animals.

Prediction
A statement that describes and explains what you think will happen in an investigation.

Pressure
A large force pressing on a small area gives a high pressure.

$$\text{Pressure} = \frac{\text{force}}{\text{area}}$$

Prey
An animal that is eaten by a predator, e.g. a rabbit is prey for the fox.

Principle of conservation of energy
The amount of energy before a transfer is always equal to the amount of energy after the transfer. The energy is 'conserved'.

Producers
Green plants that make their own food by photosynthesis.

Product
A substance made as a result of a chemical reaction.

Proportional
The link between 2 variables, e.g. the extension of a spring is directly proportional to the load on it, so if you double the load, the extension is also doubled.

Protein
Food needed for the growth and repair of cells.

Puberty
The age at which the sexual organs become developed.

Pumice
A light, porous rock formed from lava.

Pyramid of numbers
A diagram to show how many living things there are at each level in a food chain.

Qualitative observations
Descriptive evidence from an investigation,
e.g. your observations of different pieces of material
left buried for several weeks to see which are
biodegradable.

Quantitative data
Numerical evidence produced from your
measurements during an investigation.

Radiation
Rays of light, X-rays, radio waves, etc., including
the transfer of energy through a vacuum.

Reaction
A chemical change which makes a new substance.

Reactivity series
A list of elements in order of their reactivity. The most
reactive element is put at the top of the list.

Reduction
A reaction when oxygen is removed,
e.g. copper oxide is *reduced* to copper.

Reflection
When light bounces off an object.

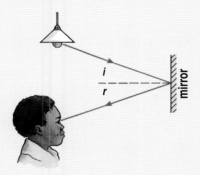

Refraction
A ray of light passing from one substance into another
is bent (refracted).

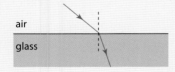

Relay
A switch that is operated by an electro-magnet.
A small current can switch on a large current.

Reliability
A measure of the trust you can put in your results.
For example, if you were to collect your data again
would you get the same results?
In some investigations it is difficult to get precise
measurements, e.g. measuring how high a ball
bounces. You can improve the reliability of your
results by repeating readings and taking averages.

Renewable energy resources
Energy sources that do not get used up,
e.g. solar energy, wind, waves, tides, etc.

Reptile
An animal with dry, scaly skin that lays eggs with soft
shells.

Resistance
A thin wire gives more resistance to an electric current
than a thick wire.

Respiration
The release of energy from food in our cells. Usually
using up oxygen and producing carbon dioxide.

glucose + oxygen ⟶ carbon dioxide + water + energy

Resultant force
The result of *unbalanced forces*. (See page 106).

Rock cycle
A cycle that means that one type of rock can be
changed into another type of rock over a period of time.

Salt
A substance made when an acid and a base react
together.

Sample size
The number of subjects included in an enquiry.
For example, in biological investigations it is difficult
to control all the variables. So you can improve
your evidence by collecting data from more plants,
animals or places. This is called increasing your
sample size.

Satellite
An object that goes round a planet or a star,
e.g. the Moon goes round the Earth.

Saturated solution
A solution in which no more solute can dissolve at that
temperature.

Scattering
When rays of light hit a rough surface (like paper) they
reflect off in all directions.

Sedimentary rock
A rock formed by squashing together layers of material
that settle out in water.

Selective breeding
Choosing which animals and plants to breed in order
to pass on useful features to the offspring, e.g. high
milk yield.

Sensor
An electronic device that detects changes.
It may be connected to a computer.

Series circuit
A way of connecting things in an electric circuit,
so that the current flows through each one in turn.
(See page 182.)

Solar System
The Sun and all 9 planets that go round it.

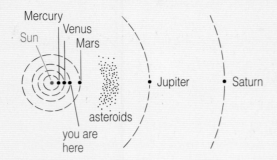

Solid
A substance which has a fixed shape, is not runny and is not squashed easily. The particles in a solid are packed very closely together – they vibrate but do not move from place to place.

Soluble
Describes something which dissolves, e.g. salt is soluble in water.

Solute
The solid that dissolves to make a solution.

Solution
The clear liquid made when a solute dissolves in a solvent, e.g. salt (solute) dissolves in water (solvent) to make salt solution.

Solvent
The liquid that dissolves the solute to make a solution.

Species
A type of living thing that breeds and produces fertile offspring.

Spectrum
The colours of the rainbow that can be separated when white light is passed through a prism: red, orange, yellow, green, blue, indigo, violet (ROY G. BIV).

Speed
How fast an object is moving.

$$\text{Speed} = \frac{\text{distance travelled}}{\text{time taken}}$$

Sperm
Male sex cell.

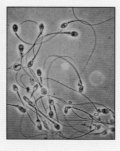

States of matter
The 3 states in which matter can be found: *solid*, *liquid* and *gas*.

Static electricity, electrostatistics
When an insulated object is rubbed, it can become charged with electricity.

Temperature
How hot or cold something is. It is measured in °C, using a thermometer.

Testis
Where the sperms are made in a male.

Thermal energy
Another name for heat energy.

Thermal transfer
When a cup of tea cools down, there is a transfer of thermal energy (heat) from the cup to the surroundings. This transfer can be by conduction, convection, radiation and evaporation.

Thinking distance
The distance travelled in a car during the driver's reaction time.

Tissue
A group of similar cells that look the same and do the same job.

Toxins
Poisons produced from bacteria and other microbes.

Trachea
The wind-pipe taking air to and from the lungs.

Transfer of energy
The movement of energy from one place to another, for a job to be done.

Transformation of energy
When energy changes from one form to another, e.g. when paper burns, chemical energy is changed to heat and light energy.

Unbalanced forces
If 2 forces do not cancel out each other, they are unbalanced. There will be a resultant force. (See page 106.) The object will change its speed or change its direction.

Universal indicator
A liquid which changes colour when acids or alkalis are added to it. It shows whether the acid or alkali is strong or weak.

Upthrust
Upward force produced on an object in a liquid or a gas. There is a very small upthrust in a gas.

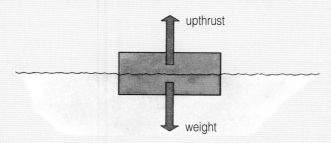

Uterus
The womb, where a fertilised egg settles and grows into a baby.

Vaccination
Protection against a disease by introducing into the body a harmless sample of the microbe that causes infection.

Vacuole
The space in a plant cell that is filled with a watery solution called cell sap.

Validity of conclusions
A measure of the certainty you can put on your conclusions drawn from the data that you collected in your investigation.

Variable
The things (factors) that can change (or vary) in an investigation.

Variation
Differences between *different* species, e.g. between dogs and cats, or between individuals of the *same* species, e.g. people in your class.

Vein
A blood vessel that carries blood back to the heart.

Vertebrate
An animal that has a backbone.

Vibrating
Moving backwards and forwards quickly, e.g. the particles in a solid vibrate.

Viruses
Extremely small microbes which are not visible with a microscope. Many viruses spread disease by invading cells and copying themselves, e.g. influenza.

Vitamins
Complex chemicals needed in small amounts to keep us healthy, e.g. vitamin C.

Wavelength
The distance between 2 peaks of a wave.

Weathering
The crumbling away of rocks caused by weather conditions such as wind and rain.

Index